# The Televisi 1 Handbook

*The Television Handbook* is a critical introduction to the practice and theory of television. Jonathan Bignell and Jeremy Orlebar discuss the state of television today, explain how television is made, and how production is organised, and discuss how critical thinking about programmes and genres can illuminate their meanings. This book also explores how developments in technology and the changing structure of the television industry will lead the medium in new directions.

*The Television Handbook* gives practical advice on many aspects of programme making, from an initial programme idea through to shooting and the post-production process. The book includes profiles giving insight into how personnel in the television industry – from recent graduates to television executives – think about their work.

*The Television Handbook* bridges the gap between theory and practice. There are chapters on the vigorous debates about what is meant by 'quality' television, how news and factual programmes are changing as new technologies and formats such as Reality TV have risen in prominence, and how drama, sport and music television can be understood.

**Jonathan Bignell** is Reader in Television and Film and Director of the Centre for Television and Drama Studies at the University of Reading.

**Jeremy Orlebar** is a television producer, director, writer and lecturer with over 25 years' experience.

# Media Practice

Edited by James Curran, Goldsmiths College, University of London

The *Media Practice* handbooks are comprehensive resource books for students of media and journalism, and for anyone planning a career as a media professional. Each handbook combines a clear introduction to understanding how the media work with practical information about the structure, processes and skills involved in working in today's media industries, providing not only a guide on 'how to do it' but also a critical reflection on contemporary media practice.

Also in this series:

# The Television Handbook

Third edition

Jonathan Bignell and
Jeremy Orlebar

Routledge
Taylor & Francis Group

LONDON AND NEW YORK

First published 2005 by Routledge
2 Park Square, Milton Park, Abingdon, Oxon OX14 4RN

Simultaneously published in the USA and Canada
by Taylor & Francis Inc.
270 Madison Ave, New York, NY 10016

*Routledge is an imprint of the Taylor & Francis Group*

© 2005 Jonathan Bignell and Jeremy Orlebar

Typeset in Times by
Florence Production Ltd, Stoodleigh, Devon
Printed and bound in Great Britain by
MPG Books Ltd, Bodmin, Cornwall

*British Library Cataloguing in Publication Data*
A catalogue record for this book is available from the British Library

*Library of Congress Cataloging in Publication Data*
Bignell, Jonathan.
    The television handbook/by Jonathan Bignell
    and Jeremy Orlebar. – 3rd ed.
        p. cm
    Rev. ed. of: The television handbook/Patricia Holland. 2nd ed. 2000
    1. Television – Production and direction – Handbooks, manuals, etc.
    2. Television broadcasting – Handbooks, manuals, etc.   I. Orlebar, Jeremy.
    II. Holland, Patricia. television handbook.   III. Title
    PN1992.5.H63 2005
    791.4502′3 – dc22                                    2005018907

ISBN 0–415–34251–1 (hbk)
ISBN 0–415–34252–X (pbk)

# Contents

...........................................

# Illustrations

# Part I

# Television today

# 1 Media literacy

..........................................................................

## Introduction

..........................................................................

Television Studies is a relatively new academic subject compared to the study of other media such as literature or art, for example, and even in its short history the emphases in the subject and the ways of teaching it have changed. Television Studies is in a continual process of development, and the ongoing production of new television programmes, made by new and changing institutions under changing conditions and with new technologies, continually generates new questions and ways of answering them. In this book we aim to take account of recent and current developments in television and in the ways it can be studied, building on the work done by Patricia Holland who was the author of two earlier editions of *The Television Handbook*.

Part I provides an initial overview of the state of television in Britain today, and some of the key areas of work in academic Television Studies. This part sets the agenda and presents some important information about contemporary television. The subsequent parts of the book focus in greater detail on the practices of television makers and the institutions they work for, and on some of the programmes and points of debate that are central to teaching about television today.

We discuss British television much more than any other national or regional television culture in this book. British television has aimed to represent a relatively unified culture, even though the nation has been divided into local TV areas like the Midlands, Scotland or Northern Ireland. The great majority of programmes shown on British TV are made in the UK, and there are important differences between the way TV is organised in Britain compared to other nations such as the US or Italy. In a similar way, the shape of the critical approaches to television taught in British colleges and universities is relatively distinctive compared to other nations. Despite the international flow of ideas (not unlike the international trade in television programming), there is a strong and healthy interest in television among British students, critics, teachers and enthusiasts. This book is for that broad constituency of people who want to participate by working in or learning about television. Although there are many books that address aspects of this field (some are listed in the Further reading at the end of this part), *The Television Handbook* balances up-to-date information, ideas and arguments in a distinctive way.

## Teaching and training

Teaching about television falls into two related but distinct approaches. In academic institutions, Television Studies has adopted a focus on the analysis of selected programmes. Television Studies emerged in the 1970s and 1980s out of several interconnected ways of discussing the medium. One of these was the discourse of journalistic reviewing (see Caughie 1984) that aimed to critically evaluate programmes broadcast in the immediate past (such as the night before) and draw viewers' attention to immediately upcoming programmes. Television Studies also adopted some of the more sophisticated discourses of evaluation used in related subjects such as literature, fine art and the emergent discipline of Film Studies. Like television reviewing's discussion of selected programmes, these approaches also focus on the analysis of individual texts or art-works. Specialist procedures of analysis, especially semiotics and narrative theory, are used to unpack the patterns of meaning-making that television texts use. And these procedures are briefly outlined in Chapter 2, and their ramifications are further explored in Part III of this book. The advantage of analysing programmes is that it makes an example accessible to television students, who can focus on a single programme and discuss selected moments in it. This approach tends to deal with issues of structure, the meanings created by interactions between images and sound, and context-ualisation in relation to programmes of similar genre and form. Clearly, the selection of what to study, and the analytical questions asked about the programme, have important effects since the expectations about what television is, and how it should be approached critically, are shaped both consciously and unconsciously by the teachers and students engaging in the subject.

Because of the deep embedding of television viewing in everyday life, Television Studies also has a strong connection with studies of the sociology of culture (see Brunsdon 1998). The sociological strand of television study addressed television in the context of a political critique of the forces of social control, since television's institutional and industrial production could be seen as the carrier of ideological values. By analysing television as one of the means by which social life is given meaning, and aspects of contemporary society are represented and debated, Television Studies with this sociological focus can contribute to social and political education. It has been especially important in considering society as a dynamic and changing thing, in which more powerful and less powerful definitions of issues, groups of people and expectations of the future compete to establish themselves as the accepted common sense understanding of the world. Analysis of television with this sociological and political agenda could therefore reveal the negotiation between the sanctioned 'official' values of a ruling elite or governmental institution and the world-views of ordinary people. Television programmes' meanings could then be regarded as a site of struggle between different 'official' and 'popular' discourses. In this analytical tradition, study of television is one of many ways to discover how social meanings are created, perpetuated or modified, and how television representation connects up with the broader media landscape of a particular historical moment, especially the present. Again, the main outlines of this kind of approach in Television Studies are presented in Chapter 2 of this book, and are debated more fully across the chapters in Part III.

The other significant strand of teaching about television is the imparting of professional skills and knowledge that enables students to understand how programmes are made technically, industrially and institutionally, providing them with the potential to find employment within the television business. However, while this kind of training may sometimes seem merely to be creating a workforce to serve the current state of the television industry, the great majority of television professionals aim for a committed engagement with the technical resources of the medium, a concern for its relationships with society at large, and an interest in the creative possibilities that are possible in television production. This assumption that working in television is creative, socially engaged and personally enriching is matched by the syllabus of many courses that primarily focus on the acquisition of professional knowledge and skills. Work in television is understood as the deployment of a body of professional knowledge, working practices and technical expertise. The key aspects of these professional competencies are outlined in Parts II and IV of this book. But the possession of these competencies is also a means for the expression of ideas and an opportunity to contribute to the evolution of the television industry and also the broader society to which that industry belongs. Television training entails the understanding of social responsibility and the recognition of opportunities for creative intervention. So television training is close to the agendas of the theoretical studies of television described above, in that it deals with questions of quality, aesthetics and politics. In this book, we take the position that the two strands of television education are mutually compatible and interrelated.

## The value of television and television studies

The legacy of educational theories developed in the nineteenth century is that education is concerned with imparting knowledge to enable students to discriminate between what is valuable and what is worthless. By means of this discriminating ability, the educated person will be able to seek out what is valuable and reject what is not, thus gaining the means to become a better person and a more valuable citizen. Clearly, this raises the question of how to judge what is good. It will also involve the assumption that what is ordinary, familiar and enjoyed by the majority of a population will probably be less valuable than what is enjoyed by an educated elite. So the discrimination between valuable and worthless subjects of study is parallel to, and supports, the discrimination between valuable people and worthless people. The formation of an elite collection of subjects to study goes hand in hand with the formation of an elite group of people who are more highly educated, discriminating and valuable as citizens than their ordinary contemporaries. This set of interconnected assumptions about the value of education has had a huge impact on the kinds of attention given to television, and to the academic study of the television medium.

   Television is the most pervasive audio-visual medium in contemporary society. Therefore, it is necessarily ordinary, familiar, and subject to the accusation that it is worthless because it is so available and integrated into everyday life. Furthermore, this argument leaves little room for extracting some of television's output from the rest and discriminating it as valuable or good. If such discriminations are to be made, there is also a problem with how to locate the criteria that support this judgement. It seems quite legitimate to claim that *The Simpsons* is a very important piece of cultural work, because of its textual complexity, its self-awareness as television, and its relevance to contemporary media landscapes and their audiences. These values make *The Simpsons* fit the criteria for quality and value, yet it is obviously part of popular culture, not least because of its familiarity and large audiences. There is clearly an unsolved problem at the moment, about how to judge the value of television in general and specific programmes in particular. Competing arguments are advanced, for and against the value of television and Television Studies, with no agreed criteria for deciding which of these arguments is the stronger, or even the more useful. We develop these ideas and debates further in subsequent chapters, and especially in relation to television drama programmes in Chapter 13.

# 2 The political landscape

...............................................................

Terrestrial broadcast television has always been regulated via Acts of Parliament. The first media related Act was the Wireless Telegraphy Act in 1904. Commercial broadcasting was started by an Act of Parliament in 1954. The BBC had a different genesis and was set up by Royal Charter in 1927. In the UK, successive governments have avoided a cut-throat and unfettered commercial market, such as that found in the US, by setting up broadcasting regulatory bodies to oversee all areas of broadcasting, including cable and satellite. These bodies maintain technical and programme standards. They ensure that broadcasters provide a mix of programmes for a variety of audiences. They ensure that programmes do not offend against what is generally considered to be good taste or decency. They require that programmes are fair, and do not incite crime or racial hatred. News should be accurate and impartial. They provide a code on the content of advertisements and regulate when and how often they can be shown. Until recently there were five different regulatory bodies covering the commercial broadcasting of radio and television, with wide ranging powers. In 2003, the Labour Government under Tony Blair passed a new Communications Act that included the setting up of a new communications regulator for the digital age, called the Office of Communications, or Ofcom. The reason for its introduction was convergence in the media and telecoms industry, and the rise of cross-media companies such as AOL Time Warner and News International.

# Ofcom

Ofcom is the new broadcasting and telecommunications regulator, with a wide brief. It was created to make the UK's media regulations more efficient and more user-friendly to viewers. It combines the functions of the previous regulators; the Independent Television Commission (ITC), the Broadcasting Standards Commission (BSC), the Radio Authority, the Office of Telecommunications (Oftel), and the Radio-communications Agency. It replaces other broadcasting watchdogs including the Broadcasting Standards Commission (BSC) which deals with taste and decency matters on TV and radio, and the Radio Authority. It oversees telephone services in the UK. Ofcom's stated aim is to 'further the interests of citizens in communication matters'. An independent regulatory body, Ofcom's responsibilities and duties were laid down in the Communications Act 2003.

## What does it do?

Ofcom is aimed at clearing up some of the confusion that broadcasters and the public have felt in dealing with different television watchdogs and regulators. It regulates the whole area of terrestrial and satellite commercial television. It regulates the use of commercials on television. It regulates the whole area of telecommunications. It is concerned with media spectrum allocation including the allocation of mobile phone wavelengths, and telephone landlines. It is formulating new rules on the mergers of media companies, such as the merger between Carlton and Granada. It can even comment on the way music is downloaded from the internet.

## Taste and decency

Ofcom will monitor the use of bad language, violence and scenes of a sexual nature on all television channels. Some commentators have argued that it has too many powers for one organisation, and may become the broadcasters' bully. Broadcasters hope Ofcom will not stifle the creation of new, and perhaps risqué TV formats and programmes, and will keep up with the times in terms of what is acceptable to an adult television audience. For the first time the official regulator is charged with looking after that difficult territory known as taste and decency in all broadcasting, including BBC programmes that have previously been regulated in this area by the BBC governors. It will police the 9.00 pm watershed on all channels.

## The cost of Ofcom

Ofcom will regulate a £44 billion industry. It forecasts that its annual running costs for its first full year will be £164 million from April 2004, but this should fall slightly in subsequent years. This is 27 per cent more than the previous five regulatory bodies cost. However, Ofcom says it now has more than 260 statutory tasks and the extra expenditure is to cover some of its new powers. It employs 880 people, over 300 fewer staff than the five bodies it replaces. It is paid for mainly by the government for managing the airwaves spectrum, and by the commercial broadcasters and the telecoms companies. The BBC also contributes.

## How does it affect us?

Ofcom is concerned with many aspects of the way digital data are transferred. It has a statutory duty to 'further the interests of consumers', and as such will be looking at, for example, the implications of the copying of music on the internet, and music piracy. Most worryingly, it seems that Ofcom can be asked to investigate the content of television programmes where it is thought the content might affect the consumer. In the past, regulators have not been able to directly alter the content of programmes before transmission, but instead they have offered advice and provided guidelines. Broadcasters regularly consult the regulators to ensure their programmes do not breach programme codes. This is unlikely to change, but some people think Ofcom should flex its regulatory muscles in a variety of new ways. For example, some MPs have suggested that Ofcom should investigate whether children's television programmes cause bullying at school, and the health implications of the marketing on television of fatty foods. Ofcom has said it will consult widely with 'consumers'. Broadcasters hope the new body will encourage good programming and not stifle creativity.

To find out more about Ofcom, you can consult its webpage and write, telephone or email: www.ofcom.org.uk; Ofcom, Riverside House, 2A Southwark Bridge Road, London SE1 9HA; Telephone: 0845 456 3000. There is an email address dedicated to student inquiries: contact@ofcom.org.uk.

## Convergence

Convergence is the coming together of multimedia digital technologies. As soon as audio and video are converted into digital data they can be transmitted by any suitable digital medium. This allows for great flexibility in delivery and storage of data. For example, a computer or a television set linked to a broadband transmission system – satellite, telephone line or cable – becomes an interactive communication module. It is able to download music, video, sophisticated graphics, pay per view films, and offer two-way interactive communication as well as receive broadcast television programmes. There are potential difficulties here for a television regulator as the dividing line between a television programme and other internet content is blurred.

## Watershed

The watershed is a voluntary agreement by all broadcasters on all channels that only programmes suitable for family viewing will be shown before 9.00 pm. This can mean that some films are censored if they start before the watershed, usually by cutting out the use of the 'F word' and reducing the amount of graphic violence. Uncut films with a 15 rating cannot be shown before 8.00 pm even on a dedicated satellite film channel. Films with an 18 rating cannot be shown before 9.00 pm on any channel.

# 3 Public service broadcasting (PSB)

Public service broadcasting is any broadcasting for the benefit of the public and not primarily for profit. In the UK, terrestrial television companies must provide some public service scheduling. This includes news and current affairs programmes and other programming that enlivens the cultural climate. Most developed countries have some degree of public service television funded by a form of licence fee and advertising. In the UK, the BBC provides a sophisticated and comprehensive television, radio and interactive website service to UK citizens solely for the cost of the licence fee, currently £126.50 per year for a colour television. All households with a television receiver are required by law to pay the licence fee. This upsets some people as it is seen as a compulsory tax. However, alternative methods of raising finance for PSB generally involve advertising or subscription fees or both. Governments do not like taxes that do not come to the treasury and are constantly looking for an alternative way to finance PSB, so far without success. A recent Parliamentary review found that funding public service broadcasting by the licence fee was the best and most cost-effective method of maintaining the range and quality of the public service broadcasting provided by the BBC.

## Ofcom and public service broadcasting

The terrestrial commercial television channels have a remit to provide some public service programming and to conform to the guidelines and codes set up by Ofcom. BBC programming on all BBC terrestrial and satellite channels comes under a public service remit regulated by the BBC governors. Ofcom regulates taste and decency in all broadcasting, including BBC radio and television programmes. Ofcom can fine a broadcaster up to £250,000 for serious or repeated breaches of its codes of taste and decency. Early in its life, in 2004, Ofcom censored the BBC for an overtly suggestive dance routine on *Top of the Pops*, although less than ten people complained. It is already being said that Ofcom is being too heavy handed in its regulation and is out of touch with modern culture. Ofcom does not have the power to regulate standards of impartiality and accuracy in BBC programmes. This continues to be regulated by the BBC governors.

In 2004, Ofcom began a comprehensive and far-reaching review of who is doing what in the public service broadcasting arena. This will involve detailed analysis of all the UK public service broadcasters: BBC, ITV1, Channel 4, Five, S4C and all related television services including the extremely popular and comprehensive BBC websites. Broadcasters have been asked to provide details of schedules, content and cost of practically all the programmes they have shown in the public service sphere since 1998. Ofcom is asking 6,000 people about what they want from public service broadcasting. The outcome of this review will feed into the government's review of the BBC Charter. Surveys show that the public always values 'good television programmes'. Public service broadcasting is one way of ensuring this. Until 1982 when Channel 4 began broadcasting there was a duopoly of broadcasters – just the BBC and ITV – with light touch regulation. Now with multichannel commercial television as a strong force there is more regulation. The 2003 Communications Act introduced quotas to ensure that certain types of programmes, such as arts, religious programmes and current affairs, do not disappear from the schedules of commercial television.

The broadcasters will try to ensure that Ofcom is not too prescriptive about exactly what constitutes a public service programme. Certain projects such as the Big Read on BBC caught the public's imagination, and the programmes were both entertaining and educational, making it an ideal public service project. Other projects offer the highest production values from script writing to casting and are both popular and come within a public service remit. For example, ITV1's faithful and excellent adaptation of Thomas Hardy's *The Mayor of Casterbridge* was transmitted in prime-time over the Christmas holidays in 2003. ITV could have placed a less expensive and more lightweight programme in this slot, and perhaps gained a greater audience, but their PSB remit was, in this case, to the viewer's advantage: first-class drama at a convenient time.

In devising their research into public service broadcasting Ofcom have divided PSB into four broad areas:

- programme quality;
- social values;
- diversity of programmes;
- the range and balance of programmes.

Key public service programmes are in the areas of education, political coverage, news, the arts, religion, and the representation of diverse social groups.

## The independence of the BBC

The BBC is an entirely independent organisation. It is run in the interests of its viewers and listeners. Twelve governors regulate it, appointed by the Queen with advice from government ministers. A TV licence fee, paid by every household with a working television set, finances the BBC. The advantage of this form of financing is that the BBC can concentrate on providing high-quality programmes, and interactive services, catering for everyone, including minority groups and organisations, without having to satisfy shareholders looking for profits.

The BBC's governors safeguard its independence. They also set its principal objectives, and approve strategy and policy. They monitor the BBC's performance, publishing an annual report. They are accountable to licence payers and to Parliament. BBC governors represent the public interest, and particularly the interests of viewers and listeners. The BBC has no shareholders and was set up by Royal Charter. The current Royal Charter and Agreement were granted in 1996, and expire in 2006. The process of Charter renewal started in 2004. Governments continue to look at alternatives to the licence fee, and reports by Ofcom on the future funding of the BBC were sent to the government in 2004. One suggestion, known as top slicing, was that 5 per cent of the licence fee should be given to Channel 4 to make public service programmes.

# The role of the BBC

All BBC public services are available to everyone. The BBC runs eight interactive national television channels, ten national radio networks, and over 50 local television and radio services. Some services are on digital platforms only. There is no advertising whatsoever on BBC channels, and editorially the BBC is independent of any commercial or political interests. The BBC receives no revenue from advertising. Commercial radio and television networks derive their revenue from various forms of advertising and commercial sponsorship. BBC programme content covers a very wide range, from distinctive local and national news to live music, original drama, documentaries, children's programmes and entertainment. The BBC is also an important provider of broadcasting and media training. It supports British production skills and talent in music, drama, film, radio and television. Surveys have shown that the BBC is perceived to provide excellent value for money, although it is not without its detractors. It provides an astonishing range of broadcasting on radio and television with two flagship national terrestrial television channels, BBC1 and BBC2.

# Why does the BBC provide online services?

In addition to broadcasting, the BBC runs an interactive online service via the website www.bbc.co.uk. When granting consent to the BBC, in October 1998, for a permanent online service, the Department of Culture, Media and Sport set out three core requirements:

a    to act as an essential resource offering wide-ranging, unique content;

b    to use the internet to forge a new relationship with licence payers and strengthen accountability;

c    to provide a home for licence payers on the internet and act as a trusted guide to the new media environment.

A BBC report to the government in 2003 said:

In the future, the BBC plans to ensure that online services, working closely with BBC Television and Radio, will fulfil their potential to enrich, connect and empower people across the UK. Uniquely among

European public broadcasters the BBC has become a genuinely tri-media organisation, with television, radio and online services all complementing and enhancing each other, enabling far greater delivery of value to licence payers than was ever possible in the age of linear media.

(BBC submission to the Dept of Culture, Media and Sport, 2003)

## News

News is the backbone of public service broadcasting. Modern international news rooms servicing domestic TV news and 24-hour news channels require large amounts of video footage each day. A TV newsroom aims to get up-to-the-minute pictures on the air as soon as possible. This is an extremely competitive business as news channels compete for the first pictures of a breaking news story. The main BBC newsroom in west London currently receives about 300 hours of video every day. The news footage comes in to a new digital newsroom, utilising the latest technology such as the Sony XDCAM disc camcorders. The advantage of the disc camera system is that it records a preview video of the recorded pictures and sound. This can be sent back to the newsroom at up to 50 times real time speed. The material can then be rapidly edited on a laptop, without the need to digitalise all the footage on the tape.

Other 24-hour news channels, such as Sky News, are similarly updating their newsroom technology, and providing faster and more sophisticated on-air and on-line services. Sky News has a particularly fast rolling graphics service.

## Funding public service broadcasting

The main terrestrial television channels available in all homes are regulated by Ofcom. They have to provide elements of public service broadcasting. For the commercial channels there is an obligation to provide a regular, quality news service throughout the day. There are other requirements to do with programmes for minorities. A bone of contention for ITV1 is that they are required to broadcast regular religious programmes, and Ofcom has indicated that it may drop this requirement in the future.

*Figure 3.1* News crew

All broadcasters agree to comply with the 9.00 pm watershed. The BBC is the only public service broadcaster with no commercial funding. It is funded by the licence fee. There have been many attempts to invent an alternative source of funding for what is seen by some as a retrogressive compulsory tax. Other countries such as New Zealand have scrapped the licence fee, and fund all channels with advertising. This has not led to a better service for the viewers. Some European countries keep a smaller licence fee and allow some advertising for their public service channels. Most commentators agree that by accepting advertising the independence of the channel could be compromised.

All the evidence is that the majority of the British public are willing to pay for BBC services at the 2005 level of the licence fee – £126.50 per annum. This guarantees the independence of the BBC and particularly its news and current affairs. Alternative sources of funding include a subscription service. This is how the public service channels in the US are funded, often woefully inadequately. Also subscription undermines the principle of universality, whereby the broadcaster's output is available to everyone. Another idea is to top slice the licence fee, and give some of the money to other broadcasters who have a public service remit. Many broadcasters oppose this as it would confuse the public's idea of what the licence fee is for, and add an intolerable level of extra bureaucracy. There is the risk that public money would benefit shareholders rather than licence payers. Another idea that is often floated is that the BBC should accept advertising. This would reduce the licence fee according to the amount of revenue generated by advertising. The main argument against this is that the revenues of the commercial broadcasters, particularly ITV, Channel 4 and Five, would be severely reduced. Other suggestions include a government grant, rather like a grant to an arts institution such as the National Theatre. It is very difficult to find a better way of funding a public service such as the BBC. Most people agree that because the licence fee is separate from general taxation, and is not a government grant, it reinforces the BBC's independence, and keeps it focused on serving the public.

There is no doubt that BBC services are very popular, reaching over 98 per cent of the UK population every week. Surveys show that viewers prefer radio and television programmes that are not interrupted by advertising. The BBC website with over 2 million pages is one of the most popular in the world, continually winning awards.

# 4 The widescreen world of digital technology

........................................................................................................

New technology has always had a profound effect on television. Television started as a black and white medium transmitting with a screen resolution of 405 lines. This is grainy and lacks impact. Colour television with a resolution of 625 lines was introduced in the 1960s, and the sharper picture and startling realism of colour was instantly a huge success, providing not only a boost for manufacturers but also for the BBC. The colour TV licence was much more expensive than a black and white licence. It generated more revenue and allowed the BBC to open a second channel – BBC2. Current digital technology is also generating changes in all areas of television. Programmes are shot in widescreen format with digital cameras, edited with digital postproduction software on a computer, and transmitted in widescreen format using digital transmission systems. The benefits of recording television pictures in a digital format are enormous including impressive quality, more compact storage, ease-of-use with more possibilities in postproduction. More and more productions are being made in the next generation of digital equipment known as HD – High Definition. In North America more and more programmes are broadcast in HD.

## Television broadcasting goes digital

........................................................................................................

The UK government plans to switch off analogue television transmission by 2012. This means that the way we receive our television pictures through an aerial will change, but this will hardly affect the consumer. Already the digital transmission system Freeview offers the mainstream, terrestrial, digital television channels (BBC1, BBC2, ITV, Channel 4, and Five) via a roof aerial to a large proportion of the UK. Freeview is as its name suggests free, apart from the modest one-off cost of a set-top decoder box. Satellite and cable services offer enhanced multichannel and interactive viewing for a monthly charge of about £20 for the basic service, rising to over £40 per month for on-demand film services and other specialist channels. Freeview offers free digital terrestrial transmission (DTT) to most of the UK. Where households cannot receive Freeview the BBC is proposing to collaborate with other suppliers to supply free TV via satellite. Sky has already announced a Freesat service. This is very attractive to the government who would like to sell off the analogue channels currently used for TV transmission.

The BBC is at the forefront of this digital revolution. In its manifesto for the future published in June 2004 in the lead-up to the renewal of its Charter in 2005, the BBC says it intends:

> to be at the leading edge of the new era and is building its case on free services … the BBC stands for public value and this may involve taking a large share of the responsibility for creating a digital Britain – not just for its own services, but on behalf of the public and the rest of the industry.

The BBC says it can help the UK become a fully digital nation because of the appeal of its content, and the trust the public has in its brand. Some people think the BBC is too large, and should only offer a narrow range of services. The BBC's manifesto for the future issued in July 2004 puts a persuasive argument for keeping the Corporation as it is: 'First there is little evidence to suggest the BBC depresses the commercial success of the rest of the UK industry. Second, the BBC accounts for fewer than a quarter of UK revenues compared with 46% nine years ago (1996)' (BBC Online).

The BBC is putting a large emphasis on education. It intends using interactive technology to transform people's ability to learn at their own pace, and in their own time. In 2006, the BBC with commercial partners will launch an online digital curriculum. This will cover the key elements of the school curriculum, and be made available, free, to every school in the UK.

## Digital technology

The term digital refers to the fingers and thumbs used in ancient times for counting, and is associated with whole numbers. Digital technology is a way of representing data – such as video pictures and sound – in a digital, binary form (information encoded using two values: one or zero, on or off). These data can be encoded in a series of electronic pulses, and in electronic circuits such as are found in a computer, switches are either on or off. Data that are encoded digitally have distinct values allowing no variables. To make a number of value greater than one, combinations of binary digits are used, known as bits. For example, two bits give four combinations of ones and zeros: 00, 01, 10, 11. Eight bits have 256 combinations of ones and zeros. So it is possible to build up a digital stream of numbers that represent any value.

These streams have distinct values, which means they are stable. With digital technology more data can be transmitted over the same physical links. These links can be cables, fibre optics, satellite or TV transmission. Fast ISDN telephone systems allow higher and more efficient internet usage. They are more accurate, with more data being transferred in shorter times. There are many important advantages of using digital technology in television and video. It allows audio and video recording with none of the electronic noise or distortion found using tape analogue systems. There is no loss of quality no matter how many copies are made from the same digital master. Pictures and sound recorded as digital data can be manipu-lated for an extraordinary variety of video effects, from wipes and dissolves to computer-generated animation (CGA) found in films such as *The Lord of the Rings*. Digital technology is now standard throughout television production, from recording through postproduction to final transmission.

## Digital video

A digital video camera or camcorder employs CCDs – typically a quarter of an inch in size – to collect and process light coming in from the lens. A CCD (charge-coupled diode) is a supersensitive light sensor that converts the light into an electric signal, and high-quality television cameras have three CCDs. A prism inside the lens barrel splits incoming light into the primary colours, red, green and blue (RGB). Each colour goes to a different CCD. This gives superb colour reproduction and image quality. Cheaper cameras have just one CCD. This is fine for domestic camcorders, but does not give a high enough resolution for broadcast TV. At the heart of a CCD is a complex grid made up of pixels which process

*Figure 4.1* Broadcast-standard digital camcorders

the electronic signals and make up the picture. Pixels vary in quality and capability. It is not always true that the more pixels in a digital camera or camcorder, the better the picture resolution.

## Digital sound recording

The digital audio recording process involves sampling sound into binary code. The sound is usually encoded into 16-bit PCM (pulse code modulation) and sampled at 44,100 Hz. This is the configuration most commonly used for compact discs. (Hertz, or cycles per second, is a measurement of the frequency, or pitch, of sound waves. Orchestras tune to the note A, which has a frequency of 440 Hz). The physical sound waves produced, by the voice of a TV presenter for example, are picked up by a microphone. The sound is sampled by using PAM (pulse amplitude modulation). This means the amplitude of the waveform is measured many thousands of times a second to produce a digital value that can be stored on tape, CD or DVD. A typical 16-bit sample will have 65,356 levels of clarity. This can be read and reconfigured as electrical waves that can be heard through a loudspeaker.

The most obvious advantage of digital audio is that the sound recorded is very hard to corrupt, compared to analogue recording systems. Digital data are measured as electrical pulses, either on or off. When different pieces of electrical equipment 'talk' to each other there is very little chance of a misunderstanding, as they deal with definite values. Therefore, the copy of a master recording will be a precise clone of the original recording. The data are digital so it is easy to copy the data in bulk. This is an extremely fast process that does not need to be done in real time, as making analogue copies does, and uses less space. Using high-end microphones and recording equipment – such as a Nagra digital recorder – the recorded sound has impressive clarity and fidelity to the original. There is no electrical noise or hum, and the equipment can be light in weight. Even using inexpensive kit, digital recording offers clarity, portability and easy transfer of data to formats such as MP3 or minidisc.

## Television transmission

The invention of radio demonstrated that sound waves can be converted into electromagnetic waves, and broadcast over great distances to radio

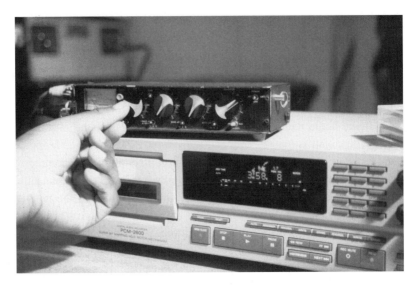

*Figure 4.2* Digital audio recorder and mixer

receivers. Similarly a television camera converts the colour and brightness information of the moving image into electrical signals that can be transmitted to TV receivers at home, or recorded in a digital domain on tape, disc or computer. These television signals are converted into frames of data, and projected at a rate fast enough so that the human eye perceives continuous motion.

There are three forms of TV signal encoding for broadcasting:

- Nearly all of Europe uses the PAL (phase alternate line) system with a resolution of 625 lines. Each separate frame is drawn line by line, from top to bottom. Using a typical European 50 hertz alternating current, it draws 50 lines per second, but it takes two passes to draw a complete frame. The frame rate is therefore 25 frames per second (fps).

- France, Russia and some Eastern European countries use the French system SECAM (Séquential Couleur Avec Mémoire).

- The US and Japan use a system called NTSC (National Television Standards Committee). This system uses 525 lines and runs at 30 fps, and was developed from the electric current used in the US, which alternates at 60 hertz.

These are all analogue systems. In the UK, the government wants to 'turn off' analogue transmission systems, and use only digital transmission by about 2010. Sky TV already transmits only in digital format. In the US, the government has said that it will switch off analogue transmission in 2006.

# Digital broadcasting

Throughout the UK and in much of Europe and the US, digital technology is now used to record and transmit television pictures and sound. An analogue to digital converter (ADC) will convert analogue signals into binary data. As in digital sound recording the process is achieved by sampling. This is also known as video capture. To view digital video on a traditional television set, the process has to be reversed. A digital to analogue converter (DAC) is required to decode the binary data back into an analogue signal that a domestic TV can understand. Digital data are more stable and use a much smaller transmission bandwidth than analogue. This frees up the airways for other uses, and makes transmission cheaper. Several digital channels can be bundled together on a digital transmission multiplex, offering higher quality vision, stereo sound, interactive services and multichannel viewing.

In 1993 in Europe the DVB (Digital Video Broadcasting) project was set up. This provides a forum for suppliers to agree specifications, which then go to existing standards-making bodies for ratification. A decision was made to use the computer digital standard MPEG-2. This operates at about half the data rate of DVD, but MPEG-2 video offers a much better picture than analogue TV. There are other benefits such as error correction that eliminates snow and ghosting. The video carried by digital TV is compressed, and is transmitted digitally in accordance with one of a number of DVB specified modulation standards. In the UK, the digital terrestrial system known as Freeview uses six MPEG-2 TV multiplexes. Each one carries around six channels. Bandwidth is also available for a Super Teletext service which promises image-rich interactive applications via MHEG3 (Multimedia and Hypertext Expert Group). The advantage of digital transmission is that it can make use of unused spectrum otherwise unsuitable for TV.

Digital TV offers many benefits for the viewer. One channel can present different programme feeds such as camera angles for a sporting event like motor racing or football. The viewer can select the point of view by changing to a different feed within the channel. Films or other programmes can be broadcast at several times during a day, offering the viewer a choice of time to view. Already, interactive TV services are proving very popular. The viewer can select a different ending to a movie, or select an answer to a question during a distance learning programme with the choice resulting in positive feedback, or a further explanation of the topic. Different camera positions can be selected during sports broadcasts, or different activities at a multisport event such as the Olympics. Digital TV's interactivity has already been used by many viewers to vote via the remote control for their favourite pop idol or celebrity game show contestant. Television today is poised at the threshold of significant changes in technology, organisation and viewing experience.

## Further reading

Bignell, J., *An Introduction to Television Studies* (London: Routledge, 2004).

Branston, G. and R. Stafford, *The Media Student's Book*, 2nd edn (London: Routledge, 1999).

Brunsdon, C., 'What is the Television of Television Studies?', in C. Geraghty and D. Lusted (eds), *The Television Studies Book* (London: Arnold, 1998), pp. 95–113.

Burton, G., *Talking Television: An Introduction to the Study of Television* (London: Arnold, 2000).

Caughie, J., 'Television Criticism: A Discourse in Search of an Object', *Screen* 25: 4–5 (1984), pp. 109–20.

Corner, J., *Television Form and Public Address* (London: Arnold, 1995).

Corner, J., *Studying Media: Problems of Theory and Method* (London: Arnold, 1998).

Corner, J., *Critical Ideas in Television Studies* (Oxford: Clarendon, 1999).

Corner, J. and S. Harvey (eds), *Television Times: A Reader* (London: Arnold, 1996).

Creeber, G. (ed.), *The Television Genre Book* (London: BFI, 2001).

Fiske, J., *Television Culture* (London: Routledge, 1992).

Geraghty, C. and D. Lusted (eds), *The Television Studies Book* (London: Arnold, 1998).

Goodwin, A. and G. Whannel (eds), *Understanding Television* (London: Routledge, 1990).

Mackay, H. and T. O'Sullivan (eds), *The Media Reader: Continuity and Transformation* (London: Sage, 1999).

McQueen, D., *Television: A Media Student's Guide* (London: Arnold, 1998).

Scannell, P., 'Public Service Broadcasting: The History of a Concept', in A. Goodwin and G. Whannel (eds), *Understanding Television* (London: Routledge, 1990), pp. 11–29.

Selby, K. and R. Cowdery, *How to Study Television* (Basingstoke: Macmillan, 1995).

# Part II

# **Working in television**

The television industry has a large variety of jobs in the production and operational areas as well as in administrative areas. It is useful to divide the jobs in programme making into two main areas: production jobs and technical jobs.

There is crossover in some areas especially in operating portable equipment such as camera and sound kit. For a production to work successfully both sets of personnel need to work harmoniously together. As multi-skilling becomes the norm on small productions there is often very little distinction between the two. However, to work in a technical area for a broadcast company, you need skills, training and television experience. If you are thinking of going into television it is a good idea to have knowledge of both areas.

# 5 Production jobs

To get a television programme off the ground you need a team of hard-working enthusiasts who can pool their skills and experience. This team is known as 'production'. Television is a producer-led medium and **the producer** is the head of a television production team. He or she starts the process of creating a show, and then goes about getting the money to make the show, and selecting the production personnel. It is the producer who selects the writer, and also picks the technical crew with the assistance of the director. The producer has overall responsibility for everything to do with the show. This includes the key matter of the budget, as well as health and safety considerations for location filming and for actually getting the programme on the air. This is a creative job for a flexible, seasoned and experienced professional, and well worth aspiring to. It is the producer who has the creative power and delivers the programmes. It is the producer who takes the blame, enjoys the fame, and accepts the BAFTA.

**The director** works closely with the producer, and is responsible for staging the show and directing performers and technical crew. The exact role depends on the genre of the show, and the way it is made.

## TV drama director

For a television drama shot on location the director will cast the actors, and direct them on the set. He or she will create the overall look of the production by working closely with the camera crew. Directing is largely about creating an enthusiastic, dynamic working relationship with a variety of other professionals who are all working hard to realise your ideas, so good communication is the key. The director needs to know exactly how a scene is to be shot, and then communicate this to the actors, and the technical team. Before coming on set the director will have fine-tuned the script, and created a storyboard. This will give everyone a clear idea of what is going to be shot, and how a scene may be cut together in editing. He or she will supervise the editing, select the music, work closely with the production manager and make sure the production is of the highest quality for the broadcast slot.

A **TV studio director**'s main job is to direct a multicamera studio set-up. This will involve creating a camera script, rehearsing front of camera talent (the performers) and some involvement with the content and look of the show. A studio show may go out live, or be recorded as live, so the director's job is crucial on the day of recording. However, much of the preproduction will be set up by a large production team headed by the producer. Before the studio day the director will create a camera script. This is a complex document that assigns each shot to a camera, and sets out precisely how each shot will look, where music will come in and how videotape inserts will be integrated into the programme. Live sports shows rely on the director's ability to follow the action, and cut to the correct camera at the right time. This is a job that needs lightning quick reflexes, a calm and measured way of working and an understanding of what the viewer needs to see at any one time. It is not for the faint-hearted.

## Factual programme director

More and more documentary and factual programmes are produced and directed by the same person. This is not just a cost-cutting development. Modern digital equipment and processes have cut down the production time needed to make a programme. One person doing both jobs can be in a better position to make fast decisions, and take quick action, especially when working with a small team on location. More independent companies are making mainstream programmes. This allows specialist programme makers to create their own style of programming and offer the networks reasonably priced factual or reality programming – e.g. all those programmes about relocating to somewhere sunny abroad.

# What makes a good director?

The main criteria for becoming a television director are the ability to understand and communicate the inner meaning of a script or programme idea, and visualise the action in a filmic way. This means seeing in your mind how each line of the script will appear on the screen. You will need to understand and be able to develop characterisation, narrative and the language of directing. You have to be able to compress ten minutes or ten years into a few screen moments. You have to give the audience clues about character and back-story without being obvious. You have to be aware of pace, timing and structure, as well as unravelling what the script is all about. You need to think of how to shoot a scene in the most economical way. Only Hollywood has huge budgets.

# Are you a TV director?

Try doing this exercise. Show how you would shoot these scenes for maximum dramatic effect. Draw stick men pictures inside a TV frame (a storyboard) to tell the story visually. There is no dialogue.

- *Drama.* A blonde woman in a mask holds up a bank while her boyfriend/accomplice waits on a motorcycle nearby. They make off with the money but leave a tell-tale object behind.

- *Drama.* A young man flies to Venice for an important business meeting. He agrees to start a mysterious job. He has to tell his girlfriend back in London that he cannot make the wedding of her best friend, set for two days' time. Work out how you can shoot this scene economically to bring out the main character's inner motivation.

- *Factual programme.* You are interviewing a well-known celebrity. You are in a major city. You can do the interview in a hotel room. Describe what other shots you need, so that you do not just have a talking head. What can you ask your celebrity to do to make the interview interesting? What locations can you use?

See Part IV for details of filming and storyboarding.

## Researcher

A researcher in television is often the first production job for a new recruit into the business. In fact, this is a demanding and absorbing job that requires a number of skills. A researcher must be good with people, able to come up with stunning ideas for a programme, and have excellent organisational skills. This is not the same as a simple academic research task such as logging on to Google and finding out who won the Oscars last year. Your main job for most factual programmes is to actually find people to take part in TV programmes. This takes patience, stamina and lateral thinking. You need an extraordinary ability to persuade people to take part in a television programme they may never have heard of.

Look at the schedules of the terrestrial broadcasters. Any day of the week includes programmes with so-called 'real' people. Diligent researchers have unearthed all these contributors. It appears to be less difficult to persuade someone to take part in a programme than it used to be, but finding suitable, interesting subjects can still take an enormous amount of telephoning. You must keep a list of anyone you have contacted. You must be scrupulous in checking facts, and checking all personal details to avoid bogus contributors.

Broadcasters and production companies require researchers with some experience to make short films or items from inception to transmission. You may be taken on as a researcher, but you must be able to think up, budget, research, shoot and off-line edit a story entirely on your own. This is multiskilling. You will need to keep the producer informed of what you are doing and how it is going at all stages. You will need to be able to write a treatment, and show that you can deliver the item for the allocated – probably very small – budget. When going for an interview it is a good idea to have a file of possible stories, and good ideas, relevant to the programme genre of the company.

## Production assistant

The PA works closely with the producer and the director on the paperwork for all types of production. She, and it is nearly always a woman, is a formidable communicator, and an essential part of every production.

She will work on the shooting schedule, set up filming and will be involved in the day-to-day activities of the production team. She may well do much of the research. On a factual programme the PA organises flights, books hotels, hires cars and deals with the budget. She will ensure contributors sign release forms, as well as organising location permissions.

On a drama the PA's role is more specialised. She will be closely involved with the production of the script. She will work on scheduling the whole shoot with the production manager. Some shoots may require her to look after continuity on set. She will be responsible for drawing up a comprehensively marked-up editing script after each day's shoot.

## Production manager

The Production Manager is in charge of resources for a production, and is answerable to the producer. He or she works closely with the director. This is an essential and important job in producing a drama. Before filming begins you need to be able to budget and schedule complex activities, and aim to save money wherever possible. Responsibilities include managing locations, scheduling the film crew, negotiating daily rates and terms of technical contracts, being responsible for health and safety and insurance, and arranging technical facilities. This means getting the crew, the actors and everyone else to turn up at the right time in the right place. Then if it rains, or a leading actor is ill, thinking on your feet and getting the whole show to another location. You need to be cool and calm under stress, and brilliant at organisation. You also need to be up to speed with the latest technical developments and costs in the industry. The PM will be involved with finding locations, drawing up the shooting schedule, the daily call sheets, and seeking permissions from land owners, the police and local authorities. For someone entering the television industry this is a job to only aspire to, as it requires a great deal of experience. One way towards becoming a production manager is to work first as a runner and then as an Assistant Director (AD). Second or third ADs are often involved in directly helping the production manager with everything from daily schedules to setting up locations.

## Profile | **Production manager**
Robin Small

**Robin Small is a production manager working on factual programmes and television drama.**

Programme making for television is a strictly accountable activity, taking place within tight deadlines. The production manager's priority is to make sure that everything happens on time and on budget. The scale of the task can vary from a full fiction shoot on an overseas location lasting several months, to a camcorder video diary shot in a day. The same basic principles apply, even though their application will be different. A good production manager will have a complete knowledge of equipment and production services, and be an excellent communicator. On occasions he or she will also need diplomatic skills to soothe troubled waters and deal with frayed nerves.

In an ideal world, production management is a planned activity, requiring much anticipation and preparation. This is fine in theory but, in practice, production for television has always involved tight deadlines and budgets. It demands a balancing act between the creative aims of the production team and the practical requirements of the executive producers who want a finished programme delivered on time, and the programme accountants who want it delivered on budget. This means that an essential skill for a production manger is to be able to prioritise on a daily basis. The skills of planning can be learnt, but it would be foolish to pretend that this is all that you need to be a good production manager. There is no substitute for experience.

## Runner

A runner works to the production manager on the set, and 'runs' for anything that is needed at the time. Many professionals working on television dramas say that this job is the best way to learn the business. Certainly, you see every aspect of the production by actually being on set nearly all the time. However, you do not usually see how a production is set up in preproduction, or the editing process in postproduction. It is worth asking for work experience in these areas.

# Assistant producer

This is a post usually found on factual productions. As the title suggests the main function is to work closely with the producer. The assistant producer on a factual series is often the director and researcher and even the editor. He or she will research and set up a story, shoot it, edit it, and then finalise the graphics and music in postproduction. On a studio-based programme the assistant producer is often the studio director. Large broadcasting companies such as the BBC employ assistant producers on many productions. The next step up for a researcher can be to assistant producer. The post is very good training to be a studio or location director, and/or a television producer.

An assistant producer needs skills and experience in television production, some of which may be gained with work experience, and on a good practical degree course in media production. This is unlikely to be a first job. If you really want to work in factual programming and for a large TV company then this is the job to aim for. It helps if you have expertise in another area. Large TV companies run factual programme strands such as science, the arts, gardening, motoring, travel, history and wildlife. Newer areas include the housing market, archaeology, leisure and tourism, collecting and antiques, and all the social areas of 'reality' TV. You may have a particular interest in British cinema, or energy and the environment, or vintage cars. This is worth highlighting on your CV. It is worth thinking up programme ideas based on any expertise you have in any area, however obscure, and writing them down as short one-page treatments.

# Assistant director (AD)

ADs are usually found on drama shoots. There are several ADs, and the nearest to an assistant producer is the important post of first AD, who does much of the organisational work on a shoot. The first AD can line up shots, set up locations, supervise rehearsals and be responsible for the actors. The first AD is assisted by the second AD, the third AD and, on large shoots, the fourth AD. Each has a specific role. Often the third AD is in charge of the extras. This can mean marshalling large crowds or making sure a few extras are in exactly the right place for a shot. The fourth AD can be a suitable job for a trainee, often helping the third AD.

## Production executives

Any large-scale television production will have an **executive producer** (EP). This is the person who has originally commissioned the programme, and has sanctioned the budget. You may never see the EP on the set, but the EP will have had an important role in setting up the show. In television the EP will probably work within a genre such as documentary, programming for young people, reality television, arts, current affairs or science. He or she will have a certain number of shows to deliver, and is always looking to commission new ideas and talent.

Another important role especially on an expensive drama is the **associate producer**. The associate producer is heavily involved in devising a realistic budget in preproduction, and has a large say in the way the budget is spent. The associate producer can be responsible for increasing funding for a particular series through co-production with a broadcaster from another country. This is important for public service broadcasters, who aim to make impressive programmes but have limited budgets. The associate producer on any production will be looking to arrange deals for technical resources, as well as ways of maximising sales of the finished product in order to bring cash into the production.

# 6 Technical jobs

## Lighting cameraperson

This role is also often known as the **director of photography** (DOP), and is the supervising cameraperson who works with the director to achieve a distinctive 'look' for a production. The DOP is in charge of the technical crew on a location set.

On a large production, such as a drama, the DOP will work with the chief electrician, and supervise the team of electricians (sparks) to set up the lighting for a scene. This may involve dozens of different lights; all need to be carefully placed not to cast shadows that may be 'in shot', and to light the area where the action takes place. The DOP will work with the **camera operator** to select the right lens, the most suitable camera mounting – dolly, tripod or steadicam, and any lens filters for a scene, as well as actually framing the shot. The camera operator will move the camera, operate the controls, and is responsible for the technical quality of the pictures. On a small production the DOP will operate the camera as well as supervise the electricians to position the lights, place reflectors, and light the scene according to the mood suggested by the director. On a small factual programme shoot for television the camera operator will operate a digital camera, and carry a set of lights to light small areas such as a room for an interview. In news, the camera operator will operate a camera with a light attached to it, or carry a battery-powered light for street interviews.

## Camera assistant

This job is a good way of learning the skills of being a good camera operator. He or she makes sure batteries are charged, loads and labels tapes or discs, and sets up the camera with the correct timecode at the beginning of the shooting day. The camera assistant might also be the **focus puller** on a shoot (setting the correct focus for a shot). He or she does a lot of carrying of equipment such as tripods, lenses and batteries.

## Sound recordist

The sound recordist is in charge of recording all the location sound. For television he or she uses a small portable sound mixer that receives the output from the microphones either by wire or radio link. The mixer is cabled to the camera. The sound is recorded onto the digital tape or disc in the camera. For drama productions made on film, the sound recordist will work with a portable sound recorder such as a Nagra and record a separate sound track. A clapper board is used to later put the recorded sound 'in sync' with the actors' lip movements. Two or more microphones can be set up and the sound monitored by the recordist on headphones. Television programmes are recorded in stereo. The sound recordist is not just responsible for sound quality. He or she ensures that there is no overlapping sound – voices talking over each other – in interviews or in drama, and that there is a good balance between background sound and speech. The aim is to deliver clean uncluttered sound to the editor, that retains the ambience of the location and the full resonance of the speech.

## Sound assistant

He or she works with the sound recordist setting up microphones, operating sound equipment in the TV studio sound gallery, and holding the mic boom on location. If you are interested in sound and have some knowledge of microphones, this can be a good first job.

## Gaffer

This is a term (deriving from feature film-making) for the chief electrician on a shoot who is responsible for all the other electricians operating lights and lighting equipment. He or she works with the DOP to light a scene. Electricians working on lighting in television are qualified electricians, or in training to qualify.

# Grip

The grip is a member of the camera crew, and works to the DOP or lighting camera operator. The main function of the grip is to set up the camera dolly, and lay the track for the dolly. The grip will also move the camera along the track smoothly at the required speed, stopping at exactly the right point. He or she needs experience and knowledge of video/film cameras.

## Profile | Camera operator and technician: a first job in television
Daniel Barnard, 22

Daniel's first job, after studying for a degree in Media Technology from Farnborough College of Technology in North Hampshire, is to work for Aerial Camera Systems. The company is currently based in Surrey and operates all over the country.

*Figure 6.1* Profile: Daniel Barnard

I went straight into this job from leaving university. I have just completed my first six months training. I really enjoy the job because it is varied and I am working on live productions. At university I learned how to set up and make television programmes, so that when I meet other professionals I know what they do and I don't get in their way. All the theory was useful too. The practical part of my degree is really useful to my work. I know how to plug up equipment. I worked on many live radio programmes on the College's radio station. I really like the flexibility and quick reactions you need for a live TV sport transmission. The TV studio work helped too – I know what the director is talking about when he calls for shots – it gives you confidence.

A typical day is to drive with a colleague in a company van to the McAlpine stadium in Huddersfield for a rugby match, with pan and tilt remote control cameras. We fit a camera in each dressing room and test them for the evening transmission. We stay overnight and then travel really early to Sunderland's Stadium of Light to fit our remote cameras behind the goal. We check the cameras all morning, and rehearse with the live match director until transmission in the afternoon. You have to be able to sort something out if it goes wrong. We work for BBC Sport, Sky Sports, ITV and C4.

I got into television because of that feeling of liveness. An inner feeling of enjoyment working to a live audience. If there is a downside it is the long hours away from home. This is a young person's job. The great thing is you concentrate hard when you are working, but afterwards you get a whole day off with no paperwork. We also do foreign trips which I am really looking forward to.

The interview for the job was quite easy. They asked me if I could operate a camera, what my interests are, and did I mind being away from home. The company get at least half a dozen CVs a week, but few people actually follow up their CV. This job was advertised on the College notice board. My work experience at Southampton FC television service helped a lot. I would really like to stay with the company as there are many opportunities to learn different skills. There are different sorts of remote controlled cameras. We have specially shock proofed cameras for putting on helicopters for movies, or the Olympics blimp. There's the computer system we have for writing on the screen. They use it on Channel 4's cricket to show where the ball has gone. Lots to learn. It's great to have such a varied and interesting job.

# 7 Working in a television studio

M aking a television programme in a TV studio involves a number of specific jobs that are only found on a multicamera shoot. Studio production is still an important part of the output of many broadcasting companies, especially ITV, BBC and Sky. A wide variety of different programmes are made in a studio. There are music shows such as *Top of the Pops*, quizzes such as *Mastermind*, celebrity interviews such as *Parkinson*, daytime chat shows, children's programmes and situation comedies. Many live sports shows come from a studio as all the technical equipment is in place to integrate the graphics, presenters and guests with the live or recorded action. News also comes from a dedicated news studio that has remote cameras and few technical staff.

## Studio floor

The studio floor is where the action that is to be recorded takes place. It is a large flat area with a grid of computerised overhead lights. Depending on the type of programme, there will be a set. This may be a 'box set' with chairs for the presenters and their guests, or a quiz show set-up, placed within a three-sided set. The cameras, usually at least five, will record the show largely from the open side of the set. There may also be an audience.

On the floor are technical operators. These are camera operators, sound assistants and lighting assistants. The **floor manager** (FM) is in charge of everything that happens on the floor. He or she liaises between the studio

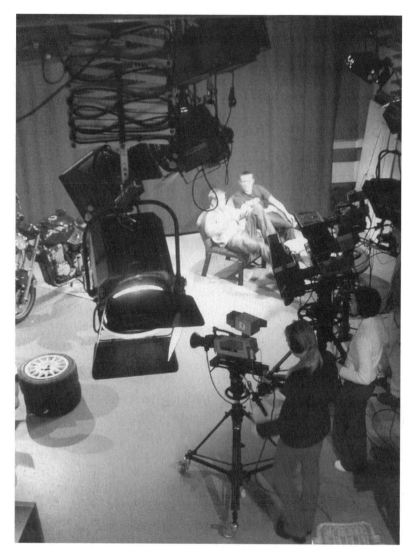

*Figure 7.1* Television studio

director and the presenters or performers, and is helped by one or more assistant floor managers (AFM). An art or design director will look after the artistic side of the set. Stage hands will move set or scenery as required. Other personnel found on the studio floor can include an autocue operator, make-up artist and costume designer.

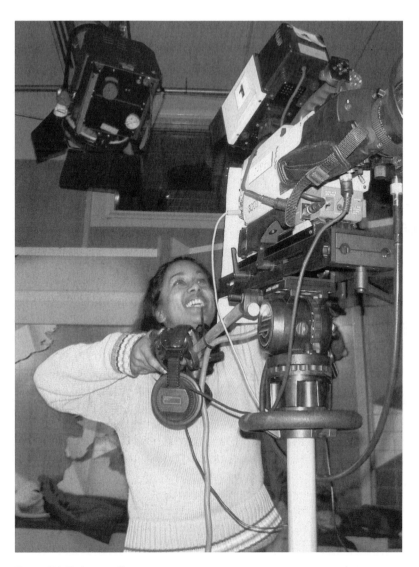

*Figure 7.2* Trainee studio camera operator

The floor manager has the very responsible job of being in charge of the entire studio floor, from health and safety to the movement of performers, and the audience. He or she communicates with the director in the gallery via a two-way headset, and can hear 'talkback' from the gallery. He or she delivers notes to the on-screen talent from the director, cues the presenter and winds up interviews when time runs out. AFMs help the floor manager by collecting guests from dressing rooms, and looking after the needs of the presenters and guests.

## Studio gallery

This is the control room of the studio floor. It is typically located in an upstairs area that looks down on the studio floor. The most striking feature of a gallery is the large bank of dozens of TV monitors facing a long curved switching desk. Here the whole production is directed by the studio director. This is a fast moving, complex job. The studio director prepares a studio script. This is a written version of the complete show. It is based around the dialogue script, and indicates where everything is positioned on the studio and all the technical requirements. It includes everything the technical team and the production team need to know to record the show. This includes the dimensions of the set, camera positions and angles, shot sizes and cut points, as well as details of previously recorded material for the show. The first thing the studio director does is to go through the script with the technical crew and the presenters. He or she gives instructions to the FM through the talkback system.

Sitting on the left of the director is the **production assistant** (PA) from the production. This is an interesting and demanding job that can only be learned through experience. Qualifications include excellent word processing, terrific sense of timing, the ability to bar count in music, and a calm disposition. You may be counting out a live programme into a live news bulletin that must run accurately on the hour.

Sitting on the right of the studio director is the **vision mixer**. The vision mixer operates a bank of high-tech buttons and switches. These are linked to the output of the studio cameras, and any other sources such as videotape machines (VT), or outside broadcast (OB) cameras. The vision mixer selects the desired picture from the bank of monitors and cuts, mixes or wipes between each picture. The pictures can be manipulated using digital video effects (DVE) to create chromakey and other visual effects. Qualities needed to be a good vision mixer include a sense of rhythm and timing, a feeling for visual composition, a clear calm temperament and ability to work live, and under pressure.

Other personnel working in the gallery area of a TV studio are the **sound supervisor**, **technical manager**, and **vision controller**. The sound supervisor operates a multi-channel sound mixing desk, usually in a sepa-rate soundproofed area, and manages the team of sound assistants who may be on the studio floor or working in the sound gallery. The technical manager is in charge of the final technical quality of the programme, and the complex technical requirements for the whole studio. This includes ordering special electronic equipment, checking the technical quality of outside links (e.g. satellite) coming into the studio, and making sure the programme is recorded onto the required format of tape or disc. The vision controller monitors the technical quality of the picture from each studio camera and other sources, and adjusts it so that colour, contrast and luminance are uniform throughout the programme.

## Specialist jobs in television

Many other personnel contribute to the making of a television programme. Depending on the type of show there will be people from make up, graphic design, costume, as well as a property buyer – for on-set moveable props – and an art designer for making and maintaining the set. Nearly all these personnel have assistants.

If you are interested in any of these areas it is often possible to gain work experience as an assistant to see whether that area of television production is for you. If you are interested then apply for a job as a full-time assistant. You will need a media friendly CV. All jobs in television attract a large number of applications especially if they are advertised in *The Guardian* newspaper, one of the main sources of media jobs. Job applications should not just indicate your interest in a job. You will need to highlight the extent of your work experience in that particular area. It is no good going for a job as a sound assistant if you know nothing about how sound is recorded, or lack basic knowledge about microphones. The company will expect you to have some experience of working with a sound recordist on location or in a TV studio. You will want to personalise your CV according to your skills, experience and qualifications. (See pp. 52–3.)

If you would like to work in television production there are various ways you can gain work experience to see whether this is the industry that appeals to you. A good place to start is at the industry's training forum Skillset, whose website is www.skillset.org. They publish *A Career Handbook for TV, Radio, Film, Video and Interactive Media*, by Shiona Llewellyn and Sue Walker.

Part of the same organisation is www.skillsformedia.com which has a lot of information about entering or progressing in the media industry. This includes case studies that offer the inside story. Skillsformedia is the UK's only specialist media careers advice service delivering individual career solutions in all areas of broadcasting, film, radio, video and interactive media. Skillsformedia is owned and managed by the audiovisual industries through Skillset, the Sector Skills Council and BECTU, the industry's trade union.

**Profile** : **Assistant video editor: a second job in television**

Matthew Loxterkamp, 23

**Matthew is in his second job in the media since leaving university. His aim is to work in the film industry, and he now works in postproduction on British films.**

*Figure 7.3* Profile: Matthew Loxterkamp

Matthew studied practical television and film at university. He was particularly interested in film studies. Looking around for a part time job in the media industry, he took on part time work at BAFTA in

London. They wanted help with organising all their archive material collected since the BAFTA awards began in 1947. When Matthew's degree course finished BAFTA took him on full time to continue putting all the photos, videos, and press cuttings into an accessible archive. He found the work gave him a chance to improve his knowledge of British film and television and work in a professional environment. He designed a database for the archive, and then in spring 2004 found himself out of a job. The BAFTA building was being completely renovated and the archive was stored elsewhere.

Wanting to keep on working with film and TV, he sent out 87 emails and mailed 41 CVs to directors, TV production managers and a few film producers. He received 20 emails in reply, but none offering him any work. They said they would keep his CV on file. Eventually he saw an advertisement for a trainee assistant video editor with Vertigo films in Kentish Town, London. This company had a good track record of editing films including *Human Traffic* and *Football Factory*. The job offered turned out to be four weeks' work experience, with only expenses paid. Learning editing techniques on Final Cut Pro and AVID, he was able to bring his experience of graphics work with Photoshop to help create press material for the company's films. This and his impressive interpersonal skills led the company to offer him a more permanent job as an assistant video editor. Matthew says: 'It helped that I know Photoshop and that I was able to show that I was competent with editing software. Even though I didn't know the particular one they were using'.

Matthew is very aware of how hard it is to get that first job: 'It's all about personality. You need to be adaptable and get on with everybody from day one. I wrote everything the editor told me down, so that I wouldn't forget anything. The editor liked the fact that I knew about film analysis and character and plot – so the media degree course was worth it just for that. He asks my opinion. He seems to like my input on the film he is editing, but I am careful what I say!'

Matthew is using this job as experience in order to move into drama production.

'My ambition is to try and work on major movies or TV dramas. I feel that if I don't give it a really good shot now then I would always regret it. You don't go into this business for the money. I only earn £200 a week, and the hours are very long. But I am getting priceless experience, and working with really nice people.'

# 8 Working in postproduction

....................................................................

M uch of the work in creating a television programme happens after all the material has been shot. This is the process of postproduction. At the core of this process is the editing of the programme. This is the stage where the fragmented shots and sequences are brought together and reassembled into the illusion of three-dimensional space that we know as broadcast television. Editing brings together different perspectives on the same scene and balances the pictures and the sound to create a cohesive whole. It is essential in creating the narrative thrust of a programme, since editing decisions guide the audience through the movement of sound and images that make up the programme.

There are many employment opportunities within the postproduction area. The main job is **video editor**. A video editor will typically have several years experience as an assistant video editor, or in some other area of video postproduction. The job requires a very good sense of narrative and picture composition, a profound understanding of the medium and some technical ability. Modern editing for television is a non-linear, digital, computerised process that allows the editor an extraordinary amount of freedom in creating the finished programme from the filmed material. There are a number of industry standard software systems for video editing. AVID is one of the best known, and has systems for editing drama, news and factual programmes. Apple produces the iMovie software, and the dedicated professional Final Cut Pro, which is popular with many editors. Adobe Premiere is an effective system for low-budget productions, or for home editing. Whether on digital video tape or disc the editor sees pictures on a monitor, and manipulates them with a mouse and a keyboard. Large broadcasting companies have their own teams of video editors both off-line and on-line.

Many people working in television production found their first job in the postproduction area. These are often at facilities houses. A facilities house is a commercial company offering a range of TV production facilities for hire on a daily or hourly rate. Some companies offer solely video editing suites and equipment, while others offer all the equipment you need for the full postproduction process including sound dubbing. An assistant may be helping with the collection of tapes, or setting up and loading videotape machines or transferring rushes for clients. Some of the work may be copying tapes, looking after clients, opening the mail, and helping around the office. It is all good experience. Postproduction also includes sound dubbing where the final sound mix is created in a specialist dubbing suite from the original rushes. There is possible work here as a sound assistant where knowledge of sound/music mixing is essential.

## Television production companies

Until the advent of Channel 4, most television programmes were made in-house by the broadcasting companies. Channel 4 is not a producer of programmes. It is effectively a publisher as all its output is contracted from outside production companies. Over 25 per cent of the BBC's television production is now made outside the organisation, and this has led to the growth of small and large production companies often specialising in one genre of programme. *Lion TV* in west London, for example, make a wide variety of factual programmes for terrestrial and satellite broadcasting companies. Other companies such as *Hat Trick* are known for their comedy output.

There are many smaller companies working on just one or two commissions at any one time. All these companies are looking to recruit enthusiastic and flexible people to work on a variety of roles on their productions. There are other more technical companies who provide camera crews for a whole range of specialist and standard types of production. These range from high-quality outside broadcast units to smaller companies hiring out low-budget DV cameras or providing camera crews and other personnel.

It is worth sending your CV to any company in your area that you think is involved in television production. Telephone them to see whether work is available, and/or send a CV that is aimed at whatever job you think they may have. Always follow up a posted CV with an email or phone call. Job vacancies can arise very quickly. Be prepared to do some work experience for a few weeks for very little money.

**SAMPLE CV**

Your name
Your address
The date

---

### TELEVISION RESEARCHER

An experienced television researcher with a particularly strong track record in researching distinctive factual programmes, finding and selecting contributors and making short films for independent television companies.

---

### TELEVISION EXPERIENCE

I have been working with independent production companies on broadcast television programmes for two years, including location programmes for Channel 4, and make-over programmes for the BBC. I find and select contributors, check that all their details are correct, make a short video about them, and recommend suitable ones to the producer. I direct short inserts for the programme. I have written, produced and directed a ten-minute short which was shown at the London film festival. I would like to work in television production management.

---

### SKILLS

I have strong interpersonal skills. This is an asset in recruiting exciting programme contributors. I am able to direct actors and presenters in single camera or multicamera formats, and film sensitively with members of the public. I have a good knowledge and understanding of digital video equipment.

What is the job you have most experience at doing?

Describe in one or two sentences what you do best in television.

I have experience and expertise in developing scripts, and shooting short dramas and factual programmes. I have a range of experience working with non-linear audio and video editing systems such as AVID and Premiere.

## TRAINING

SKILLSET researcher's course (4 wks)
Writing for the media LFS
Equal Opportunities in Broadcasting BBC

## EDUCATIONAL QUALIFICATIONS

BA (Hons) Film with television studies (2:1), Warwick University.
Three A levels: Media Studies (A), Business Studies (B) and French (B)

## RESEARCH

'The Daring Task of Literacy in India'
Research study of literacy in southern India, undertaken in gap year.

## INTERESTS

I enjoy the Arts: theatre, music and film.
I also participate in active leisure. I play tennis regularly.
I take colour and B & W photographs for publication in books and periodicals. I have an informed interest and concern for the countryside.

Your CV should be no more than two pages long, preferably one. Notice that any television experience and skills you have acquired at university or on work experience are at the top of the page, before your qualifications.

# Definitions of postproduction terminology

**Non-linear editing**   This is computer video editing. All the material shot on video can be loaded onto a computer hard disc via a digital link such as Firewire or a USB port, and edited using suitable software such as Adobe Premiere or AVID. The process is non-linear because picture and sound can be accessed separately, and each frame or scene can be viewed, moved or rearranged into any order easily and quickly. The sequence can be altered, copied or changed indefinitely without losing the original rushes, and with no deterioration in technical quality. Video effects such as dissolves and wipes can be added and any number of versions created. Depending on the power of the computer and the type of software, a whole programme can be edited and the soundtrack mixed, and then rendered and copied to a video recorder for broadcasting.

**Off-line edit**   Off-line is a low cost form of video editing that uses non-linear computer editing to make a rough cut, or early version, of a programme. The rough cut can be shown to a client or editor and, after adjustments to the programme, an edit decision list (EDL) is created. This is a computer disc with the data of all the edit decisions made in the fine cut. This can be taken to an on-line edit where the high-quality original pictures from the rushes can be conformed using data from the EDL to create a broadcast-quality final version.

**On-line edit**   This is the highest quality editing of video tapes in a dedicated editing suite, often in a facilities house, where video effects, captions, credits and other visuals are added to create the final edit master. For a longer programme an off-line edit will have produced an edit decision list on disc that can then be conformed in an on-line edit.

**Rushes**   All the film or video footage shot each day is known as that day's rushes. The term comes from the early days of cinema when the footage shot each day was rushed to the labs for processing overnight so that it could be viewed early the next day before shooting began. This is still how it is done on feature films. For TV production on digital videotape the term 'rushes' is still useful as a way of referring to original video footage before it has been edited.

**Sound dub**    This is where the various audio elements of a programme are blended and mixed together to produce the final audio track(s). Using a sophisticated sound mixing desk, speech, actuality, atmospheric sounds ('atmos'), music and sound effects (FX), and commentary if required, are balanced to create a harmonious audio master for the programme.

# Further reading

Hart, C., *Television Program Making* (Oxford: Focal Press, 1999).

Millerson, G., *Video Production Handbook*, 3rd edn (Oxford: Focal Press, 2001).

Orlebar, J., *Digital Television Production* (London: Arnold, 2002).

Orlebar, J., *The Practical Media Dictionary* (London: Arnold, 2003).

Tunstall, J., *Television Producers* (London: Routledge, 1993).

Tunstall, J. (ed.), *Media Occupations and Professions: A Reader* (Oxford: Oxford University Press, 2001).

# Part III

# **Television theory**

# 9 Genre and format

## Introduction

Genre derives from the French word meaning 'type', and can be defined as the sharing of expectations between audience and programme makers about the classification of a programme. Much television output can be regarded as generic in this sense, and there has been a proliferation of genre-specific channels in recent years, such as the Sci-Fi Channel, CNN or The Cartoon Network. Generic television recognises and uses the expectations of the viewer, for, as the writer David Edgar has observed, genre 'involves a transfer of power. It is the viewer saying to the producer, I possess key elements of this event before it's begun ... If foregrounding the customer is the end, genre is the means' (Edgar 2000: 75). Genre is, in this respect, a democratic concept, since it takes account of viewers' preconceptions, expectations and demands of television. Genre television (such as soap opera, police or hospital drama, or game shows) is attractive to television executives because a popular generic programme has a brand identity. In the same way as casting a known television personality or performer, the recognition of familiar genre conventions provides both security and appeal for the audience.

The term 'format' is more commonly used within the television business than in academic writing. It refers to the features of a programme that define its uniqueness, such as the premise, type of setting, range of characters or performers, and genre. For example, some of the key aspects of *Big Brother* include the house, the group of 'ordinary' contestants, the process of nomination and voting-out, the hidden cameras and the role of Big Brother as the unseen authority. Once a programme format has been

defined, it can be traded like a product, and sold to another production
company in another country, for example. If another programme maker
produces a 'copycat' programme using the same format without permission, a format owner could take the issue to court and claim that the format
has been 'stolen'. The concept of format is not only useful when making
programmes, to lay down the basic components that the production team
are going to use, but it also has a legal and commercial status. Both genre
and format are ways of pinning down the essentials that make a programme
what it is, but these two terms are used in rather different ways.

Genres allow for change. Programme makers try out forms and modes
of address in one genre that are adopted from apparently different genres.
In semiotic terminology (semiotics is the study of signs and their meaning),
the mixing of genre elements is a form of intertextuality, consisting of the
borrowing in one programme text of signs from another. Since each
individual programme is surrounded by others in different genres before
and after it in the schedule, and by competing programmes on other
channels at the same time, it requires both similarity and difference from
these alternatives to establish its own identity. The process of borrowing
across and between genres is part of a continual negotiation of identity
for programmes, and leads to generic instability. Programme makers
and television institutions continually imagine audience needs and desires,
and attempt to address these and target them. If particular programmes
seem to catch an audience constituency that shows up in the ratings, or
generates press coverage, items on radio phone-ins or on other television
programmes such as talk shows, they quickly acquire generic centrality,
economic value and public visibility. Television genre is negotiated
between texts, institutions and audiences in a radically flexible way that
suggests both television's specificity and also its connection with other
media and with culture in general. This chapter begins by discussing
selected television genres that have been relatively stable, then considers
programmes where genre characteristics are mixed together.

Soap opera is a relatively stable and identifiable genre. Multiple storylines built around a large group of characters living in the same location
produce an impression of rapidly occurring events. The scenes and
sequences in an episode are likely to involve several different combinations of characters, and scenes involving different combinations of
characters follow each other rapidly, producing forward movement in the
storylines. But on the other hand, any one episode of a soap opera usually
occurs in a very short space of represented time such as one day or even

just a few hours. The exchange of information between characters through gossip and conversation, and the withholding of information that has been revealed to the audience also encourages the viewer to be aware of developments a long time in the past. Viewers speculate about future events, and experience pleasurable uncertainty about which of the numerous occurrences in any one episode will have effects on the relationships between the characters. But many of the features mentioned here are also evident in other programmes that are not squarely in the genre of soap opera. For example, hospital drama series such as *Casualty* or *ER* share many of the same features. The most significant difference between soap opera and television hospital drama is in the degree of narrative closure in individual episodes. Hospital drama and police drama are characterised by narratives in which transitional characters appear and produce a disruption to the social space, and at the end of an episode this storyline is completed.

## Where genre comes from

Some of the most established television genres derive from types found in other media. For example, soap opera began in radio, where continuing serials were created to address the mainly female daytime audience by focusing on emotional relationships. These serials were sponsored by companies producing domestic products such as soap. News and current affairs television share conceptions of news value, and the institutional structures of reporters and editors with newspapers and news radio. Sketch shows and situation comedy have roots in music hall and variety, which were adapted for radio and later for television.

The study of genre is based on the identification of the conventions and features that distinguish one kind of work from another. The study of genre allows theorists to link the conventions and norms found in a group of texts with the expectations and understandings of audiences. Genre studies explain how audiences classify television according to features of the text itself, such as cues that they identify in programme titles or aspects of form such as setting and narrative structure. As Steve Neale (Neale and Turner 2001: 1) notes: 'Most theorists of genre argue that generic norms and conventions are recognised and shared not only by theorists themselves, but also by audiences, readers and viewers.' Genre is also signalled by the supporting information about programmes in listings publications, trailers and advertising. The identification of genre may also be apparent through the prominent presence of writers or performers associated with a particular genre.

However, theorists of genre have struggled to pin down where genre resides. It can be argued that genre forms arise from the properties of texts, so that identifying genre means listing elements of a text that determine its membership in one genre rather than another. However, the listing of constituents is not always reliable. In news, for example, interviews are coded in the same ways as in sports programmes. The address to camera in news can also be seen in sports or quiz programmes. News programmes contain actuality footage accompanied by a voice-over, as in documentary, current affairs or wildlife programmes. One of the difficulties in television genre study is identifying unique genre features and the boundaries of a genre.

Genres are also categories used by the producers of programmes and in the institutional division of creative staff in television institutions. Large organisations such as the BBC divide their staff into departments based on genres, such as drama, light entertainment, news or sport. However, some kinds of programme, such as sitcoms for instance, are clearly dramas but are made by the staff of light entertainment departments. Another possible means of deploying the concept of genre is to regard it as a category brought by audiences to the programmes they watch. Some viewers might regard *The Kumars at No. 42* as a talk show, since it features celebrity interviews, while others might regard it as a variant of the sketch show genre because of its scripted ensemble comedy routines. Wherever we look, we find genre being used to categorise programmes, but when we look deeper into how genre is used, it becomes clear that its meanings are complex and ambiguous.

The ideological functions of programmes cross genre boundaries. Television police series are structured around the opposition between legality and criminality. The central detective or policemen is a personal representative of legality, against whom the otherness of crime and its perpetrators are measured. The television audience is encouraged to identify with the central figure, whereas the criminal is established as an outsider responsible for disruption. In television news, a similar opposition is established between the public, the news presenters and the institution of television news on one hand, versus the other nations, public institutions, perpetrators of crime and the impersonal forces of chance, the weather, and natural processes which produce the disruptions and disorder reported in the news. Although these are different genres, the ideological oppositions between order and disorder, continuity and disruption, structure both.

Theorists of genre have a particular interest in programmes that transgress the boundaries of genre, considering them to be more valuable and interesting because they draw attention to the conventional rules of television genre by breaking or blurring them. Programmes that are firmly within the boundaries of a genre tend to be regarded as formulaic and of lesser significance. Nevertheless, all texts participate in genre to some extent, and often several simultaneously. Programmes become interesting and pleasurable by working against genre conventions as well as with them.

## Genre: the sitcom

The sitcom has a history that spans most of the post-1945 period, and is one of the most popular and enduring of television genres. Not only do new sitcoms figure prominently in the schedules of terrestrial television, but 'old' examples of the form are a staple of cable and satellite channels as well. Nostalgia and familiarity have enabled 'classic' sitcoms to retain an important position in the schedules despite some outmoded and sometimes embarrassing assumptions in them about race or gender for instance. Indeed, certain sitcoms have such a hold over the popular imagination that they can still gather audiences in the millions some time after their first screening: a repeat showing on BBC1 of an episode of *Dad's Army* (1968–77) in 2001 attracted 6.6 million viewers (Nelson 2005). But both British and US sitcoms have recognised the need to engage with cultural change, especially the changing position of women (see Hallam 2005), if only as a response to broadcasters' need to deliver a new generation of affluent and confident women consumers to the advertisers who sponsor or support programmes.

Some components of sitcom can be identified as key elements of the genre, but even these are not exclusive to it. Sitcoms have a situation, like a house or workplace where the action happens and where characters seemed trapped together. Audience laughter provides cues for the audience about what is expected to be funny, such as jokes and comic actions or a contrast between what characters say and what they do. Yet some sketch shows, variety, and cartoons also have this feature. The genre of sitcom is a particular combination of elements such as scripted fictional narrative, self-conscious performance by actors, jokes and physical comedy, and studio audience laughter. Focusing on performance discourages the audience from judging speech and behaviour according to the norms of everyday behaviour. The violence of the BBC sitcom *Bottom*, for example, in which characters attack each other with furniture and domestic objects, is made safe by being performance rather than realistic narrative. The BBC sitcom *The Office* lacks the laughter of a studio audience on the soundtrack, normally a generic marker of sitcom, and also appears to be shot with a single camera, as if it were a docusoap. But it has a situation, jokes, physical comedy, and a script, so it is a variant of the sitcom genre.

Sitcom is a genre that has evolved with relatively rigid boundaries that are now blurred and transgressed in some programmes. The most interesting sitcoms exploit the constraints of genre by drawing attention to the circularity of narrative in them. By definition, the situation that gives a programme its setting and main characters must be preserved no matter what challenges are introduced in a particular episode. So there are firm limits on the possibilities for change, and only limited narrative progression that would affect subsequent episodes. However, as Barry Langford (2005) points out, certain sitcoms such as *Steptoe and Son* (BBC 1962–65 and 1970–74), *Porridge* (BBC 1974–77) and *The Office* (BBC 2001–03) have made room for some narrative progression that reflects on and challenges the series' premise. When the circularity of narrative within the sitcom genre becomes part of the drama as well as a framework for it, sitcom is able to engage viewers at a very sophisticated level.

## Genre: the police series

Narratives in the police and detective genre begin with a disturbance in the social world of the programme, such as a murder or a robbery. It is the task of the policemen or detective to restore the equilibrium of that world. This is achieved by a sequence of processes that usually occur in a fixed order. First, the police find the explanation for the disturbance by collecting evidence and interviewing witnesses and suspects. This enables them to remove the disruptive force, usually by arresting the person who has committed the crime. This provides the conditions for the restoration of order. However, the fictional world of the police genre is unstable. Conflicts within the central character, among the workers in the police institution, and conflicts between the upholders of the law and the criminals they pursue are often equally of interest, and reduce the cosiness and security of the fictional world. The central characters of police and detective series often work in teams of two or more, to provide opportunities for explaining plot points, evaluating the behaviour of witnesses and suspects, and assessing evidence. The differences between one central character and another not only serve to create possible tension for the audience but also enable each character to make up for the insufficiencies of the other. Buddy teams in police series might be, for example, a younger and an older man, a man and a woman, a married woman and a single woman, a black man and a white man. Some recent programmes in the police genre use the audience's awareness of these genre conventions in order to question them.

World Productions' BBC series *The Cops* was overseen by the producer Tony Garnett, and his work for television over more than 40 years has challenged conventions of television realism, genre and narrative form. *The Cops* not only signalled conventional expectations of the police genre, but also sought to manipulate these through negotiation with genre and the audience expectations that it mobilises. At the opening of the first episode, the main character Mel was introduced in plain clothes, with no indication that she was a policewoman, and was seen snorting cocaine and dancing the night away in a club. The distinctions between the upholders of the law and those whose criminal activities make them the object of police attention were blurred right from the beginning. As the series progressed, the young police officers learned more about the inhabitants of the local housing estate who they were often called upon to deal with. They developed increasingly caring attitudes to these people and greater understanding of their problems, and the easy identification of perpetrators and victims, heroes and villains, was made increasingly difficult. Scenes in *The Cops* were shot with a single camera, always following the police characters into action, rather than establishing a scene before their arrival. The single camera was often hand-held, moving with the police as they moved through the corridors of the police station, through the streets, and into houses, to give the impression of unrehearsed action occurring in real time. This camera convention is used in documentary, and its effect was to generate a sense of realism in following action as it occurs. It also deprived the audience of the dramatic contrasts which would structure narrative in conventional police drama, and the interpretive voice-over that would be expected in documentary. The effect was to demand more active viewer attention. *The Cops* both signalled genre conventions but also blurred them. The series put into question any easy distinction between 'us' and 'them', police and perpetrator, and creatively pushed the boundaries of a very established television genre.

## Profile

## Drama producer
Tony Garnett

Mark Thomson, now the Director General of the BBC, has described Tony Garnett as 'probably the finest drama producer British television has produced' (*Guardian*, 10 November 1997).

Well known and applauded for his collaboration with directors such as Ken Loach on television dramas and films, he helped to create a loose, naturalistic, vérité style that used everyday speech and location filming with a deceptively documentary look. His television dramas reveal social injustices and explore political issues. He produced the influential *Cathy Come Home* (BBC 1966) which instigated the setting up of the homeless charity Shelter, and later *Days of Hope* (BBC 1975) a drama series spanning the First World War and the 1926 General Strike. Tony Garnett still produces television dramas that explore issues, and are filmed with a gritty sense of realism. His own production company World Productions has come up with some remarkable new dramas including *This Life*, *Cardiac Arrest*, *The Cops* and, in 2004, *No Angels* for Channel 4. This series deals with the lives of four feisty nurses, uncovering their sexy and fast living social life. He has also written a TV series, *Buried*, a hard-hitting prison drama for Channel 4.

'In my opinion television should be a bloody great circus with lots of acts. Many years ago at the BBC when we were asking ourselves what our function and role should be, I argued that our job was to tell the truth. Not The Truth, because only God, if he or she exists, knows The Truth, but our job should be to tell our truth, to bear witness, whether through a situation comedy, a news programme, or a drama. That's what the public expect of us. But my truth or anyone's truths is partial, in both senses of the word, so we need a whole range of truths on television all the time. I used to say that all drama is political, only some drama *knew* that it was. I have had a lot of fun trying to create good entertainment, but it's the political ones that are remembered because they created a controversy. The kind of television drama that should have a place, and I would like to be part of it, is the drama of social criticism, the drama of anger. I'd like to see a drama that, through the experience of the characters, invites the audience to imagine an alternative, politically, socially and in the way that institutions are run, as we did in *The Big Flame.* I think the action now is in the long running series. I turned to series partly because that is now the reality of the industry, but then I discovered I was really excited by the challenge. Series are enormously difficult to keep fresh. It's easy to be repetitive and formulaic and it's easy to turn them into a branch of manufacturing. But if you fight very hard against those things there are enormous benefits. The long series is the natural form of television, the equivalent of the nineteenth-century episodic novel.'

Garnett has a deserved reputation for working with and nurturing young talent, especially writers:

'From my point of view as a producer we're always hungry for good writers. They don't need to know how to write a screenplay. If someone can create a believable world and the characters come off the page, they can be taught the rest. Part of what I do now with a generation growing up is to try to create a secure atmosphere for them.'

He has distinctive views on young television directors, and believes they should have more experience working with actors:

'The problem with the film schools is that new directors emerge with the technical stuff coming out of their ears, very interested in how the camera moves, but with virtually no interest in or experience with actors. Orson Welles said you can learn all you ever need to know about directing a film in an afternoon, and he was right.'

On the future of television, Garnett was one of the first to embrace digital shooting and editing. He argues that technology tends to predicate social and cultural change:

'Forget the idea of the audience as the nation gathered together round the camp fire, listening to the same story. That was born of channel scarcity. Think publishing – anyone can do it, but a handful will end up being dominant. One thing is unchanging. We must adapt to these changes and ride them. The alternative is certain oblivion. We must continue to keep our ideas alive and use the screen to argue them.'

Some of this critical reworking of the police genre is already there in the confusions between legality and deviance that the genre already contains, even in its most conventional forms. The characters and actions of the perpetrators of crime can be very similar to those of the policemen or detective. Lying, casual violence and disrespect of authority are all found both in the central characters and the criminals they pursue. What distinguishes the policeman or detective from the criminal is the effectiveness of their methods, and the aim that justifies their behaviour. John Fiske and John Hartley (1978: 29) have argued that this similarity between police and criminal, and the value placed on efficiency, are means of presenting ideological conflicts – conflicts in the taken-for-granted political assumptions about everyday reality:

> What the police versus criminal conflict may enact symbolically, then, is the everyday conflict of a competitive society in which efficiency is crucial. . . . The common concern that television police are becoming more and more like the criminals in their methods and morals, means that the few factors that distinguish them take on crucial significance. Of these distinctive features, efficiency is the most marked.

The police and detective genre establishes some activities as criminal and excessive. Breaking the law is the misapplication of the principles that underlie a law-abiding society. The representation of crime on television is a means of defining the boundaries between the legal and the illegal in terms of the reasonable versus the excessive, though the desires and motivations behind legal and illegal behaviours may be exactly the same.

## Talk as entertainment

Talk shows are a television version of public debate where issues of the day are picked up and discussed, on the assumption that the television audience are interested and potentially involved in the discussion. Of course 'issues' can be very varied, from problems of childhood obesity to the release of the latest celebrity's cookbook. But talk shows are part of television's creation of a 'public sphere' – a space for rational debate, using the shared assumptions about putting arguments and views in public that originated in ancient Roman cities. Television's public sphere simulates democratic debate, both keeping alive the sense of participation and also substituting for the absence of places to meet, talk and argue with strangers in highly developed societies. Talk shows rose to prominence in the 1970s with American programmes such as the *Oprah Winfrey* show and *Donahue*. The format was exported to Britain, and hosted by television personalities including Esther Rantzen and Gloria Hunniford. In its original form, the talk show focused on individual guests who represented a larger minority constituency which sought a voice. For example, black single mothers, the disabled, or people struggling with drug addiction were able to individualise the problems of that group in person. This was a mechanism of empowerment and resistance. The contributions of experts on talk shows connected the experiences of the guests to institutional discourses such as those of medicine, psychoanalysis and civil rights. The translation of personal experience into institutional discourses was also a mechanism of empowerment, although it served to convert anger and protest into more socially acceptable forms.

But the talk show has shifted its generic identity, especially in US versions, and become a form of light entertainment. Audience preferences lead to the creation of new genres, and the reshaping of old ones. Graeme Turner (Neale and Turner 2001: 6) notes that 'the cumulative effect of repeated tweaking of the format and content amounts to a change in genre' as 'more finely grained, and more readily available, viewing figures have the effect of influencing content, format and, ultimately, genre'. American television talk shows such as the *Jerry Springer* show and the *Morton Downey Junior* show had become, by the 1990s, as internationally successful as Oprah Winfrey had been, but with a very different and much more aggressive attitude to their guests. The hosts of these programmes are much more inclined to make accusations against the opinions and behaviour of their guests than to support them. The most commented-upon feature of these programmes is the prevalence of aggressive physical behaviour when guests confront each other in front of the cameras and the audience. The role of the host, who has always functioned both as a representative for social norms represented by the collective audience behind him or her as well as a mediator between the guest, the audience and experts, has become instead an orchestrator of confrontation and a ringleader encouraging the audience to vent its condemnation of one or more of the studio guests. The prominence of experts has diminished in parallel with this, so that the conversion of social exclusion and violent emotion into the rational terms of institutional discourses is much less evident. A remnant of the liberal discourse of empowerment remains at the end of the *Jerry Springer* show, however, when Jerry delivers his weekly three-minute address direct to camera, containing a more considered homily on the foibles of human nature. Nevertheless, the ideology of talk shows has become increasingly focused on the reinforcement of social norms, where audiences (represented by the studio audience) close their ranks against perceived deviance. Dramatic conflict, staged forms of exaggerated behaviour, and reinforcement of social norms each draw the talk show genre towards light entertainment.

# Reality TV

New genres emerge at the same time as old ones change. The genre that has most recently become the subject of viewers', reviewers' and academics' interest is Reality TV. Reality TV is a generic hybrid: it adopts constructed situations (like holding the contestants in the specially built *Big Brother* House), and is thus like sitcom in being based on a particular setting and featuring characters who cannot escape from it. Reality TV is obviously like documentary, inasmuch as it is a factual form with an ostensible concern to investigate human behaviour and relationships using a 'fly-on-the-wall' camera style. It is also like drama in its sequential flow based around detailed exploration of character. It is like the game show in being based on competition, where contestants compete to stay on the show and usually compete for a prize. It is like the talk show in being a means for reflecting on social issues (like how contestants will react to someone of a different sexual orientation or someone with a very different social background) and usually foregrounds opportunities for the contestants' personal confession (as in *Big Brother*'s Diary Room). It is like lifestyle television in its emphasis on making and changing the persona, and showing that people can change and learn from their surroundings and from each other, and that social relations are changeable.

Reality TV also has generic relationships beyond the television medium. The exhaustive observation of the contestants by hidden or ever-present cameras recalls the permanent surveillance that characterises contemporary public and private buildings and the public space of town centres. In making 'stars' of some of its contestants, Reality TV is part of the celebrity culture that shapes public understanding of personalities such as film stars, football stars and pop music performers. Reality TV has only recently crystallised from being a variant on the documentary to becoming a recognised genre in its own right, and there are many debates about which of its constituent elements are the essential criteria for defining a programme in this newly recognised genre. Even so, Reality TV is significant as an example of how genres mix and develop, and how the expansion of an apparently marginal television form can give rise to the recognition of a new programme category.

In Reality TV, as well as in other programme formats involving live coverage, unpredictability and threats to the format are in themselves part of the format. For example, contestants on *I'm A Celebrity Get Me Out of Here* (series 2), led by the TV chef Antony Worrall Thompson, rebelled because of late and insufficient deliveries of food to the programme's jungle location. With eight episodes to go in the run of the series, the contestants threatened to leave all together as a group, which would stop the series. They confronted the producers on camera and were rewarded (after some heated and protracted negotiation) by being given steak for dinner. This conflict both threatened the show but also made more exciting television for the viewers, thus serving the ultimate interests of the producers, the contestants and the audience. In another case, the Irish television reality show *Cabin Fever* involved participants sailing a boat around Ireland and the unfortunate amateur sailors were caught up in an unforeseen storm, putting them in great danger. The boat later ran aground and broke up, and the contestant-crew had to be rescued by helicopter. Two weeks later, six of the nine contestants returned to the programme when a new boat was found and the run of episodes continued. In this example, developments that could not have been predicted by the producers or the contestants provided exceptionally dramatic 'real-life drama'. These kinds of memorable moments demonstrate how the constraints of format and genre in Reality TV are also founded on television's ability to witness events live (or almost live) and the risk that this involves to both participants, programme makers and audience expectations. Reality TV exploits the unpredictability and excitement that older genres have sometimes lost.

# Further reading

Bignell, J., 'Television and Genre', in *An Introduction to Television Studies* (London: Routledge, 2004), pp. 113–34.

Brunsdon, C., 'Structure of Anxiety: Recent British Television Crime Fiction', *Screen* 39: 3 (1998), pp. 223–43.

Clarke, A., '"You're Nicked!": Television Police Series and the Fictional Representation of Law and Order', in D. Strinati and S. Wagg (eds), *Come on Down?: Popular Media Culture in Post-War Britain* (London: Routledge, 1992), pp. 232–53.

Creeber, G. (ed.), *The Television Genre Book* (London: BFI, 2001).

Edgar, D. 'Playing Shops, Shopping Plays: The Effect of the Internal Market on Television Drama', in J. Bignell, S. Lacey and M. Macmurraugh-Kavanagh (eds), *British Television Drama: Past, Present and Future* (Basingstoke: Palgrave Macmillan, 2000), pp. 73–7.

Feuer, J., 'Genre Study and Television', in R. Allen (ed.), *Channels of Discourse, Reassembled* (London: Routledge, 1992), pp. 138–60.

Fiske, J., *Television Culture* (London: Methuen, 1987).

Fiske, J. and J. Hartley, *Reading Television* (London: Methuen, 1978).

Hallam, J., 'Remembering *Butterflies*: The Comic Art of Housework', in J. Bignell and S. Lacey (eds), *Popular Television Drama: Critical Perspectives* (Manchester: Manchester University Press, 2005).

Kidd-Hewitt, D. and R. Osborne (eds), *Crime and the Media: The Postmodern Spectacle* (London: Pluto, 1995).

Lacey, N., *Narrative and Genre: Key Concepts in Media Studies* (Basingstoke: Macmillan, 2000).

Langford, B., '"Our Usual Impasse": The Episodic Situation Comedy Revisited', in J. Bignell and S. Lacey (eds), *Popular Television Drama: Critical Perspectives* (Manchester: Manchester University Press, 2005).

Livingston, S. and P. Lunt, *Talk on Television: Audience Participation and Public Debate* (London: Routledge, 1994).

Neale, S. and F. Krutnik, *Popular Film and Television Comedy* (London: Routledge, 1990).

Neale, S. and G. Turner, 'Introduction: What is Genre?' in G. Creeber (ed.), *The Television Genre Book* (London: BFI, 2001), pp. 1–7.

Nelson, R., '"They do like it up 'em": *Dad's Army* and Myths of Old England', in J. Bignell and S. Lacey (eds), *Popular Television Drama: Critical Perspectives* (Manchester: Manchester University Press, 2005).

Rose, B. (ed.), *TV Genres: A Handbook and Reference Guide* (Westport: Greenwood, 1985).

Shattuc, J., *The Talking Cure: TV Talk Shows and Women* (London: Routledge, 1997).

Sparks, R., *Television and the Drama of Crime* (Buckingham: Oxford University Press, 1992).

Wagg, S. (ed.), *Because I Tell a Joke or Two: Comedy, Politics and Social Difference* (London: Routledge, 1998).

# 10 Schedule and audience

## Introduction

The emphasis in this chapter is on the ways that the scheduling of programmes in British television attempts to match the perceived interests and demands of the audience. But as well as explaining how scheduling can be approached critically as a mechanism for shaping audiences and the ways that audiences watch television, the chapter also debates how audiences may be incompletely understood, and how audiences may evade or resist the attempts by television institutions to determine how the meanings of programmes are perceived and used.

Before beginning this discussion of audience and schedules, it is worth noting that television is not only a delivery system for television content, but also a physical object that is embedded in the domestic household. It is important to consider not only what people watch, nor even which organisations bring television to the viewer, but also what the physical presence of a television within a household means. Television viewers' experience of television is partly determined by their social positions in society, and differences between individual viewers and household audiences are significant within cultures and nations as well as between them. The uses of the television in the household, and the programmes watched on it, are affected by, and have effects on, the sense of social identity constructed by individual viewers and their fellow viewers. Keeping wedding photographs on top of the television, placing it prominently as a symbol of affluence, or concealing it inside a piece of furniture, might each tell us a lot about the household and how television supports or conflicts with that household's self-image and self-presentation to visitors and other family members. The television set, its programmes, and the objects around it, form a complex set of negotiations with the past and the present, public and private life, technology and everyday routines of behaviour, and the household's family members and their absent relatives and friends. The study of television in this anthropological sense shows that it is not just programmes that are significant to television's place in culture, but also the embedding of TV in everyday life as a way of understanding identity and community.

## Scheduling practices

Scheduling comprises selection and combination. John Ellis (2000: 25) has argued that the composition of a television schedule is parallel to the operations involved in editing:

> Instead of combining shots and sounds into a sequence and sequences into a programme, as an editor does, the scheduler combines whole programme units into an evening's flow, whole evenings into a week, whole weeks into a season, and whole seasons into a year.

Some programmes have connections between them while others are placed next to programmes that have a quite different genre and format. While in the early years of television production the lengths of programmes and their interrelationships with each other were subject to little overall planning, by the 1980s standard programme lengths such as 30 minutes and one hour had produced grids of time slots such as were already common in the US.

The problem of placing new programmes arises in part from a vicious circle that affects schedulers' use of audience data from the Broadcasters Audience Research Bureau (BARB):

> The success or failure of a particular scheduling strategy is measured by the same methodology that suggested it in the first place. A problem with audience size or composition produced by a particular programming policy is identified through using the BARB figures. This leads to changes in that policy, whose success is measured by using the same BARB data.

(Ellis 2000: 35)

This makes television schedulers wary of taking risks by making decisions that run counter to their expectations about time slots and the positions of programmes within television seasons.

One way of deciding on the scheduling of a new programme is to test the idea for the format, or a completed sequence or whole programme by setting up focus group discussions. For example, focus group participants might be asked whether they would prefer to watch the new programme at 7.00 pm or 8.00 pm, and whether it would be best placed on a weekday or at the weekend. Finding out whether viewers might prefer the new programme to a competitor on another channel can enable schedulers to make decisions about whether the new programme should aim to inherit the same audience as a competitor, and whether to place the new programme directly against the competitor. Since the majority of viewers watch television accompanied by other members of their household, the focus group might also be asked whether they would be embarrassed to watch with their children, their parents, or their spouse. Clearly, focus groups represent very small samples of the total viewing audience, and the results can be unreliable. Viewers tend to make judgements based on what they already know, which is why television broadcasters are criticised for producing a diet of television that seems always the same. However, surprising successes can result from placing programmes in unexpected ways. The scheduling of *Big Brother* in the summer, for example, has been successful for Channel 4, and gathered large and young audiences. Its placing in the summer period is surprising since summer programming is usually made at low cost per hour and the schedule involves numerous repeats.

By re-evaluating audience figures, channel controllers and schedulers identify patterns of audience movement. For example, a 'pre-echo' is an audience group intending to watch a programme starting shortly, thus increasing the audience for the programme scheduled just before the one they are interested in. 'Echoes' are audiences inherited from a programme that has just been broadcast. Now that British programmes tend to fit into the grid of half hour and hour-long slots, there are more 'junction points' at which large numbers of viewers may switch from one channel to another. For example, at 10.00 pm, news is broadcast on both BBC1 and ITV1, and the 9.00 pm watershed is a point at which programmes aimed at a more adult audience can begin, so there is a tendency for all channels to change the kinds of programme available at 9.00 pm or 10.00 pm, thus producing a junction where audiences may choose to move to one channel or another. 'Tent pole' programmes are those that can be relied on to gain a large audience, thus lifting up the trend line showing audience size, like the ridge pole of a tent. Schedulers might also position a programme with a relatively small audience between two popular ones, hoping to inherit audiences from the preceding programme and to pick up audiences expecting to see the following one. This is called 'hammocking', whereby a less popular programme is held up by those on either side.

The arrival of the personal video recorder and multichannel television signals the possible demise of this kind of planned scheduling. Because interactive television makes it easy to view a programme at a variety of different starting times (because the same programme is being streamed by perhaps three or four different channels, starting at for example, 7.30 pm, 8 pm, or 8.30 pm) the viewer's chance to catch a programme is greatly increased. Correspondingly, the power of television schedulers to control when audiences watch diminishes, and television viewers become schedulers themselves. Digital television also changes the nature of the programme itself, so that different viewers could be seeing different programmes as a result of the interactive choices they make. Viewers can call up additional information about programmes, and access brief television segments that support the programme they are watching. Wildlife programmes, for example, may have supporting material giving further information about the animals seen in the programme, or providing further footage that was not included in the eventual edited version. The technology of picture in picture allows this material to appear in smaller windows within the television screen, or for the viewer to see what is being broadcast on another channel. It has been suggested for a long time that it will also be possible for viewers to see alternative endings of drama programmes, or to change the relationship between narrative sequences, in a way that is already possible in retail DVD systems where the 'chapters' comprising the film can be viewed in any order. With a range of up to 200 available channels, conventional schedule listings are difficult to use, and instead, electronic on-screen programme guides list available programmes in a time slot. Electronic programme guides are easiest to use when programmes are of standard lengths, and it is likely that interactive television will produce greater standardisation of programme lengths for this reason. Interactive television both challenges conventional scheduling, since viewers have more choices among and within programmes, and also standardises the lengths and formats in which programmes are produced.

# Television for the family

Schedules are planned on the basis of assumptions about the nature of the television audience and the ways audiences watch. Television schedules have for a long time been planned around the ways that hypothetical family audiences organise their time. Television still often assumes that the audience is a family group with gender and family roles that are reinforced by TV programmes. So television's ideological effect is therefore to reinforce the family values on which capitalism is based politically. Children come home from school at the end of the afternoon, meals are usually eaten in the early or mid-evening, children are expected to go to bed at around 9.00 pm. In general, the early evening contains shorter and more diverse programmes, while the later evening offers adult viewers longer and more complex forms and formats. Across the year as a whole, new programmes are traditionally introduced around September, when the holiday season has finished and family routines get back to normal as school time begins. In the summer, people watch less television because they are more likely to be outside in the warmer weather, so the summer period contains more repeated programmes and fewer high-profile programmes. At a particular point during the year, expected events such as the football cup final, the Eurovision Song Contest or Christmas celebrations will require the schedule to be rearranged and specially planned.

Different decodings are produced by viewers who occupy different social positions. Women in Western societies are expected to be emotional, caring and community forming (as opposed to the masculine characteristics of adventurousness, aggression and individualism). The negotiation of the meanings of television programmes is affected by the social status of the viewer. Audience responses are not only determined by the text, but also by the social environment in which talk about the programme among friends, workmates and family members takes place. Viewing context, such as watching television with other members of a family, or with friends, for instance, affects viewing experience. People watching with their families will often be persuaded to watch something they do not enjoy, whereas watching a favourite programme with a group of friends might help to confirm a person's shared relationships with members of that group. John Storey (1999: 114) summarises this social role of television viewing by arguing:

> Watching television is always so much more than a series of acts of interpretation; it is above all else a social practice. That is, it can be a means to isolate oneself . . . or to make contact with other family members. . . . In these ways, the cultural consumption of television is as much about social relationships as it is about interpretations of individual programmes.

John Ellis (2000: 26) goes as far as to say that the schedule is

> the locus of power in television, the mechanism whereby demographic speculations are turned into a viewing experience. And it is more than that as well, for any schedule contains the distillation of the past history of a channel, of national broadcasting as a whole, and of the particular habits of national life.

For example, programmes about home improvement are likely to be shown at times when people are considering doing work on their houses, for example on Fridays and Saturdays, when major DIY superstores will be open for people to purchase materials: ITV1 is unlikely to show DIY programmes on Sundays when viewers will already have completed their shopping for such items. This British situation is different from that in the US, where programmes are generally scheduled in strips, for example, soap operas in the afternoon, sitcoms in prime-time, drama in the late evening. Each American network channel's schedule is similar to its competitors, with much less variety and unexpectedness than in Britain.

Audience research about who talks about television, to whom, where and how reveals the different roles television can play in making, breaking and maintaining social relationships. Researchers have looked at how 'television viewing is generally a somewhat busy activity, interrupted by many other activities and routinely accompanied by talk, much of it having nothing to do with the programme being watched' (Storey 1999: 16). For the discipline of Television Studies in general, a shift of interest onto viewers and audiences rather than on television programmes as texts has focused on 'active' rather than 'passive' viewing, and provided good reasons to value kinds of viewing and kinds of programme that have been considered of low quality. Rather than being passively positioned by the meanings of television programmes, watching television requires viewers to draw on their personal histories, their cultural, class, racial, economic or sexual identities, and to use their cultural competence, gained from media knowledge of comparable programmes and the various information sources available to them, to construct a relationship with the television programme in the context of their cultural lives.

# Family and feminisation

Inasmuch as television audiences are regarded as domestic and members of a family, television is also a feminised medium in that it adopts this domestic tone and form. Television programmes are dominated much more than cinema, for example, by people talking and interacting in familiar situations, just as life for viewers at home is often centred around these activities. Much of the theoretical work carried out in the 1980s on the domestic context of ordinary viewing focused on women viewers, and on programmes attractive to female audiences. Indeed, the genre of soap opera in particular became a focus of attention because the textual characteristics of the genre were argued to map closely onto traits conventionally recognised as feminine. Soap opera works primarily through dialogue, both between the characters in the programme and between members of the audience who are invited to speculate about what will happen and to make judgements about the moral and emotional problems experienced by the characters. Talk and gossip are recognised by sociologists as an important component of women's lives, as ways of constructing community and shared experience. Soap operas provide both a representation of this community, and material that actual women can discuss with each other.

Furthermore, since narrative information is conveyed largely through dialogue in soap opera, it is possible to watch soaps with what Jeremy Tunstall (1983) called secondary involvement, getting on with other tasks and looking occasionally at the screen. Tunstall distinguished between primary, secondary and tertiary involvement with media. Primary involvement is close concentration to the exclusion of any other activity. The kind of attention where viewers are sometimes distracted is secondary involvement, where the viewer may also be doing something else at the same time. Tertiary involvement is only momentary attention while engaged in another activity, scarcely seeing any of the images on the screen and only occasional sound. The level of involvement makes a lot of difference to the meanings that viewers can make, and while some television programmes (such as news) are constructed in order to attract primary involvement, soap opera and other genres aimed at female audiences can be satisfying with secondary or even tertiary involvement.

The production of viewer talk is encouraged and mirrored by talk in programmes themselves. Programmes as diverse as *EastEnders* and *Big Brother* consist largely of sequences of conversation between the performers or participants, representing familiar interaction and conversation which could then be talked about by viewers. The frequent use of close-up shots of faces in soap opera and in Reality TV, and on television in general, reinforces this sense of intimacy between the viewer and what is shown on television, and contributes to an apparent equivalence between the ordinary world of reality and the constructed worlds of television. This way of using and experiencing television gives the illusion of physical closeness, and invokes rules of social interaction that demand attention and create social proximity. Soap opera has been discussed in these terms for a long time. Press coverage of *Big Brother* built up a selection of character-types, and the producers' selection of outgoing and dominant contestants provoked dramatic conflict and performance comparable to soap opera fiction, so that participants in the programme could become familiar figures, and become the topic of social talk and gossip.

But family audiences are no longer the only predominant audience addressed by schedulers and programme makers. For example, Reality TV shows focus much more on individuals in specially formed groups or in workplace groups. Contemporary audiences watching increasingly in same-generational groupings rather than inter-generational family groupings, are interested in programmes that are also about same-generational groups. So the contestants in the *Big Brother* house for example, tend to be of similar age to each other and to the young audiences addressed by the programme. The contestants in *Big Brother* do not have visible families, except as something distant that they may desire but that they and the audience will almost never see during the series. The sociability of Reality TV is what we might call 'parasociability', comprising temporary same-generational groupings that are often goal oriented, not communal, and not familial. If Reality TV is an image of contemporary society, that would be a very unhappy situation. But, in fact, it is a representation of broadcasters' imagination of the audience, not of society as a whole at all. Reality TV, like other contemporary programme forms, selectively represents the imaginary relationships between broadcasters and audiences.

# Immediacy and intimacy

Jostein Gripsrud (1998) writes about the opposing ways we might think of television. The first of these is immediacy versus intimacy. Television, in news for example or live broadcasting of sport, claims to bring immediately occurring events to its viewer, and obviously television's heritage of live broadcasting is crucial to this. Intimacy, on the other hand, has more to do with relationships of identification, with an exchange not only of information but also of feeling between viewers and what they see on the screen. Television's intimacy is also based on a sense of closeness of connection between the viewer and what he or she is watching. Gripsrud pursues this point by contrasting the two functions of the window and the mirror. Television can function as a window on the world, and again news, current affairs and documentary would be appropriate examples here. But television can also function as a mirror. Its representations of domesticity and the family, documenting ordinary life and the ways that culture functions in the present, all have to do with television's mirroring function. Factual genres like documentary have a special claim to presenting the world outside to the viewer, but television has also been significant in shaping the domestic space of the viewer simply by virtue of the presence of the television set in the room and the ways that TV affects domestic life. TV has also been significant in representing the family, and particularly perhaps women and the notions of gender relations that circulate in culture. Reality TV is a subset of documentary, so it would be expected to emphasise immediacy, the function of the screen as a window, and representations of the world outside the viewing space. However, that is the opposite of what many Reality TV shows seem interested in. Reality TV emphasises intimacy, it mirrors aspects of the lives of some of its viewers, and it not only represents but also debates the meanings of domestic space and the interrelations of people who inhabit the same space. Thinking about immediacy and intimacy, window and mirror, are useful ways of understanding what programme genres and formats do.

# Marketing, scheduling and regulation

Television is increasingly considered as a market in which providers of programmes give their publics what they seem to want. With multiple channels it no longer seems necessary for each channel to expose the audience to the full range of both 'accessible' and 'difficult' programmes.

This marks a change from a paternalistic notion of the viewer as a member of a collective national audience to the notion of the viewer as an individual consumer, offered multiple TV choices by a proliferating number of channels. Rather than leading the viewer towards 'better' taste and informed citizenship, television institutions increasingly offer either mixed programme schedules that attempt to satisfy perceived desires and capture audiences through entertainment, or diversify their offerings into themed channels that offer related programme types to small niche audiences.

The power to commission new programmes is in the hands of broadcasting executives, but schedulers have an important role to play in identifying programmes that are likely to gain audiences, based on information schedulers have about what audiences have watched in the past. So schedulers provide recommendations to commissioning executives and thus influence which programmes are made. The attractiveness of Reality TV formats to schedulers can be seen in the UK in relation to Channel 4's placing of *Big Brother* on both its terrestrial and cable/satellite channel. Once the *Big Brother* format had made an impact in the UK during the first series in 1999, Channel 4 used the programme as a means to attract audiences to Channel 4's new paid cable, satellite and digital channel E4. Different regulations affect the scheduling of programmes on non-terrestrial channels, as well as different strategies developed by broadcasting institutions to use them as add-ons, alternatives, or groundbreakers for their terrestrial free-to-air services. Terrestrial broadcasters have for a long time agreed on a 9.00 pm 'watershed', before which programmes that could be offensive or disturbing to children will not be broadcast. The additional coverage of Reality TV programmes in non-free-to-air channels is not subject to the same watershed rules that are enshrined in the guidelines on Taste and Decency. The ITC Programme Code states: 'The decision to subscribe to a specialist channel available only to those who have specifically chosen it, carries with it an acceptance of a greater share of responsibility by parents for what is viewed and the watershed on such channels is set at 8 pm rather than 9 pm' (ITC Programme Code, 2002). This allowed E4 to broadcast more, and less controlled, coverage of *Big Brother* than on the parent channel, thus attracting new audiences to the recently introduced digital channel.

The issue of taste and decency is closely connected to the imagining of television audiences, and the mechanisms of scheduling. The BBC Producers' Guidelines recognise this when they state in the 'Taste and Decency' section:

Context is everything: scheduling can be vital to audiences accepting difficult material. It is vital to consider the expectations that audiences have of particular programmes and timeslots. The widespread availability of material in other media, or on other broadcasters is not reason enough to judge it acceptable.

(BBC Producers' Guidelines, 2003)

In this statement, it is worth noting that a 'me too' argument is not regarded as a justification for causing offence to some audiences. The fact that an ITV company or Channel 4 might broadcast a challenging or offensive programme is not regarded as a justification for BBC to follow suit in one of its own formats or in a programme acquired from abroad.

The representation of sex and violence on television in Britain has been problematic because of the location of viewing. The fact that the TV set is physically located in the home leads to the fear that unsuitable material may be watched by children, and cause embarrassment to adults watching with them. The informal codes of behaviour governing family life that are imagined by the producers and regulators of television mean that bad language, sexual scenes and violence are considered to be outside the norms of family behaviour. However, attitudes to sex on television have liberalised over the decades of television's existence. Evidently, what is offensive to standards of taste and decency depends on the norms of a culture at a particular time, and in a particular location. Taste and decency are the products of ideology, which changes according to the social and political character of a given group or national population.

The discussion of sex, especially in a documentary or in ironic comedies on youth television, has become common. The youth audience was offered, for example, *Ibiza Uncovered* by Sky in 1997, in which the relatively uninhibited desire of a group of young British holidaymakers to have as much sex as possible in their fortnight away was documented in some detail. The eroticised youthful body has become a commodity for the attraction of youth audiences, and also a source of titillation for the older viewer. The launch of Channel 5 depended on the depiction of sexuality since the channel had very small amounts of working capital, not all of the UK population could receive its signal, and it had a very small budget to spend on programmes. In order to gain the 5 per cent audience share required to satisfy its backers, the channel concentrated on what its first chief executive, Dawn Airey, called 'films, fucking and football'.

But children's sexualities, and the possibility that children may be objects of sexual desire for adults, is significantly absent on British television. In July 2001 the current affairs comedy spoof *Brass Eye* screened a programme satirising hysteria over paedophiles, and was much criticised in the press. Government ministers, including Tessa Jowell (Minister of Culture Media and Sport), criticised the programme but refused to view it. The Independent Television Commission ruled that Channel 4 gave inadequate warnings to viewers. Much of the regulation of television is based on the perceived need to protect children from programme content that may be disturbing to them. Although this may seem to be a straightforward notion, it is worth considering how the idea of childhood is constituted. In the developed nations of the Western world, childhood is seen in two contrasting ways. Our current conceptions of childhood began to be developed around the beginning of the nineteenth century. On one hand, children have been regarded as irrational, immoral and in need of adult guidance. But on the other hand, children are also regarded as innocent, naturally predisposed to be good, and uncontaminated by adults' problems. There is a continuing conflict between these two quite different meanings of childhood, and when considering how television regulations protect children, it is important to remember that the meanings of childhood are both contradictory and the product of adult thinking.

Protecting children from television is connected to assumptions about how other vulnerable groups in society can be adversely affected by it. Since programmes and regulations have been largely made by well-educated and socially powerful elites in society, the ideology of television regulation has considered the less socially powerful and less well-educated mass audiences of television as vulnerable and prone to bad influences in the same way that children might be. There is a long tradition among commentators on television to consider mass audiences as 'them' in contrast to the more sophisticated 'us' represented by those commentators themselves. The mass audiences of television have been regarded as childlike and in need of protection. One of the ideological assumptions behind television regulation is that viewers (or at least some of them) are not able to discriminate for themselves between programmes that have socially positive meanings, and programmes that could encourage anti-social or dangerous behaviour. The way that broadcasting regulations refer to children or to vulnerable adults can be regarded as a way of justifying the ability of a small group in society to legislate for what the majority are able to understand.

# Active audiences

John Fiske (1987) made an important argument about how audiences make all kinds of meanings out of watching television, rather than just consuming what they are given. This suggests that attempts to regulate how audiences watch, and to determine what they get from what they see, will never wholly succeed. Fiske argued that the television text will exhibit resistances to coherence and internal contradictions, such that no single meaning can be imposed or received, and instead meaning is produced by programme makers and understood by audiences in a wide range of ways. Viewers actively connect the separate shots and segments of a programme and bridge the gaps between them. They also remember and connect what they see with the previous episodes of a series or serial, or between the images on different channels as they zap from one to another. For Fiske (1987: 95) television offers a 'semiotic democracy', meaning that the signs and meanings in television's images and sounds are interpreted with a certain freedom by each viewer.

Furthermore, since television is not the property of a particular segment of the population, it escapes the control of elites and is sometimes incorporated into resistant subcultures by its viewers. Television Studies theorists began to regard the television audience not as a uniform mass but as a complex set of overlapping groups with different allegiances, backgrounds and interests. This shifted the object of study from the television programme as a text, to the television audience responding to this text. The key concepts of plurality and difference were applied not just to the many possible meanings of programmes, but to the different ways audiences might interpret them. By focusing on the audience, often by setting up situations in which researchers listen in person to the talk of actual viewers, Television Studies granted more power and authority to viewers, in particular viewers belonging to ethnic subcultures, women and children. Audience studies also provided an opportunity to find new sources of potential resistance to the ways that the television business is organised, and to the conventional and ideological meanings discovered by close analysis of programmes. Rather than just looking for instances of resistant programme texts that might make new and politically radical meanings, researchers looked for groups of resistant and radical viewers.

Landmark studies conducted by feminist television studies academics showed how programmes often regarded as of low quality (such as soap opera) could be central to the experience of women viewers, who themselves were in a position of relatively low social power (see, for example, Ang 1996, Geraghty 1991). It became possible to see how viewers might actualise the many meanings in a television text. The primary emphasis of research on soap opera, and of much audience research by Television Studies academics in general, has been on the viewer's pleasure in television, and methodologies have been developed to engage viewers in talk and discussion about their everyday viewing experiences and their reasons for watching and enjoying particular programmes or genres.

Ethnographic audiences studies ask how television functions in relationships between people, and affects the ways that daily lives and self-understandings are formed (see Geraghty 1998). Yet ethnographic audience studies are most often carried out by talking to respondents who have voluntarily put themselves forward, and are therefore likely to have something to say. The methods used to find respondents can give rise to a number of problems. Some researchers have used 'snowballing' in which one person finds another who will participate, then that person finds another, and so on. This methodology is less artificial than selecting a representative panel, but it inevitably produces a self-selected group. Other researchers have placed advertisements in magazines, for example, and reviewed the responses they receive. Those people who respond have something that they wish to communicate, and adopt the formalities of letters, such as politeness. Talking can present some of the same problems, when respondents give answers they think may be most interesting to the researcher, or that present them in the most interesting light. Nevertheless, interpreting audiences reveals the intricate, singular and different ways in which people make interpretations of their world and think about their own cultural behaviours.

Specific cultural groups, such as the resistant television audience groups studied in media audience research, are imaginary communities. The theorist of fan cultures, Henry Jenkins (1992), conducted studies of the attitudes to *Star Trek* of a range of different groups including science students and members of the gay *Star Trek* fan group The Gaylaxians. Jenkins points out that MIT students largely share the ideological values of the programme, such as faith in science and human progress, and are hardly a resistant audience. In his study of The Gaylaxians, Jenkins (1992: 264) notes that:

Resistant reading can sustain the Gaylaxians' own activism, can become a source of collective identity and mutual support, but precisely because it is a subcultural activity which is denied public visibility, resistant reading cannot change the political agenda, cannot challenge other constructions of gay identity, and cannot have an impact on the ways people outside the group think about the issues which matter to the Gaylaxians.

The more that an audience is identified by researchers as an emblem of resistance to the dominant norms of television and contemporary society, the less likely it is that this audience group will be able to exert any actual power to create change in either television or society.

In a discussion of some of the many studies of women viewers of soap opera, for example, Ien Ang and Joke Hermes (1996) have pointed out that researchers have a tendency to assume that the responses of particular research respondents are representative of the larger group made up of women viewers in general. The impetus behind much audience research is to value the voices of viewers in a dominant television broadcasting culture which largely excludes them, and thus to claim power for the audience. Since research is always carried out with an explicit or implicit research agenda, or set of research questions, there is a tendency for academic publication of audience research to find the answers that it has already aimed to find. This problem is the same as the one identified above in relation to broadcasters' audience research, where interpretation of ratings information or focus group responses tends to validate the decisions made in the television industry in the past, producing inertia and circularity rather than innovation.

# Further reading

Allen, R., 'Audience-oriented Criticism and Television', in R. Allen (ed.), *Channels of Discourse, Reassembled: Television and Contemporary Criticism* (London: Routledge, 1992), pp. 101–37.

Ang, I., *Watching Dallas: Soap Operas and the Melodramatic Imagination* trans. D. Couling, revised edition (London: Routledge, 1989).

Ang, I., *Desperately Seeking the Audience* (London: Routledge, 1991).

Ang, I., *Living Room Wars: Rethinking Audiences for a Postmodern World* (London: Routledge, 1996).

Ang, I. and J. Hermes, 'Gender and/in Media Consumption', in I. Ang, *Living Room Wars: Rethinking Audiences for a Postmodern World* (London: Routledge, 1996), pp. 108–29.

Bignell, J., 'Writing the Child in Media Theory', *Yearbook of English Studies* 32 (2002), pp. 127–39.

Bignell, J., 'Shaping Audiences' and 'Television in Everyday Life', in *An Introduction to Television Studies* (London: Routledge, 2004), pp. 253–302.

Bruhn Jensen, K. (ed.), *News of the World: World Cultures Look at Television News* (London: Routledge, 1998).

Buckingham, D., *Public Secrets: EastEnders and its Audience* (London: BFI, 1987).

Buckingham, D., *Moving Images: Understanding Children's Emotional Responses to Television* (Manchester: Manchester University Press, 1996).

Dickinson, R., R. Harindranath and O. Linné (eds), *Approaches to Audiences: A Reader* (London: Arnold, 1998).

Dovey, J., *Freakshow* (Cambridge: Polity, 2000).

Drummond, P. and R. Patterson (eds), *Television and its Audience: International Research Perspectives* (London: BFI, 1988).

Ellis, J., 'Scheduling: The Last Creative Act in Television', *Media, Culture & Society* 22: 1 (2000), pp. 25–38.

Geraghty, C., *Women and Soap Opera: A Study of Prime Time Soaps* (Cambridge: Polity Press, 1991).

Geraghty, C., 'Audiences and "Ethnography": Questions of Practice', in C. Geraghty and D. Lusted (eds), *The Television Studies Book* (London: Arnold 1998), pp. 141–57.

Gray, A., *Video Playtime: The Gendering of a Leisure Technology* (London: Routledge, 1992).

Gripsrud, J., 'Television, Broadcasting, Flow: Key Metaphors in TV', in C. Geraghty and D. Lusted (eds), *The Television Studies Book* (London: Arnold 1998), pp. 17–32.

Hallam, J. and M. Marshment, 'Framing Experience: Case Studies in the Reception of *Oranges are Not the Only Fruit*', *Screen* 36: 1 (1995), pp. 1–15.

Jenkins, H., *Textual Poachers: Television Fans and Participatory Culture* (London: Routledge, 1992).

Lewis, L. (ed.), *The Adoring Audience: Fan Culture and Popular Media* (London: Routledge, 1991).

Liebes, T. and E. Katz, *The Export of Meaning: Cross-Cultural Readings of 'Dallas'* (New York: Oxford University Press, 1990).

Lull, J. (ed.), *World Families Watch Television* (London: Sage, 1988).

Morley, D., *Television, Audiences and Cultural Studies* (London: Routledge, 1992).

Petrie, D. and J. Willis (eds), *Television and the Household: Reports from the BFI's Audience Tracking Study* (London: BFI, 1995).

Ruddock, A., *Understanding Audiences: Theory and Method* (London: Sage, 2001).

Storey, J., *Cultural Consumption and Everyday Life* (London: Arnold, 1999).

Tulloch, J., *Watching Television Audiences: Cultural Theories and Methods* (London: Arnold, 2000).

Tulloch, J. and H. Jenkins, *Science Fiction Audiences: Watching Doctor Who and Star Trek* (London: Routledge, 1995).

Tunstall, J., *The Media in Britain* (London: Constable, 1983).

# 11 | Approaches to narrative

## Introduction

A nalysing narrative requires the distinction between story and discourse. Story is the set of events that are represented. They could potentially be told in any order (chronologically, or in flashback for example) and with any emphasis. Discourse is the narrating process that puts story events in an order, with a shape and direction. In any medium, someone or something must be doing the storytelling, and this agency is the narrator, whether it is a voice, on-screen performer, or simply the agency that viewers reconstruct as the force that controls the arrangement of camera shots, sound and music that deliver the story. Some fictional and non-fictional programmes have voice-over narrators throughout, or in particular sequences. *Star Trek: The Next Generation* begins with the familiar scene-setting narration for the programme as a whole, beginning with the 'Captain's log' where a voice-over narrates the setting and situation at the start of each episode's story. This is followed by the narration at the start of the title sequence, beginning 'Space, the final frontier . . .'. Narration can sometimes be found in the title songs of programmes, as in *Fresh Prince of Bel-Air* and *One Foot in the Grave*. Series like *ER* may open with voice-over reminding the audience of scenes in a previous programme. A few drama programmes include a voice-over narrator or an on-screen narrator within scenes, as in *Sex and the City*. Non-fiction programmes such as wildlife programmes, history programmes like *Time Team*, commercials, cooking programmes, and Reality TV such as *Big Brother* or *Survivor* have narrators. In each of these examples, the function of the narrator is to establish a link between the audience and the programme narrative, by inviting the viewer to involve himself or herself in the ongoing progress of the story.

Although some programmes make the function of narration explicit in these ways, all television narratives rely on the more complex narration made up of camera shots in a narrative progression, often with music linking shots together into sequences and giving them an emotional point of view. Sarah Kozloff (1992: 79) notes that: 'Music, in film and in television, is a key channel through which the voiceless narrating agency "speaks" to the viewer.' The viewer is aligned with point of view shots of characters or performers, alternating with apparently neutral shots that observe the represented space and the figures in it. The performers in television fiction behave as if the viewer is absent, making it more evident that the camera is the agency conveying their actions to the audience, whereas factual programmes perhaps make narration less obvious because the camera appears to be more a neutral observer. But in each case, there is an implied narrator composed from the different camera positions.

The significance of narration is partly that the viewer is necessarily positioned by the changing sequence of camera shots, the words of on-screen or off-screen narrators, and the accompanying music. The position of the viewer is the place to which all of them are directed and from where they can make sense as a coherent whole. Television viewers make an identification with the audience position laid out for them. In other words, the television viewer has occupied the role laid out for him or her by television, which is doing the looking on his or her behalf. It is often hard to specify what this institutional narrator is, whether for instance it is the production team who made the programme, or the channel on which it is broadcast. Both of these vague collective agencies seem to make claims to be overall narrators by virtue of the credits and copyright ownership information in the end titles of programmes, the narrating voice of off-screen announcers who connect programmes with each other, and by the channel idents and logos that appear between programmes and are sometimes superimposed in the corner of the screen. This narrating discourse hails an individual viewer to constitute himself of herself as part of an audience.

## Semiotics

Semiotics is a method of study that gets its name from the Greek word that means sign, and it analyses how signs communicate meanings (see

Bignell 2002). Semiotics started by working on language, made up of signs (such as words) which communicate meanings. More recently semioticians have turned their attention to all kinds of other things that communicate meanings and can be studied in the same way as linguistic signs, using the same methods of analysis. In television, the images of people, places and things are termed iconic signs, which means that they resemble what they represent. A TV image of a tree looks like a real tree. But of course the image is two-dimensional, in a frame, with a certain composition, colour, depth of focus and perspective. The way the image of the tree has been constructed can shape the viewer's understanding of its meaning. Perhaps the shot will make the tree seem beautiful, magical, mysterious or threatening, especially if music or sound effects have been added to the shot. Signs give form and meaning to thought and experience instead of just showing what was already there, so the study of television signs in semiotics is a crucial tool for explaining how meanings are made.

The key questions semiotics asks include how an image or sequence represents something. Showing something is called denotation, but TV images never simply show in a neutral way. They always suggest shades of meaning, as in the example of the tree above. These shades of meaning are called connotations, and semiotics concerns how these connotations appear in single shots and how they are connected with the connotations of the shots before and after, and in comparable shots, sequences, whole programmes or whole genres.

The meanings conveyed by signs often have much to do with how they are used according to the rules or conventions of a code. The word code is used here in a similar way to the phrase 'dress codes', to refer to the appropriate choice to make in a certain situation. For example, a television sequence of a newsreader behind a desk gains its meanings by drawing on recognisable codes. The newsreader looks into the camera, and addresses the viewer. He or she normally wears formal clothing, and speaks in a controlled and unemotional way. These aspects of shot type, costume and mode of address are all signs that belong to the conventions of news TV, the codes of news television programmes. Different codes constrain the way we might shoot and understand a drama sequence showing cowboys shooting at each other on the main street of a western town. Codes of camerawork, costume and language would be different from TV news, and looking closely at how the visual and aural signs in the programme are used will tell us how the meanings of the programme are made. The semiotic concept of code is useful in dividing signs into groups, and working out how their meaning depends on their membership of codes. Individual signs become meaningful because of their difference from the other signs that could have been chosen in any shot or sequence. But the role of signs as members of code groupings means that many signs are heavily loaded with a significance that comes from the code in which they are used.

When analysing television narrative, using semiotics is an essential starting-point that reminds us to identify exactly what choices have been made to communicate a meaning. Semiotic methods would involve asking why a certain shot was selected at this moment rather than another shot, and what the effects of the selection are. By thinking about whether a certain shot or sound conforms to the conventions of a code, it is possible to show how viewers are predisposed to interpret a shot, sound or sequence according to their knowledge of television codes. If you want to describe how a shot or sequence is funny, exciting, mysterious or boring, semiotics provides the means to do this. The meanings of television depend on the selection and combination of visual and aural signs, and how these signs connect with codes that viewers recognise.

## Flow

The academic and novelist Raymond Williams was the television reviewer for the BBC magazine *The Listener* between 1968 and 1972. In 1973 he wrote about his first exposure to American television in the previous year (Williams 1990: 91–2). Williams claimed that

> in all developed broadcasting systems the characteristic organisation, and therefore the characteristic experience, is one of sequence or flow. This phenomenon, of planned flow, is then perhaps the defining characteristic of broadcasting, simultaneously as a technology and as a cultural form.
>
> (Williams 1990: 86)

He was less interested in analysing specific programmes or forms of programme than in the experience of television itself. The flow of material constitutes the experience of television, and also carries a flow of meanings and values deriving from culture and expressing that culture's characteristic modes of thought.

Williams wrote about his experience of American television as if it were typical of all television, and this made some of his conclusions questionable. Rick Altman (1986) argues that flow is not a characteristic of television itself but part of a specific cultural practice of American commercial television, where audiences are measured and sold to advertisers, and flow is required to ensure that the television is switched on even if audiences are not watching it. Altman's critique of Williams's insight draws attention to the fact that programme flow does not illuminate anything about the texts that are part of the TV flow, or the ways in which audiences actually respond to them. Williams's concept of flow confuses a property of the text (the continuing flow of images) and a form of audience response (a flow of feelings and experiences). Williams regards the flow of television as irresponsible, and John Fiske (1987: 100) has argued that this is a result of Williams's background as a literary critic and academic, specialising in the analysis of the novel and drama. For Fiske, Williams was articulating a desire that a named author should take responsibility for a text and provide a principle of unity that organises it. John Ellis (1982: 112) also revisited Williams's concept of flow and argued that Williams regarded the individual programme as the basic unit of television and thereby underestimated the significance of the segment: 'small sequential unities of images and sounds whose maximum duration seems to be about five minutes.' The links between segments are not causal but instead they have relations of juxtaposition and sequence. Ellis emphasised the real and potential liveness of television broadcasting, and argued that television's direct address produces a relationship of intimacy where the separation and immersion of cinema is replaced by glancing and overhearing. So although Ellis's argument distances television from cinema and the novel, and clarifies the notion of flow to some extent, it also reduces the difference between the genres and forms of television, such as factual and fictional forms, in favour of the similarities between segments and the similar modes of attention and address in different kinds of programme.

Nevertheless, these examples of later writers pointing out errors and omissions in Williams's idea have not diminished the fundamental significance of the idea of flow in studying television. The idea is still very commonly thought of as a key way of distinguishing TV from other media such as cinema. The concept of flow opened the way for numerous later studies of how television programmes follow each other in an unbroken schedule through the day, and how viewers experience TV as flow of images, sounds and meanings.

# Ideology

Ideology refers to the 'natural' and common sense values that keep civil society running. It was an idea most thoroughly developed by radical Marxist writers who looked for ways of explaining how social injustice can continue without people recognising it and changing things. What ideology does is to make ways of thinking about ourselves and others seem self-evidently right, whereas a more careful analysis of the way things are might reveal that there is much that should be changed. In relation to television, the study of ideology looks at how people and ideas are represented in programming, to identify whether such concerns as race, gender, age group or ethnicity are being distorted in ways that need to be modified. It also considers how television is organised as a business, for example to determine whether it is controlled in the interests of the audience or for the benefit of an elite group of owners and shareholders. The pattern of television broadcasting that dominated the twentieth century and continues today was neither natural nor necessary. But it suited modern societies characterised by democracy and citizenship, and participation in a consumer society where owning a television means also being the recipient of commercial advertising messages. The home is not only the location of private leisure and family life, but also the site where ideological meanings are consumed and expressed through watching television and desiring or buying the commercial products and services advertised on it. Television in the home provides access by government and industry to private space and private life. This ideological conception of the place of television in people's lives and homes focuses on television's cultural role: it emphasises how television has become embedded in people's lives, in the places they live, the social structures to which they belong, and how television forms and reinforces the expectations about home, work and leisure that they hold.

In the police series, the task of the policemen or detective is to assemble evidence and information into a narrative of the crime. So the narrative of the programme is occupied with the construction of this other narrative whose events occurred usually either before the beginning of the programme, or in its opening few minutes. The closure of the narrative and the resolution of the programme are achieved when the policeman or detective has completed the assembly of the narrative of the crime. This narrative of the crime is presented to the perpetrator, or perhaps to a court or to the detective's superior. The programme can end when this narrative of the crime is confirmed as true, most often by the confession of the criminal. At this point, the ideologically correct positions of the characters can be established: the criminal is captured, justice is done for the victims, the policeman or detective has done his or her job, and the superior officer is satisfied. The stability of society and the security of the positions occupied by the various characters are confirmed. For the ordered structure of the narrative, its movement from beginning to middle to end is, itself, a kind of proof that the assumptions and actions of its central characters are justified. The world of the police show is set up so that the events in that world justify the behaviour of its central characters. The structure of the narrative supports the structure of ideology.

In an apparently very different example, *Big Brother* can be seen as a coded representation of the ideological conditions of contemporary society (like the fictional novel by George Orwell, *Nineteen Eighty-four*, from which its title derives). In *Big Brother* and other examples of Reality TV, individuals pursue self-interest and try to win a prize, but to do this they have to participate in a community. There is a tension between self-interest and participation. A structure of rules is imposed on the contestants, devised and enforced by the producers who act as a ruling elite who possess the power to punish or exile contestants from the show. Participants are required to work at tasks or undergo challenges in order to receive essential supplies and gain rewards. These components of the programme are evidence that *Big Brother* and other competitive Reality TV formats are variations on a metaphor for contemporary capitalist society. *Big Brother* substitutes the house for society at large, and sets up the tensions between freedom and restraint, individual and community, and work and pleasure, which characterise contemporary ideology. *Big Brother* is not a critique of the ideology that it reproduces, and ideological analysis demonstrates that Reality TV both shows and conceals, reflects and distorts, the realities that it represents.

## Realism

As John Corner (1992: 98) notes, realism has been regarded as 'television's defining aesthetic and social project'. The notion of realism operates as a standard of value within television institutions and for audiences, since each of these regard the connection of television programmes with reality as a basis for judging the value of television programmes. Raymond Williams (1976, 1977) discriminates between different definitions of realism, and first notes that the term 'real' is used in contrast to 'imaginary', to refer to the material existence of something in contrast to an unreal or fantastical world. This first definition concerns a notion of representation as reflection. Realism as reflection is connoted not only by what is represented, but also by the level of apparently redundant detail included in a programme's *mise-en-scène* (which means the choices of casting, lighting, sound, music and shot composition it uses). Redundancy consists of the inclusion in the narrative of a number of signs that have a contextual or supporting role, to provide texture and tone. Details of setting, costume, much of the detail of dialogue, and some of the narrative action is likely to be redundant from the point of view of the story. But in programmes claiming to be realistic, redundancy has the crucial effect of embedding the story in a fully realised world. Furthermore, one of the ways that narratives can be most pleasurable and interesting is when the relationship between redundancy and functional narrative components is changed in the course of the story. In detective narratives and whodunits, for example, an apparently redundant detail that seemed simply to lend texture to the fictional world might turn out to be a crucial clue. In science fiction television, redundancy is crucial to establishing a futuristic environment as realistic, in the sense that it has the detail and texture for it to be believable.

In a second meaning of realism, Williams points out that 'real' contrasts with the 'apparent', and refers to a hidden truth that might be revealed beneath the surface of what is communicated. This meaning of realism refers to revelation or analysis. Nineteenth-century notions of representation assumed that the real world could be adequately explained, and could be satisfactorily represented. Williams argues that this produces three features in realism: it is contemporary, it is concerned with actions that can be explained and that take place in the material world and, third, it is socially extended in that it has an ambition to represent ordinary people. As a consequence, a fourth element of realism is its ambition to interpret the world in relation to a certain political viewpoint in order to produce understanding. Williams was a literary critic, and noted that naturalism in literature is a descriptive method that observes the detail of reality whereas, in contrast, realism aims to produce the experience of dynamic struggle over what reality is like, in order to provide an understanding of contradiction and causality. So realisms are possible inasmuch as they admit that they are partial. Realist representations in this critical sense are not deceptive appearances or figments of someone's imagination, they take on the task of representing the real world and confront it without being able to resolve its contradictions. For television, detailed representations of a real-seeming world can be found in dramas such as literary adaptations, or in documentaries such as *Blue Planet*, and these would be more naturalistic than realist. The interest in competing world-views and how events are caused in programmes such as *The Cops* or the drama-documentary *Dirty War* about a terrorist attack, make these examples realist.

## Identification

Narrative depends on a shifting pattern of identification between the viewer and the programme. Viewers can identify with both fictional and non-fictional performers but also distance themselves from a performer (in order to find him or her funny, for instance). In some genres, viewers can also identify with a studio audience, taking up a shared position in relation to what the studio audience and home audience have seen. Narrative requires the shifting of the viewer's position into and out of the television programme, and a rhythm of identification and disavowal of identification. Narrative lays out positions for its viewers, offering signs and codes that invite them to make sense of and enjoy what they see and hear. But whether or not viewers actually occupy the position of being-an-audience, and how they inhabit this position, depends on the many variables comprising each viewer's social and psychological identity. In consequence of this, television theory has drawn, sometimes with reluctance, on an account of identification developed by psychoanalytic criticism and used to discuss cinema (as well as other media).

The pleasure of seeing images on TV brings with it an awareness of absence, that 'I' am separate from what I see, and am not 'you', 'he' or 'she'. Narrative offers numerous images of other people, places and things, and keeps repeating the pleasurable moment of identifying with others who the viewer is not, and the displeasure of recognising otherness forever beyond him or her. Wanting to watch television is part of the viewer's desire for the other, which narrative keeps displacing onto the next moment in the succession of images and sounds that it presents. This psychoanalytic account of pleasure in watching television has therefore argued that there are several identifications that viewers make. The first of these is an identification with the television medium, as something that delivers images that promise to satisfy viewers' desire to see and imagine themselves differently. There are also identifications with all the figures on the screen, the performers who stand in for the viewer and play out the roles that the viewer might desire to play. There are identifications with the fictional and non-fictional worlds presented in television, just as in a day-dream or fantasy we might imagine and place ourselves within fictional worlds. Narrative texts are constructed from a network of looks: relations between the looks of the figures, the look of the camera, and the viewer's look. The movement of television narrative in this way is analogous to fantasies that allow for mobile patterns of identification across different positions. All the possible roles in the narrative are available to the viewer: he or she can imagine being the one who looks or the one who is looked at, and can occupy a position outside the scene, looking on from a spectator's point of view. The disjuncture between these looks and positions is parallel to the cutting and juxtaposing of different views in TV narrative to defer complete knowledge and total vision to the viewer, thereby stimulating the desire to keep on looking. Television narratives work by offering, connecting and partially fulfilling the viewer's many divergent identifications and understandings of the programme, and binding them into coherence.

This psychoanalytic model offers a very complex understanding of the processes of watching television, whereby it can be understood in terms of mobile processes of making sense, experiencing pleasure and displeasure, and giving and withholding interest. The approach was developed for understanding film spectatorship, where film viewers are much more likely to be immersed in narratives. The dark space of the cinema, the large size of the screen, and the choice to place oneself in the position of a viewer among an audience of other viewers, all militate in favour of much greater involvement in film than viewers often experience watching television. John Ellis (1982: 137) pointed out this distinction by describing the viewer's look at television as a glance, rather than the concentrated gaze of the film spectator. In response to this distinction, television theorists have increasingly moved away from psychoanalytic accounts of television viewing, and instead examined how television narratives offer audience positions for viewers who may be often disengaged glancers rather than immersed spectators.

## Structures

The predominant structures used in television narrative are the series and the serial. Serials consist of a developing story divided into several parts, and television soap opera is a special case of the serial form where the end of the story is infinitely deferred. The series form denotes programmes in which the settings and characters do not change or develop, but where new stories involving the continuing characters and setting are presented in each episode. Contemporary television programmes now frequently combine the series features of a single setting and new stories in each episode, with the developing characters and stories that occur in serials. Robin Nelson (1997) has coined the term 'flexi-narrative' to denote fiction such as this which adopts the short sequences of action and rapid editing that occur in television advertisements, along with the developing characters and stories found in television soap opera, and the new stories each episode that are found in television series. The flexi-narrative form is a case of the combination of television structures.

The hospital drama series *Casualty* is a flexi-narrative, whose narrative is patterned to include periodic bursts of rapid action interspersed with more leisurely character development, and the programme as a whole is segmented into a large number of relatively short scenes. The longer and slower scenes of character interaction draw on the conventions of soap opera, in which reaction by one character to events in the life of another are represented by frequent close-up, emotional cues provided by music, and an emphasis on the viewer's memory of past events in the characters' lives to enrich what is happening in the narrative present. By contrast, the shorter scenes of rapid activity, usually scenes in which the doctors respond to the arrival of an injured person, use rapid hand-held camera shots and rapid editing. These action sequences use conventions deriving from observational documentary or news footage of action caught on the run by the camera, adding to this the uses of dramatic music and complex sound found in action drama series, such as police shows. The US hospital series *ER* does similar things in a more extreme way. Flexi-narratives such as *Casualty* or *ER* are borrowing conventions and narrative structures from other programme genres, a technique of allusion for which the theoretical term is intertextuality. Intertextuality is essential to television, and it is one of the means for programmes and advertisements to establish their similarity and difference from other programmes and advertisements, and from other media texts.

Binary oppositions underlie the narrative structures of many television programmes, for example oppositions between masculine and feminine, or young and old. The tradition in British sitcom, for example, is to oppose: masculinity and femininity, work and domesticity, rationality and emotionalism, intolerance and tolerance. Humour derives from contrasting these values when they are each embodied in a character, and also from aligning a character who might be expected to represent one side of binary with the other side. For example, Victor Meldrew in *One Foot in the Grave* was masculine and intolerant, but redundant from his work and in an enforced domestic setting that is conventionally regarded as feminine. This offered numerous occasions to create comedy from his sense of being 'out of place' in a situation. *Frasier* adds to this by setting up oppositions between sophistication and crudeness, youth and age, so that Frasier's and his brother Niles's sophistication and relative youth can be contrasted against their father's crudeness and elderliness, for example. The simplified character-positions in sitcom are too excessive to be 'realistic' because it is important to the comedy for a character's place in a system of binary oppositions to be clear in contrast to another character. Sitcom narrative sets up oppositions and connections, which by the end of an episode have been laid to rest. The movement of sitcom narrative keeps repeating and developing incompatibilities and compatibilities, playing on the already established position of each character in the system of binaries. But the audience's pleasure partly derives from the anticipation that these conflicts will be resolved satisfactorily. The audience needs to recognise the narrative codes of sitcom and the stakes of the binary oppositions in order to accept the surprising reversals and conflicts in it. The interruption of laughter and close-ups on the performers' facial expressions are important narrative turning-points where the viewer is invited to recognise a conflict or reversal among the binary oppositions, and measure its effect on the characters by reading their expressions. The bursts of laughter in the narrative set out the rhythm and pattern in each scene, and punctuate the narrative with stopping-points. This rhythm of stops and starts keeps confirming the position laid out for the viewer to make sense of the narrative and find it funny.

## *Mise-en-scène*

Human vision is binocular. Having two eyes close to each other but in different positions provides two slightly different images of the world which the brain interprets as a three-dimensional image with depth and perspective. TV cameras mimic many features of human vision, but television pictures are noticeably flatter so that techniques of lighting, sound and shot composition are used to produce the impression of depth and coherence. Programme makers have in mind the relationships of one shot to another, and shots that 'will cut' are those where the point of view of the camera and the relationships that comprise the shot composition fit the conventions of editing. Shots that will not cut are those where conventions are not being followed and for the viewer there will appear to be a leap from one represented space to another, from one camera point of view to another. In drama, for example, the conventions of a 'shot reverse-shot' will allow alternations of point-of-view between speakers so long as the camera does not break the 180 degree rule.

Shot composition allows the relationships between people, and between people and things, to be expressed in spatial terms. More interesting uses of shot composition contribute to narrative progression and the tone and meaning of television sequences. The distance between speakers in two-shots, for example, and the relative closeness of each of them to the camera, can be manipulated to signify the quality of their relationship and to generate dramatic tension between them. Similarly, positioning characters in frames within the camera frame (such as doorways, windows or mirrors) can create spatial relationships that connote entrapment, or produce a feeling of distance between the audience and the character.

For example, *Attachments* was a BBC drama serial about a company constructing a website, seethru.co.uk (the website actually existed, and followed the fictional story of the programme). The camera style of *Attachments* evolved from decisions by Simon Heath (the producer) and Tony Garnett (head of World Productions) to match the static environment of the company office with no moving camera work, to emphasise the close attention to details on computer screens that the characters' work involved by using a lot of close-up shots, and to allude to the very wide shot size of webcams by including wide shots covering the entire office space. Simon Heath commented in an unpublished interview with Helen Quinney in 2001:

> The energy of the show would come from its cutting style, which itself was a product of having lots of different angles on a scene. We were going for big wide shots which would take in the whole of the office, and then an ordinary close-up, and then a much tighter close-up that

would highlight eyes, or mouth – the sort of detail you don't neces- sarily get on television but that you sometimes get in cinema. And then by fast cutting between different sizes and different angles and different characters in the scene, we'd generate an energy in the same way that a panning camera gave us the energy in *This Life* [World Productions' earlier hit drama serial].

The aesthetic of *Attachments* allows figures to be shot in profile, some- times with objects masking them, and even shooting through window blinds. By breaking some of the rules of television camera technique, the drama found an aesthetic appropriate to the setting, characters and subject.

Shot composition is inseparable from point of view, where the camera's closeness to or separation from the action is extremely influential on the audience's relationship with the action and the characters. For instance, the sense of being involved in the action or kept separate from it, the sense of being given information transparently by the camera or being denied it, are produced by the interactions between shot composition and point of view, and the relationship between one shot and those before and after it. The tone and meaning of television sequences can be further enhanced by the use of lighting, sound and music. No single element of a shot or sequence carries an intrinsic meaning; it attains its meaning by its interaction with the other elements of the programme. Tone and meaning depend on all the elements that contribute to *mise-en-scène*: the lighting, music, sound, shot composition, props and objects in frame, costume, and camera movement.

Sound adds dramatic perspective to images by providing a 'sound point of view' on the action: action in long shot can be accompanied by sound appearing to bring the action much closer to the audience by its volume and clarity, or on the other hand close-up action can be distanced from the audience by muting or blurring sound. In documentary, background sound will be captured by the sound recordist, as well as the speech or other sync sound, for use to cover edits, and provide a background sound- scape for the programme. In drama, sound can subtly suggest off-screen intrigue, or provide a rhythmical foundation to the programme, as in the ticking of a clock or approaching footsteps. Contrasting sound and image provokes moods and tones that shape interpretation for the audience, while sound montage opens up a whole range of meanings when running parallel with montages of images.

Television genres have their own codes that enable viewers to recog- nise and expect particular kinds of meaning and pleasure. While many genres use extreme long shots (ELS) at the beginning of scenes and sequences to establish a physical location, close-up (CU) is very often used to denote emotion signified by performers' facial expressions. In general, the greater a genre's emphasis on emotional reaction, the greater the proportion of close-up shots. But while close-up is a signifier of performance in television *mise-en-scène*, and seems highly dramatic, the shot-length in soap opera and other emotionally focused dramas is relatively long. Shots are held in order to observe characters' reactions to each other, whereas in action dramas such as police or hospital programmes, there is less close-up and shorter shot length. Action dramas also use codes of shot composition differently, since static composition allows space to contemplate performance in soap opera versus the dynamic moving shot composition in police and hospital dramas such as *NYPD Blue* or *ER* which focus on disorientation, disorder, and seem to capture action as it is 'naturally' occurring. Colour choices are also significant to *mise-en-scène*, for example the sitcom *My Family* connotes the warm and comfortable environment of middle-class suburbia with yellow, red, and brown, while other programmes (such as *The X Files*) use the conventionally colder colours of blue, grey and black to signify a more threatening and uncertain environment.

# Further reading

Altman, R., 'Television Sound', in T. Modleski (ed.), *Studies in Entertainment: Critical Approaches to Mass Culture* (Bloomington: Indiana University Press, 1986), pp. 39–54.

Bignell, J., *Media Semiotics: An Introduction*, 2nd edn (Manchester: Manchester University Press, 2002).

Bignell, J., 'Television Texts and Television Narratives', in *An Introduction to Television Studies* (London: Routledge, 2004), pp. 85–112.

Corner, J., 'Presumption as Theory: "Realism" in Television Studies', *Screen* 33: 1 (1992), pp. 97–102.

Ellis, J., *Visible Fictions: Cinema, Television, Video* (London: Routledge and Kegan Paul, 1982).

Fairclough, N., *Media Discourse* (London: Arnold, 1995).

Fiske, J., *Television Culture* (London: Routledge, 1987).

Fiske, J. and J. Hartley, *Reading Television* (London: Methuen, 1978).

Hall, S., 'encoding/decoding', in S. Hall, D. Hobson, A. Lowe and P. Willis (eds), *Culture, Media, Language* (London: Hutchinson, 1980), pp. 128–38.

Kozloff, S., 'Narrative Theory and Television', in R. Allen (ed.), *Channels of Discourse, Reassembled: Television and Contemporary Criticism* (London: Routledge, 1992), pp. 67–100.

Lacey, N., *Narrative and Genre: Key Concepts in Media Studies* (Basingstoke: Macmillan, 2000).

Nelson, R., *TV Drama in Transition: Forms, Values and Cultural Change* (Basingstoke: Macmillan, 1997).

Seiter, E., 'Semiotics, Structuralism, and Television', in R. Allen (ed.), *Channels of Discourse, Reassembled: Television and Contemporary Criticism* (London: Routledge, 1992), pp. 31–66.

Tolson, A., *Mediations: Text and Discourse in Media Studies* (London: Arnold, 1996).

Williams, R., *Keywords: A Vocabulary of Culture and Society* (London: Fontana, 1976).

Williams, R., 'A Lecture on Realism', *Screen* 18: 1 (1977), pp. 61–74.

Williams, R., *Television, Technology and Cultural Form* (London: Routledge, 1990).

# 12 Factual television: tabloid TV?

## Introduction

Television audiences are invited to experience the lives of other people through factual TV forms, so factual television carries assumptions of both realism and social responsibility. Factual programmes play a key role in the public service commitment to disseminate information about contemporary events, and the range of attitudes and ways of life among the population. Television documentary and other factual genres aim both to mirror society to itself and to show the diversity that exists within that society. Documentary was initiated in the film medium and was designed to be socially responsible, and to be an art of record in contrast to cinematic fantasy. In television, documentary especially is able to take up the requirement for public service by focusing objectively and with authority on public events. Its realism is a particular form which not only denotes a real world but also makes it public and explains it. Documentary makes an argument and centres on evidence, and this usually includes some reliance on narration and interpretation. In other words, documentary always has a point of view, even if it claims to be a neutral one.

Television has always placed great emphasis on the moment of the present, especially in its factual output, partly because live broadcasting has been so significant throughout the development of the medium. There are plenty of factual programmes about the past (such as *Time Team*), but even in those there is usually some connection with the present. *Time Team*'s archaeological digs take place against the clock, and the site is always shown first in the modern present before the digging into the past begins. Programmes about historical figures suggest parallels and contrasts between ancient kings and modern-day rulers, or between ordinary people's ways of life in the past and the way most people live in Britain today. Television has always been used to relay events (such as sporting events, royal weddings and general elections) live across the country, thus keeping people in touch with what is thought to be significant. Contemporary television still devotes much of the available broadcast time to factual programmes, though now they are rarely live. Both factual and fiction programmes seek new kinds of realism to engage the audience in up-to-the-minute ways. All of this derives from the assumption that television informs a national audience about the actual state of society, and that knowledge about what is happening now is essential to a democratic and humane culture. This kind of assumption about what television is for can be seen in BBC Producers' Guidelines (2003), for example, which include this general principle: 'The BBC has a responsibility to serve all sections of society in the United Kingdom. Its domestic services should aim to reflect and represent the composition of the nation.'

Reflecting the nation means representing both what is considered normal and ordinary as well as what is deviant and exceptional. Since the late nineteenth century, photographic media have been used for collecting criminal evidence, and to record scenes of crime. Factual television continues this tradition, by both representing people who might be 'just like me' in *What Not to Wear* for example, and also people who seem very different from the norm (in *Too Posh to Wash*, for instance). There is still interest in representing the special kind of deviance that constitutes crime, perhaps by using surveillance footage as the raw material for programmes. But because documentary and factual programmes have this role of reflecting reality and representing society, there are continual debates over whether individuals, groups or issues are represented fairly. The medium of TV introduces the notion of a restriction of vision as well as a privileged vision, since the camera can select and emphasise particular shots, and editing and postproduction in general will inevitably construct meaning and point of view through selection and combination of images and sound.

## Documentary forms

In order to produce the impression of realism in television documentary, several very unnatural procedures have to be carried out. The documentary subject will almost always be aware that he or she is being recorded, witnessed or even pursued by the camera operator and often also by a sound recordist. Once the footage has been gathered, the documentary maker will edit the footage together in order to produce a coherent argument or a narrative. While the finished programme may acknowledge the presence of the documentary maker, it is often the case that documentaries imply that the subject is behaving 'naturally' or at least representatively. There is a tension between producing a documentary that is representative and 'accurate' and providing the audience with a programme that conforms to the conventions of argument or storytelling.

Paradoxically, the impression of reality in documentary television can often depend on supporting narration, testimony or expert commentary that provides an interpretive context for the observational denotation of the camera and diegetic sound. These devices link documentary with other factual genres, where the authority of a narrator provides coherence and continuity, such as in motoring programmes where an on-screen or off-screen narrator explains the features of a new model. In documentary, testimony of members of the public supports the authenticity of the programme, as it also does in some television commercials, where members of the public declare their preference for a certain brand of headache pill for example. Expert commentary provides backing for the assertions and arguments of the programme maker or the figures appearing in the programme, and this can also be seen in sports programmes, science programmes, nature programmes and current affairs. So although documentary always makes claims to represent a real world, it borrows some of the codes and conventions from various other kinds of factual and fiction programmes.

Some documentary conventions connote unmediated reality, such as hand-held cameras, 'natural' rather than expressive lighting, and imperfect sound, while other conventions connote drama, argument and interpretation, such as voice-over, narrative structure, and contrastive editing. The grainy images from closed circuit television in some factual programmes carry powerful political and social connotations. They police the boundaries between normal and deviant or criminal behaviour, and provide evidence of it. Whereas documentary has a history of representing and arguing for those in society who are the least privileged, the most vulnerable to exploitation and the most marginalised, the use of footage from closed circuit television in factual television can reinforce marginalisation, deprive deviant behaviour and deviant people of the opportunity to explain and provide contexts for their actions, and remove their actions from larger social and political contexts. The pleasure for the audience is in seeing something hidden, seeing the very moment when something shocking and disturbing is happening, and the provision of this pleasure or the generation of anxiety take greater precedence than the investigation and exploration of the behaviour portrayed.

The device of metonymy in documentary enables part of reality to stand for the larger real world: metonymy is a term derived from linguistics that means using one thing to stand in for something else it is part of, or that is related to it. One day in the life of an airline worker in *Airport* metonymically stands for any other day. The work of a rural vicar in *A Country Parish* stands metonymically for the everyday experiences of all rural vicars. Specific images or sequences, or specific documentary subjects, have metonymic relationships with the reality of which they are a part. This device is one of the unstated assumptions that enable television programmes to claim implicitly that they represent society to itself, and connect the specific subjects of programmes to larger social contexts. But creating this kind of realism in documentary depends on the relationship between the codes of the programme and the codes available to the audience for interpreting it. Kilborn and Izod (1997: 39) refer to the shaping of documentary programmes to accord with the assumed knowledge of the audience, and they call this 'accommodation'. Documentaries about airlines or vicars accommodate themselves to some extent with ideological assumptions about airlines and vicars that circulate in society, and in other television programmes. Television documentary's claim to represent the real rests on negotiating with the ideologies that already shape reality for the audience.

Accommodation is a key feature of factual forms that not only rely on found footage, but also use covert surveillance systems in order to generate actuality. Programmes such as Granada Television's *Rattrap*, *Nannies from Hell* and others in the *from Hell* series such as *Neighbours from Hell* or *Plumbers from Hell* have adopted this technique. Programme narrators provide tips and information on how to spot inferior and overpriced work, and give guide prices for what particular common jobs should cost. There is an assumption that they are engaged in a public service, so that for example the company names of plumbing companies are shown on screen to inform viewers which businesses have been exposed. These programmes feature only the most disturbing and shocking incidents, and are necessarily unrepresentative. But they are successful as formats that can gain large audiences in comparison to traditional forms of documentary. The audience for the first programme in the *from Hell* sequence of series, *Neighbours from Hell*, was 11.5 million in 1997. This is a much larger audience than is conventionally gained for documentary programmes in their more traditional forms. By contrast, conventional documentary series such as *Storyville* have lower audiences and later and later positions in the schedule.

Recent variations on documentary have been very successful. For example, Channel 4 factual programmes drew a high proportion of viewers from the valuable ABC1 social groups (professional, managerial and skilled workers) who are attractive to advertisers: *The Kama Sutra* got a 54 per cent share of ABC1s, and *The 1940s House* 53 per cent. Factual programmes are scheduled in evening prime-time partly because they gain large or valuable audiences cheaply. They require few personnel and limited equipment: the Channel 4 documentary series *Undercover Britain*, for instance, needed just one person covertly operating a concealed button-sized camera, and no performers. Fiction drama cost about £650,000 per hour to make in the late 1990s, versus about £125,000 per hour for documentary. Quasi-documentary factual programmes have increased their appeal by focusing on the dramatic. One of the interesting consequences of this is the reduced importance of professional expertise in making sense of the issues denoted in programmes. The discourse of expertise tends to value middle-class virtues such as specialist knowledge, rationality and institutional solutions to problems. Newer documentary formats modify this with greater emphasis on personal stories, set-up situations, competition and inter-personal rivalry. They have borrowed some of the characteristics of drama and game shows.

The drama-documentary is of course a hybrid genre, and combines the codes of observation, witness and analysis from documentary with the narrative structure, focus on key 'characters' and movement towards resolution that derive from dramatic codes. Television drama-documentary re-tells events, often recent events, in order to review or celebrate them. The key figures and turning-points of the story are often familiar to the audience, and opening statements and captions make clear that they are based on fact. On the other hand, disclaimers may state that some events and characters have been changed, amalgamated or invented. Derek Paget's (1998: 82) definition of drama-documentary is that it

uses the sequence of events from a real historical occurrence or situation and the identities of the protagonists to underpin a film script intended to provoke debate. . . . The resultant film usually follows a cinematic narrative structure and employs the standard naturalist/realist performance techniques of screen drama.

Drama-documentary offers a single and personalised view of a dramatic situation, in which identification with central figures allows access for the audience, but where the documentation of a historical and situation 'objectively' sets these identifications into a social and political context. Narrative provides the linkage between the forms of documentary and of drama, as John Caughie (1980: 30) describes: 'If the rhetoric of the drama inscribes the document within narrative and experience, the rhetoric of the documentary establishes the experience as an experience of the real, and places it within a system of guarantees and confirmations.' British docudrama is based in carefully researched journalistic investigation, and follows the conventions of journalistic discourse such as the sequential unfolding of events, and the use of captions to identify key figures.

## Documentary, docusoap and quality

Co-production is increasingly common in the making of 'quality' documentary and factual forms, and more generally in all genres of television production. This is not only the case with major broadcasters such as the BBC, which has a long-standing track record of co-production agreements with the US and regional broadcasters in Germany and other European countries. Independent production companies in Britain also seek to finance documentaries by making agreements with programme financiers in a range of countries such as Canal Plus in France, the ABC network in Australia, and a range of smaller institutions worldwide. In factual television, certain genres such as the nature documentary are well-established formats in which co-production contributes significantly to the budget. In the case of nature programmes, the key production expense is filming on location, spending large amounts of time and money seeking interesting footage despite difficulties in locating rare animals, coping with difficult weather conditions, working without adequate technical support, and recruiting local staff on an ad hoc basis to support the production. But if good-quality footage can be obtained, the resulting film will be adaptable for translation of its commentary into innumerable languages, and can be sold to a large number of international buyers.

Docusoap combines the observation and interpretation of reality found in documentary with the continuing narrative centring on a group of characters in soap opera. In 1998 the ITV docusoap *Airline* achieved a 50 per cent average audience share, with 11.4 million viewers, while BBC1's *The Cruise* (aboard a cruise liner) and *Animal Hospital* attracted 10 million viewers and shares of 40 per cent each. BBC1's first prime-time factual programme, *Airport* (1998) attracted a 44 per cent audience share, and in response ITV moved their competitor, the fire service drama *London's Burning*, to a different placing in the schedule. But docusoaps have been criticised for lacking the depth of insight into character or situation that television documentary has conventionally aimed for. Formally, docusoaps use rapid cutting between scenes and characters to maintain audience interest, and do not adopt the sustained focus on the subject that has signified television documentary's quest for understanding. Perhaps the best-known (and controversial) docusoap of the turn of the twenty-first century was the BBC's *Driving School*, which was scheduled against the popular ITV police drama *The Bill* yet attracted twice as many viewers, peaking at 12 million.

The narrative codes of television fiction structured *Driving School*, and it featured quirky 'characters' experiencing dramatic moments and changes of fortune. Learner driver Maureen and her husband Dave became celebrities appearing on talk shows and in tabloid newspapers, after Maureen was represented nearly hitting other cars, weeping when she made mistakes, and arguing with her husband. The dramatic turning points, conflicts and moments of comedy were embedded in a narrative provided by voice-over narration. The emphasis on 'real-life drama' in *Driving School* was the subject of controversy when it was alleged that scenes had been 'faked', effectively scripted like drama rather than observed as in documentary. When Maureen was seen waking Dave in the early hours of the morning to go practising, this was a re-enactment, a fictionalised reconstruction. *Driving School* producers were also attacked for selecting subjects such as Maureen who were likely to exaggerate their emotions for the camera, and seemed keen to become celebrities. The 'objectivity' of documentary seemed to have been exchanged for 'entertainment', perverting the expectations of realism in factual television genres. For Graeme Burton (2000: 159), docusoap 'stands for a growing use of viewers to entertain the viewers – an approach familiar from the game-show genre and the use of studio audiences. It creates the illusion that television recognises its audience and works for its audience'. This inclusion of the audience and its perceived demands is even more striking in relation to the factual genre of Reality TV.

## Reality TV

The first 'people shows' or Reality TV formats in the US were driven by institutional concerns about audiences. In the US in the 1980s, the competition between four networks, cable channels, and the attractions of home video led to smaller sectors or 'niches' of the audience being targeted by programme makers and schedulers, defined either by age group, interest (such as sport), or social class. This was when MTV began, the channel that introduced the Reality TV format in its series *The Real World*. The same problems and opportunities that enabled Reality TV to come to prominence in the US emerged in Britain during the 1990s as new channels, cable and satellite began to erode and segment traditional audiences. In Britain, the term Reality TV was first applied to the combination of surveillance footage, reconstruction, studio presentation by presenters, and actuality footage in programmes such as *Crimewatch UK* and *Police, Camera, Action*.

*Crimewatch UK* both represents recent crimes in realistic ways, and also, as John Sears (1995: 51) has argued, performs 'a social function by helping to solve crime, and drawing on the collective responsibilities, experiences and knowledge of the viewing audience in order to do so'. This monthly BBC1 mid-evening programme has been running since 1984, and often features crimes that have been reported already in television news and newspapers, borrowing intertextual meanings from other media such as news and action drama. Fictionalised reconstructions of crimes aim to achieve change by dramatising events, emphasising particular details, sometimes shocking the audience and drawing them into the dramatic narrative of solving crimes. *Crimewatch* reduces its codes and conventions, and the problems it addresses, to a few highly coded images and devices which engage viewer knowledge derived from other genres of television, particularly crime drama. E-fits (images of suspects derived from witnesses' reports), photographs of stolen property, security camera footage and physical clues also appear in television police fiction. These coded images are metonyms, parts of the narrative of the crime that are connected with each other and stand in for the crime. Conversely, reconstructions on *Crimewatch* are metaphors that parallel the facts of the crime but are fiction. Although the programme constructs a sense of community, and works on behalf of society in general, it individualises its address to the viewer, and the crimes it features. The presenters of *Crimewatch* address viewers directly with questions such as 'Were you there that morning? Did you see him? Can you help?' The individual action requested from viewers is represented as a response to crimes perpetrated by individuals against individuals. Abstract and structural problems such as the complex of factors that cause crime, and crimes perpetrated by corporate bodies or government agencies are never represented in *Crimewatch*. The 'reality' of crime for *Crimewatch* is that it is committed by a small group of deviant outsiders, against certain unfortunate individuals. The consequence of this emphasis on individuation in *Crimewatch*, in common with many other programmes concerned with social problems, is blindness to the large-scale factors of social class, economics and ideologies of gender or race.

*Police, Camera, Action* is a factual programme which has connections with both news and police drama. It consists of a collection of extracts from police camera footage linked by the narrating voice of Alastair Stewart, a former newsreader, and the programme gains some of its connotations of public service by his association with the values of objectivity, seriousness and reliability that derive from television news. The footage in the programme mainly comprises shots from the cameras installed in police cars, as they follow or chase drivers either engaged in criminal activities (such as making a getaway from a robbery) or committing dangerous driving errors. The car chase is a conventional element of police drama, and normally occurs as a prelude to the capture of the criminal. Car-chase sequences in *Police, Camera, Action* do not have several camera set-ups available in drama, nor shots of the drivers of the police car or the drivers being pursued. The visual quality of the police camera footage is less polished and there is little alternation between points of view or manipulation of narrative time. But despite these differences, the function of the chase is still as an action sequence as a prelude to the capture of an offender. Since police pursuit drivers give a running commentary on their actions, there is also a diegetic soundtrack that helps to explain the action and provides access to the police understanding of events. Dramatic music is used, and the voice-over narration by Alastair Stewart mediates the pursuing police's commentary. Stewart points out the stupidity of errors made by drivers, the recklessness of criminals attempting to escape, and the danger posed to other road users. *Police, Camera, Action* draws connotations of public service and authority from news; it draws music, the narrative functions of the car chase and pursuit from the police drama series; and the visual conventions of the surveillance camera and found actuality footage from documentary.

The term Reality TV was then extended to include constructed factual programmes such as *Castaway* where situations were devised for the purpose of filming, and also extended to docusoaps such as *Airport* that impose on real events the editing techniques of parallel montage, character-focused narrative structure, and basis in a single geographical space and community, that are all found in fictional soap opera. Docusoap launched Reality TV as a more widely used and public term by grabbing large audiences throughout the 1990s. From docusoap, Reality TV has emerged as a term that describes programmes characterised by a controlled environment, free of documentary's heritage of social issues. It is closer to entertainment, and increasingly replaces entertainment in evening schedules. The result is not the authenticity and explanation of documentary, but rather the spectacle of the everyday and an emphasis on the performance of identity. But Mark Andrejevic (2002) argues that the artificiality of these scenarios in reality programmes is countered by their use of non-actor participants, no scripts, and a temporal progression that is close to the linear unfolding of lived daily time.

## Performance and Reality TV

Reality TV programmes claim a kind of realism by demonstrating how contestants attempt to keep up the façade of the persona they want to create, and yet reveal a kind of authenticity beneath this. Reality TV therefore borrows, perhaps surprisingly, some of the values attributed in drama to 'realistic' acting, and connects this to documentary's revelation of current social issues by means of telling personal stories. In terms of format, the casting of reality shows demands outgoing people and some possibility of conflict, so producers select people who will annoy each other. They test contestants physically (as in *Lad's Army* where contestants endured the hardships of 1950s National Service) and dramatic highpoints occur when occasionally contestants break down or are physically injured. Like drama, Reality TV programmes make use of character types, such as the villain exemplified by 'Nasty Nick' Bateman who plotted to get other contestants to vote against each other in the first series of the British *Big Brother*. The contestants found out and Big Brother ejected him from the house, but Nick became a celebrity and received about £150,000 from the tabloids for his story.

In Reality TV, the key moments in individual programmes are when the performance façade of the contestant falls away. This seems to reveal the real person, since the audience is aware that the rest of the time the contestant is performing the self that they wish to project. The most interesting participants are those who project a big personality and are interesting as characters, but the other side of this is that the audience wants to see those big characters reduced to ordinariness, thus re-connecting them with the audience. In drama, actors perform their identities as stars who the audience think they know, whereas contestants in Reality TV programmes perform both a public persona and also take on the role of ordinary people who are implicitly as fallible as the viewer.

Reality TV programmes claim to reveal insights into human behaviour in general, and attitudes among specific groups such as young adults. This claim of representativeness is enhanced by the use of newly developed techniques of live broadcasting, such as webcasting, and viewer interaction. *Big Brother*, for example, uses television's capacity to relay events live or almost live, and this has been one of the distinctive attractions of the medium since its invention. But documentary conventionally uses individuals as representatives of a social group. As Stella Bruzzi (2001: 132–4) and others have noted, reality programmes emphasise character and personality to the extent that individuals become relatively free of social determinants. Bill Nicholls (1994) argues that Reality TV distances the audience from reality, rather than seeking to represent and interpret it. Nicholls demonstrates that the American series *Cops*, beginning in 1989, was one of the first Reality TV programmes and seeks to control the disorder of reality by aligning the camera with the police so that threatening crimes and criminals become banal, and the abnormality and danger that many viewers perceive in the outside world is tamed.

## Reality TV and the identity of the medium

John Ellis (2000) has argued that one of the notable features of contemporary television is its focus on witness. What is at stake in debates about Reality TV is the relationship between television as a technology of record that can bear witness to an authentic truth, and television as a separate arena from actual life. If documentary is legitimate because it witnesses and records what would have been there anyway, Reality TV cannot be documentary because it creates what it records. However, documentary filmmakers and commentators very often confirm that this ideology of transparency was never more than a myth, or perhaps an alibi. Documentary and Reality TV both select and treat what they film, so the boundary between them suddenly melts away. The general question of boundaries and separation is central to the arguments about Reality TV. The question of why Reality TV matters depends on identifying what it is, and this identification is problematic. The problem occurs partly because of Reality TV's assimilation of elements of various fictional and factual television forms, partly a matter of its audience address, partly a matter of its institutional position in broadcast output, for example. Reality TV poses a question of definition, and encourages viewers, theorists and programme makers to ask what television is and what it is for. Does Reality TV mean TV that records reality? TV that makes a reality so it can be filmed? Is it the Reality of TV? And it asks about the generic boundaries between programmes and genres. In Reality TV we see television bearing witness to, and worrying over, fundamental questions of representation.

The presence in the television schedules of various forms of reality programming, often in combination with generic elements drawn from drama and other light entertainment forms testifies to the continuing demand for new generic combinations and new formats to provide novelty and engagement for the television audience. But it also represents a cultural preoccupation with the increasingly blurred boundaries between authenticity and performance. New consumer video shooting and editing technologies and the ability to exchange images over digital communication networks have led to an increased familiarity among the audience with the production practices, technical codes and structural conventions of film making. Recent years have been marked by debates about video surveillance, and the expectation, particularly among younger people, that they are subject to surveillance in many areas of public space. Blurring the boundaries between events that would have happened anyway and events performed for the purpose of recording is already a characteristic of television factual genres that have been around for a long time, such as the semi-staged interactions on television talk shows. Reality TV has been blended with genres such as the game show, soap opera, documentary and factual light entertainment programmes (home-improvement, cookery and gardening, for example). This can be regarded as a perpetuation of a process that is endemic to what television is. Television is both an external witness to, and a participant in, reality.

# Further reading

Andrejevic, M., 'The Kinder, Gentler Gaze of Big Brother: Reality TV in the Era of Digital Capitalism', *New Media and Society* 4: 2 (2002), pp. 251–70.

Bignell, J., 'Television Realisms', in *Media Semiotics: An Introduction*, 2nd edn (Manchester: Manchester University Press, 2002), pp. 131–54.

Bignell, J., 'Television Realities', in *An Introduction to Television Studies* (London: Routledge, 2004), pp. 183–208.

Bondabjerg, I., 'Public Discourse/Private Fascination: Hybridization in "True-Life-Story" Genres', *Media, Culture & Society* 18: 1 (1996), pp. 27–45.

Bruzzi, S., *The New Documentary: A Critical Introduction* (London: Routledge, 2000).

Bruzzi, S., 'Docusoaps', in G. Creeber (ed.), *The Television Genre Book* (London: Routledge, 2001), pp. 132–4.

Burton, G., *Talking Television: An Introduction to the Study of Television* (London: Arnold, 2000).

Caughie, J., 'Progressive Television and Documentary Drama', *Screen* 21: 3 (1980) pp. 4–35.

Corner, J., *The Art of Record: A Critical Introduction to Documentary* (Manchester: Manchester University Press, 1996).

Dovey, J., *Freakshow* (Cambridge: Polity, 2000).

Ellis, J., *Seeing Things: Television in the Age of Uncertainty* (London: IB Tauris, 2000).

Kilborn, R. and J. Izod, *An Introduction to Television Documentary: Confronting Reality* (Manchester: Manchester University Press, 1997).

Nichols, B., *Representing Reality: Issues and Concepts in Documentary* (Bloomington: Indiana University Press, 1991).

Nichols, B., *Blurred Boundaries: Questions of Meaning in Contemporary Culture* (Bloomington: Indiana University Press, 1994).

Nichols, B., *Introduction to Documentary* (Bloomington: Indiana University Press, 2001).

Paget, D., *No Other Way to Tell It: Dramadoc/Docudrama on Television* (Manchester: Manchester University Press, 1998).

Sears, J., '*Crimewatch* and the rhetoric of verisimilitude', *Critical Survey* 7: 1 (1995), pp. 51–8.

Winston, B., *Claiming the Real: The Documentary Film Revisited* (London: BFI, 1995).

# 13  Drama and 'quality'

## Introduction

In television, quality might depend on the production values and monetary investment made in a programme. Or it might be a function of the apparent seriousness, creativity or originality of the production. Within the television industry, quality refers to lavishness of budgets, the skill of programme makers and performers, and the prestige accruing to programmes because of their audience profile and seriousness of purpose. But within the academic discipline of Television Studies, quality has a broader meaning that also focuses attention on popular television that might be regarded by insiders as merely commercial and generic work that has little aspiration to cultural or artistic value. While the question of quality applies to all television forms and genres, this chapter explores it in relation to drama. One of the reasons for this is that drama is the most expensive and usually the most prestigious kind of television, so it has a special relationship with understandings of quality.

In drama, the writer has traditionally had a higher profile than either the director or the producer. Writers are considered as uniquely creative originators of programmes, whose work is then realised by the production team. This has two consequences: first that judging the quality of drama often means judging the quality of the writing rather than the other aspects of a production. Second, as a result, it means that the criteria of quality have a lot in common with the criteria often used in literary criticism, where there is an emphasis on structure, a 'personal vision' or style, and the expectation that a drama has something to say about humanity or society. Academic thinking has moved away from these literary kinds of

levision Studies, because they seem to consider writers as
ged elite and neglect the crucial role of the teamwork that
ble, and also the role of the audience in making meaning
ers and other creative personnel have produced. Because
es of authorship, academic studies of television have
focused less on drama than other genres in the last couple of decades
because of the concern that studying drama, with its literary associations
with authorship, will entail the celebration of authors.

Within the television industry, particular authors have been elevated
to high status, and publicised to attract audiences and claim prestige for
channels and television companies. An author can function as a brand, a
familiar name that alerts the audience to styles and themes that a writer
has explored in the past, and distinguishes the programme from the
competitors scheduled against it and around it. But the establishment of
this authorial prestige is difficult, and only occurs when there are cultures
with a television production institution that will support it. In Britain, the
marketing of authors as brands occurred in the 1980s and 1990s in
relation to dramas by Lynda LaPlante for example (*Prime Suspect*, *Trial
and Retribution*), and classic novel adaptations by Andrew Davies (*Pride
and Prejudice*, *Emma*, *Middlemarch*). A few producers have occupied this
authorial branding role, such as Tony Garnett (*The Cops*, *Attachments*)
and the American Steven Bochco (*Murder One*, *NYPD Blue*). At the end
of this chapter a Profile of Lynda LaPlante provides an overview of this
writer's contribution to quality TV drama. But this chapter also considers
kinds of drama that are not associated with authorship, such as British
soap opera, and discusses how questions of quality might relate to them.

## Popular drama and 'quality'

The sociologist Pierre Bourdieu (1984) argues that the cultural products
regarded as the best are in fact those that are preferred by the most educated
and wealthy segment of a population. Because of their social power, the
elite are able to claim their tastes as superior, and as a result, the cultural
products that the elite prefer also validate the superior taste of the elite.
In this context, academic commentators have looked for ways of discriminating between good and bad television. This becomes especially
important in relation to arguments about television policy that seek to
counter the consumerist view that broadcasters should simply provide what

the largest number of viewers seem to want. Charlotte Brunsdon (1990: 70) asks: 'What are we going to do about bad television? Nothing, if we're not prepared to admit that it exists.'

The debates about how to judge quality result in critics attempting to define it in different ways (see Brunsdon 1997: 134–6). It may refer to the public service function of a programme, or aesthetic criteria of visual or structural kinds, or relationships with the avant-garde or experimentalism or the arts. Or quality could be defined by the ways in which a programme exploits the apparent fundamental properties of the television medium. Or quality might refer to the professional expertise of the makers of the programme, and the exercise of highly developed crafts skills. Or a programme could be described as quality television because of its contribution to definitions of national culture or a perceived heritage of excellence. As channels compete by attempting to challenge a competitor's superiority in one programme genre or format, the values associated with each channel's drama brand can gradually shift. Costume adaptations of nineteenth-century literature, long regarded as the province of the BBC, are an established form of drama that channels have used in order to claim that they are making plenty of quality television. But classic adaptations have been deprioritised by BBC in recent years in favour of adaptations of modern literature. By contrast, ITV's drama productions have included *Micawber*, a prequel to Charles Dickens' nineteenth-century novel *David Copperfield*, and an adaptation in modern dress of Shakespeare's *Othello*. Indeed, it is notable the extent to which, in the early years of the twenty-first century, ITV1 is aiming to present itself differently to its current audience, and trying to attract newer audiences by making programmes that are publicised as quality television.

The idea of quality is convenient in its suggestion of fixed standards and allows for a hierarchy of what is of interest and significance, but academic studies of culture assume that hierarchies of value conceal unacknowledged assumptions (see Brunsdon 1997, Mulgan 1990). Rather than setting up a single hierarchical list in which, for example, a made for television film is superior to an episode of a soap opera, academic studies of culture ask about the purpose against which a programme is judged, and about the aims and position of the person making the judgement. John Caughie (1986) argued that the field of cultural studies arose in the context of an argument over the meaning and value of mass culture, one of whose components is television. The argument that mass civilisation produced a mass culture in which cultural value had been lost was applied particularly to American commercial culture and its TV. This commercial culture had already been regarded by powerful voices in the intellectual elite as exploitative and was stigmatised for encouraging the audience to succumb to emotional appeal rather than reason and discrimination. The inauthenticity of mass culture was argued to be the result of its nature as a business where creators of culture exercised instrumental technical skills rather than artistic creativity and originality. Mass culture seemed to overwhelm society and drive out quality. In contrast to this, theorists of television (especially in Britain) looked for ways of valuing the quality of popular, commercial television as well as prestige authored drama.

Academic commentators have argued that in fact real viewers make distinctions about quality all the time in their viewing, and that these distinctions are different from the issues of whether viewers are interested in programmes or enjoy them. Simon Frith (2000: 46) argues that viewers judge quality 'in terms of the technical (good acting, sets, camera work) the believable, the interesting, the spectacular, the satisfying – terms that echo but do not exactly match the professional concern for originality, authenticity and innovation'. The attribution of quality may depend on the response of viewers, either in terms of audience size or composition. The television industry is a self-enclosed world, with powerful internal hierarchies and codes of shared knowledge, status, competition and gossip. So indicators of success deriving from the industry itself are relatively more significant than indicators deriving from more public sources. The key indicator within the television industry is the size of the audience, but also the audience share, and the distribution of age groups and social classes. The audience for ITV's terrestrial programmes has been getting older for many years, and has a typically lower average income than BBC's audience. In terms of the standard measures of income and status, the professional, managerial and skilled sectors of society, who tend to have the highest incomes, are the ABC1 group. It is evidently very important for broadcasters that their audience contains a high proportion of the most economically and socially powerful people in the national audience. Channel 4 has addressed this audience by buying American 'quality' programmes such as *ER* and *The West Wing*, and has commissioned original British drama addressed to the ABC1 audience such as the serials *Queer as Folk* and *Never Never*.

ITV1 has made various attempts to attract younger viewers, and viewers with the higher disposable incomes that are attractive to advertisers. Paul Marquess is a television producer who had formerly worked as a story editor on *Coronation Street*, a producer of *Brookside*, and is the creator of the successful drama about the British football scene *Footballers' Wives*. He was recruited by Thames Television and ITV to turn the police drama series *The Bill* into a serial:

> ITV and Thames had decided the serial bits were very successful and the audience research supported that. I arrived with a clear brief – to turn *The Bill* into a serial. They'd have serial elements, but they were mixed with stand-alone episodes, so you'd watch the story of Page and Quinnan's affair for six hours and then that six-parter would finish and the next time you saw them in a scene together, there'd be no eye-contact, no acknowledgement they'd ever had an affair. That dissatisfied me as a viewer.
>
> (quoted in McLean 2002: 8)

In the episodes produced by Marquess, seven regular characters were swiftly killed off, to be replaced by actors with track records in soap opera such as *EastEnders* and *Coronation Street*. Marquess's aim was to address a younger and more valuable audience for ITV: 'It still gets 7 million viewers as it is, but if you look at *The Bill*'s core demographic, it is white men over 50.' The aim was not to increase the audience for *The Bill*, but to change its composition to make it more valuable as a commodity that could be sold to advertisers. While Marquess was quite open about this when interviewed about his work, it is significant that he describes his intention by framing it as a matter of quality: to make *The Bill* 'more satisfying' by altering its characteristics as drama.

In relation to the already valued television form of the authored drama series, quality depends not only on the production values of a programme but also on its contribution to the politics of representation and the debates over public issues that are the province of public service broadcasting. For example, Peter Billingham (2005) regards the Channel 4 drama series *Queer as Folk* as an authored intervention in the representation of homosexuality. The series drew on Channel 4's institutional remit to address new configurations of audience and hitherto under-represented social groups, and established patterns of relationships between characters that explored gay identity and the tensions and contradictions around sexuality. In relation to a much more generic and 'popular' programme, Jonathan Bignell (2005) has also argued that the science fiction series *Doctor Who* has drawn on a tradition of science fiction in film, television and other media that distances it from expectations of quality, but also claims to offer both realist representations of scientific subjects and historical facts that give the programme seriousness of purpose. *Doctor Who* also has a heritage of drawing on new television technologies to emphasise the visual revelation and spectacle that are conventional markers of quality. The meanings of quality shift and draw on different criteria, and are defined in relation to aesthetic forms, institutional constraints and the expectations of audiences.

## Realism and quality

Realism is a particularly ambiguous term. One meaning focuses on television's representation of recognisable and often contemporary experience, such as characters the audience can believe in, or apparently likely chains of events. This kind of realism relies on the familiarity of the codes that represent a reality, and allows viewers to say that a programme has quality if it conforms to their expectations. But another meaning of realism would reject the conventions of established realistic forms, and look for new and different ways to give access to the real. Television has a 'language of realism' that programme makers and audiences share. Finding new ways to deform or undercut that 'language of realism' is a marker of quality too, since it pushes the boundaries of audience expectations and encourages viewers to think about television representation in new ways.

The dominant form of realism in television drama, labelled by theorists 'classic realism', is usually what people mean when they describe programmes (especially dramas) as realistic and use this is a criterion for judging that they are high in quality. It can be seen in the majority of television fiction programmes, and also affects representation in factual programmes and documentary. Individuals' character determines their choices and actions, and human nature is seen as a pattern of character-differences. These differences permit the viewer to share the hopes and fears of a wide range of characters. Classic realism represents a world of psychologically consistent individuals, and assumes that viewers are similarly rational and psychologically consistent. The drama will offer identification with the characters and storylines it shows. The viewer's varied and ordered pattern of identifications makes narrative crucial to classic realism, for the different kinds of look, point-of-view, sound and speech in narrative are the forms through which this communication between text and audience is produced.

Realist television discourse resolves contradictions by representing a unified and rational world of causes and effects, actions and consequences, moral choices and rewards or punishments. It distances the viewer from the contradictory and ambiguous aspects of reality and suggests that political action to intervene in the ways that reality is produced day to day is unnecessary. Things are the way they are, and human nature doesn't really change. On the other hand, television could draw the attention of the viewer to the non-equivalence of television and reality. Since television cannot be a 'true' representation, it could draw the viewer's attention to his or her relationship with the medium and make him or her recognise the social relations that this relationship involves. So perhaps the strangeness or unrealistic nature of television versions of reality, when familiar recognitions and identifications break down, might draw the viewer's attention to the fact that he or she is watching a representation and not a reality. This strategy of 'critical realism' involves recognising a relationship between television and reality, yet resisting television's apparently neutral transcription of that reality. Drama like that would reveal the work that television representation does, and show that TV realism is not natural but cultural and constructed.

Television drama does not usually reveal the production of an illusion of reality in fiction. However, television is an unusual medium in sometimes making its own production, and the failures in its production, part of a drama or a subject for non-fiction television programmes. But this revealing of behind-the-scenes information about how drama is constructed, and drawing attention to mistakes in production, is confined to particular kinds of text. In situation comedy, episodes may end with a compilation of out-takes, but it is very unlikely that a costume drama would do this.

Nevertheless, the increasing teleliteracy of the audience makes it less easy for television creators to manufacture realism, because of the audience's awareness of the conventions and codes that it involves. The recognition that television programmes play on their own and each other's conventions of realism is one of the components of postmodernism. This theoretical term rose to prominence in Television Studies in the 1980s, as a way of distinguishing how programmes since that time appear to be more self-conscious and sophisticated than before, indicating a rise in the quality of TV. One of the most useful components of postmodernist critiques of television is the concept of reflexivity to describe the textual and narrative characteristics of programmes. The study of reflexivity entails discovering features of television that display self-consciousness, irony, and the pastiche or imitation of familiar conventions, formats and structures. Examples of this in drama include the pastiche of science fiction conventions in *Red Dwarf* and *The Hitchhiker's Guide to the Galaxy*, or the pastiche of television and film conventions in *The Simpsons*. The term can also be used to signify a more general shift in television culture, and culture in general, away from classic realism and towards the debunking of illusion. The eventual result of this trend, it is argued, is the scepticism and cynicism that audiences display in their attitudes to the media as a whole.

## British soap opera

The continuing serial, more commonly referred to as the soap opera, is a crucial means for channels to attract and retain audiences from week to week, and potentially to bring audiences to programmes scheduled before and after a 'must-see' soap episode that viewers have tuned in for. The value of soap opera can be seen in the recent increase in the number of episodes of the most popular soaps that are broadcast each week. In 2001, for example, BBC's most popular prime-time soap *EastEnders* began broadcasting four episodes per week, and BBC also compiled the week's programmes into an omnibus edition at the weekend. Similarly, the ITV1 network has always relied on its main soap opera *Coronation Street* to act as a 'banker' programme at the beginning of mid-evening prime-time, and as a 'tent-pole' programme that holds up audience levels in the evening and can also attract 'echo' and 'pre-echo' audiences for the programmes scheduled before and after it (for discussion of these terms, see Chapter 10). For ITV, the motivation for increasing the number of *Coronation Street* episodes each week is directly economic: ITV income from advertising was £1,966 million in 2000, but is now falling. The downturn in advertising income is likely to affect the ITV spend on programmes, which was £747 million in 2001 for all genres. The network has increased the proportion of its income that is spent on the production of soap and other drama, since this is the biggest draw for audiences and the most prestigious aspect of its output. ITV1 screens about 650 hours of drama per year including soaps, at a cost in 2001 of £270 million. The network invested in drama partly by contracting six or seven major television stars such as Robson Green and Sarah Lancashire (a former *Coronation Street* regular) who are paid between £1 million and £2 million each for their exclusive services. Soaps are a mainstay of drama production, and also act as a proving-ground for performers who will subsequently graduate to series and serial drama with bigger budgets and higher profile. So although soaps are not part of quality television in its usual sense, they are a sort of nursery for performers (and also writers) who may go on to 'better' things.

Soap opera has conventionally been regarded as a low-quality genre because of its exaggeration of emotion, its departures from realist conventions, and its comparatively low budgets. Its dramatic form is a kind of melodrama, a term originally signifying dramas accompanied by music, and now used to denote precisely those features of emotionalism and lack of realism. The supposed lack of quality in soap opera dramas is a reflection of the low value given to melodrama as a dramatic form. But melodrama can also be understood as a very effective way of dramatising conflicts of morality and the functioning of community. To force characters into conflict and keep them within the dramatic space for an extended period, restrictions of physical space are placed around them. The significance of space and setting to the soap genre can be seen in the titles of *Coronation Street*, *Brookside*, *Emmerdale* and *EastEnders*. Location functions as a force linking characters with each other, not only as a positive basis for community but also as a boundary that characters find it difficult to transgress. Characters in soap opera are in a sense trapped by their location, and their proximity to each other within the space creates not only alliances but also rivalries and friction. The categorisations linking characters together in soap opera include family or work relationship, age group, race or gender. They function in a similar way as either a positive ground for connection or a source of rivalry and tension. The overlapping of these categories among each other also produces possible stories in soap opera, since one character is likely to belong to several different categories, perhaps working in the local shop, belonging to a family, and pursuing solidarity with other characters of the same age group. Soap opera narrative manipulates these connections and distinctions, changing them over time, thus producing different permutations of connection and distinction that form the basis of storylines.

The expression of emotion is an important part of soap opera, and as David Lusted (1998) notes, it is both a marker of femininity and of working-class culture. While masculine values entail the suppression of emotion in favour of efficiency, achievement, and stoicism, feminine values encourage the display of emotion as a way of responding to problems. Similarly, elite class sectors value rational talk and writing as means of expression, versus emotional release. These culturally produced distinctions, have been important to work in Television Studies on the relationship between gender and the different genres of television, where news and current affairs are regarded as masculine, and melodrama as feminine. On the basis of these gender, class and genre distinctions, the role of emotional display takes on increased significance in relation to quality. Because soaps are focused on what seems to be feminine and working-class behaviour, and usually feature a high proportion of women and working-class characters, it is not surprising that they are not thought of as quality television. Quality has associations with masculine seriousness and middle-class attitudes, so soap opera has little chance of achieving it.

But on the other hand, soaps also contribute to public service aims to represent society to itself, and deal with issues of current concern. Phil Redmond (quoted in Nelson 1997: 114–15), the creator and producer of Channel 4's soap opera *Brookside* set in Liverpool, explained that when the programme began in the early 1980s, 'I wanted to use the twice-weekly form to explore social issues, and, hopefully, contribute to any social debate. . . . From the outset one of my main aims was to try and reflect Britain in the 1980s'. In this respect, the sometimes contrived storylines that would seem to distance soaps from notions of quality can by contrast be regarded as evidence of responsibility and social purpose, an alternate notion of quality. Soap opera realism allows this transfer between fiction and reality, and enables soaps to claim social responsibility and public service functions.

The balance in soap opera storylines can tip from plot to character and back again, but a focus on either of these tends to reinforce the negative evaluation of soap opera as a low-quality drama form. *Coronation Street* did not perform too well in 2001. Its stories were driven largely by plot rather than character, despite a cast of more than 50, and its recently arrived executive producer Carolyn Reynolds decided to concentrate more on the core characters. Reynolds had worked on the programme for over 20 years, as a production assistant, then producer, then as executive producer in the mid-1990s. As executive producer she had a strategic remit to integrate *Coronation Street* with Granada Television's other drama output, with the producer Kieran Roberts (formerly working on *Emmerdale*) running the programme week to week. Granada Television's new director of programmes, John Whiston, explained:

There are tensions between storyliners, who want a story that gets them logically and clearly to a particular point, and writers, who want to free up enough time for their characters to be what they want them to be. If the balance swings too far to the storyliners, you get a very plot-driven show that is a bit ploppy and for my money there has been too much emphasis on the storyliners.

(Moss 2002: 2)

The background to this shift in power from storyline (plot) to characters (script) is audience ratings: *Coronation Street* was challenged strongly by *EastEnders* in 2001. Partly because *EastEnders* has an omnibus edition at the weekend, *EastEnders'* ratings have almost always exceeded those of *Coronation Street*. Granada TV executives, and the programme's producers, make strategic management decisions about the programme based on their perceptions of audience demands and the balance of power between the staff in their production team. But the more the producers succeed in attracting large audiences, the more likelihood that the soap will be evaluated as low quality, since the thrills of melodrama and the popularity of programmes are each reasons to categorise it in this way.

## Profile | Writer
Lynda LaPlante

**Lynda LaPlante is the best known and most successful woman writer in the popular genre of the police series.**

She began with the serial *Widows* for Thames TV/Euston Films in 1982, and her drama *Prime Suspect* for Granada (1991) has the most enduring reputation among her works. Her work is notable since the police genre is associated with masculinity and yet LaPlante has investigated and critiqued masculinity within the genre at the same time as adopting some of its conventions. As a woman writer, her dramas focus on violence and the graphic depiction of bodily harm, which has been the subject of criticism, and in some of her work she has drawn on the conventions of melodrama, a form associated with the feminine. Like all drama authors, LaPlante has worked in the context of the collaborative culture of television production, and institutional constraints led her to form her own production company in order to retain greater control of her work. Questions about the relationship between truth and fiction, dramatic creation and authenticity, are also raised by LaPlante's insistence that all of her fictional writing is very closely based on extensive research and interviews conducted with people such as police, lawyers and convicted criminals.

*Widows* was the first crime serial drama written and produced by a female team (see Hallam 2005). Its central characters are the wives of a gang of criminals who take over their former husbands' role as criminal masterminds, and the drama is unusual in depicting the successful outcome of their robbery plan, rather than centring on the investigation of crime by detectives on the right side of the law. LaPlante collaborated on *Widows* with Verity Lambert, one of the few women working in television at the time, and despite being scheduled against *Dallas* in the prime-time 9–10 pm evening slot, *Widows* gained 11 million viewers. The seed of the idea began when LaPlante played a small role in the ITV series *The Gentle Touch* (ITV 1980–84), the first television drama centred on a female detective, and LaPlante offered four story outlines that were all turned down. One of these outlines was the storyline that became *Widows* and secured LaPlante's initial reputation as a television dramatist.

*Prime Suspect* was commissioned by Granada in 1990. Its central character, Detective Chief Inspector Jane Tennison (Helen Mirren), is a senior female detective whose gradual rise to greater success among the male centred London police force is charted in a series of two-hour double episodes transmitted in mini series form. In the first series of *Prime Suspect*, the masculine culture of the police is demonstrated in an aggressive contest between two male policemen who box each other as part of a charity benefit, and the violence against the pursued killer's female victims is demonstrated by forensic photographs of their mutilated bodies, and the evidence of iron manacles and blood stains on the walls of the garage where they were killed. The main character's dispassionate examination of mutilated bodies in the mortuary and of the crime scene are mechanisms for demonstrating the apparently masculine traits that allow her to succeed as a police detective, while her feminine attention to the appearance of female victims, including their clothing and fingernails, enables her to discover clues that male policemen have missed. This contrast between masculine and feminine characteristics, paralleled by her success at work in contrast to the messiness of her personal life, made *Prime Suspect* a subject of attention both for the popular press and for academic critics interested in gender and representation (see Brunsdon 1998, Eaton 1995, Hallam 2005, Jermyn 2003, Thornham 1994).

After the success of the first *Prime Suspect*, LaPlante produced the storyline for its sequel *Prime Suspect 2* (Granada 1992), but did not write the script, while the third sequel *Prime Suspect 3* (Granada 1993) was written by LaPlante. *Prime Suspect 4, 5* and *6* (1995) were produced subsequently by Granada, without LaPlante's direct involvement. The BBC producer Ruth Caleb commissioned LaPlante for the series *Civvies* (BBC Wales, 1992), about former paratroopers. This developed alongside an ITV drama series by LaPlante about a female prison governor, *The Governor* (LaPlante Productions/ITV 1995).

LaPlante started her own production company in 1994, one of the results of the Broadcasting Act of 1990 that shifted production from the broadcasting companies themselves to independent companies that created drama to be sold to broadcasters. The shift in the broadcasting landscape produced not only organisational changes, but also facilitated representations of a wider range of characters in drama and the creation of new forms, as a new cohort of writers and producers gained access to the airwaves. *Trial and Retribution* (1997) detailed the investigations and court procedures following the murder of a young child, and used split screen format to offer a variety of competing images and narrative. While split screen was criticised for being too demanding on viewers, it is the first significant example of the sustained use of split screen in television drama, and set a precedent for this technique in later work by other writers, such as the film *Timecode* (2000) and the American drama series *24* (2001). The combination of serious issues relating to sex equality, paedophilia, and the internet in some of LaPlante's dramas, established her as a key writer in the British television drama culture of the time. LaPlante adopted the role of writer and producer that is common in the US, for the series *Supply and Demand* (LaPlante Productions/ITV 1996, 1997), *Killer Net* (LaPlante Productions/Channel 4 1997) and *Mind Games* (LaPlante Productions/ITV 2000). These series were made for UK transmission but also aimed to penetrate the American television market. LaPlante's position at the top of the British drama hierarchy was demonstrated when she won the Dennis Potter Award for television writing in 2001. This recognised the respect she had gained from her peers among television dramatists, and also from the television institutions that were using her name 'above the title' as a brand that connoted both quality and appeal to large audiences.

# Further reading

Allen, R., *Speaking of Soap Operas* (Chapel Hill: University of South Carolina Press, 1985).

Ang, I., 'Melodramatic Identifications: Television Fiction and Women's Fantasy', in C. Brunsdon, J. D'Acci and L. Spigel (eds), *Feminist Television Criticism: A Reader* (Oxford: Oxford University Press, 1997), pp. 155–66.

Bignell, J., 'Space for "Quality": Negotiating with the Daleks', in J. Bignell and S. Lacey (eds), *Popular Television Drama: Critical Perspectives* (Manchester: Manchester University Press, 2005).

Bignell, J. and S. Lacey (eds), *Popular Television Drama: Critical Perspectives* (Manchester: Manchester University Press, 2005).

Bignell, J., S. Lacey and M. Macmurraugh-Kavanagh (eds), *British Television Drama: Past, Present and Future* (Basingstoke: Palgrave Macmillan, 1999).

Billingham, P., 'Can Kinky Sex be Politically Correct? *Queer as Folk* and the Geo-ideological Inscription of Gay Sexuality', in J. Bignell and S. Lacey (eds), *Popular Television Drama: Critical Perspectives* (Manchester: Manchester University Press, 2005).

Bourdieu, P., *Distinction: A Social Critique of the Judgement of Taste* (Cambridge, MA: Harvard University Press, 1984).

Brunsdon, C., 'Television: Aesthetics and Audiences', in P. Mellencamp (ed.), *Logics of Television: Essays in Cultural Criticism* (London: BFI, 1990), pp. 59–72.

Brunsdon, C., *Screen Tastes: Soap Operas to Satellite Dishes* (London: Routledge, 1997).

Brunsdon, C., 'Structure of Anxiety: Recent British TV Crime Fiction', *Screen*, 39: 3 (1998), pp. 223–43.

Brunsdon, C., *The Feminist, The Housewife, and the Soap Opera* (Oxford: Oxford University Press, 2000).

Buckingham, D., *Public Secrets: EastEnders and its Audience* (London: BFI, 1987).

Caughie, J., 'Popular Culture: Notes and Revisions', in C. MacCabe (ed.), *High Theory/Low Culture* (Manchester: Manchester University Press, 1986), pp. 156–71.

Dyer, R., C. Geraghty, M. Jordan, T. Lovell, R. Paterson and J. Stewart, *Coronation Street* (London: BFI, 1981).

Eaton, M., 'A Fair Cop?: Canteen Culture in *Prime Suspect* and *Between the Lines*', in D. Kitt-Hewitt and R. Osborne (eds), *Crime and the Media: The Postmodern Spectacle* (London: Pluto, 1995), pp. 164–84.

Frith, S., 'The Black Box: The Value of Television and the Future of Television Research', *Screen* 41: 1 (2000), pp. 33–50.

Geraghty, C., *Women and Soap Opera: A Study of Prime Time Soaps* (Cambridge: Polity Press, 1991).

Hallam, J., *Lynda LaPlante* (Manchester: Manchester University Press, 2005).

Jermyn, D., 'Women with a Mission: Lynda LaPlante, DCI Tennison and the Reconfiguration of TV Crime Drama', *International Journal of Cultural Studies* 6: 1 (2003), pp. 46–63.

Lusted, D., 'The Popular Culture Debate and Light Entertainment on Television', in C. Geraghty and D. Lusted (eds), *The Television Studies Book* (London: Arnold, 1998), pp. 175–90.

McLean, G., 'Corner Shop to Cop Shop', *The Guardian* Media Section, Monday 18 February 2002, pp. 8–9.

Mulgan, G. (ed.), *The Question of Quality* (London: BFI, 1990).

Murdoch, G., 'Authorship and Organization', *Screen Education* 35 (1980), pp. 19–34.

Nelson, R., *TV Drama in Transition: Forms, Values and Cultural Change* (Basingstoke: Macmillan, 1997).

Thornham, S., 'Feminist interventions: *Prime Suspect 1*', *Critical Survey* 6: 2 (1994), pp. 226–33.

# 14 News and current affairs: the public sphere

## Introduction

Television news, because of its liveness or potential liveness is usually the medium that viewers turn to when major news stories are breaking, in order to see pictures of the events and discover the most recent developments. There is a hierarchy of news value in which live actuality pictures are the most attractive to the producers of television news programmes, followed by actuality pictures that have been pre-recorded and, finally, those stories that cannot be illustrated by actuality footage or another visual form such as an interview are the stories that are least likely to appear. Television news claims to denote events objectively and immediately, offering a neutral and transparent channel of communication. The iconic quality of television images, which appear simply to record what is unfolding in front of the camera, are key signifiers of this mythology of transparency. When news events such as election results or the Olympics are broadcast live, or when a national event such as a royal wedding or the occurrence and aftermath of disasters are broadcast, it is the accidental detail and unpredictable unfolding of events that are fascinating.

Contemporary networks of electronic mediation allow digital news images to be circulated around the world from television news crews back to their producers at home, and also to the news agencies which sell packages of news pictures to broadcasters. Television technologies are not neutral, and the selection of news and the forms in which it is represented have political effects. One example of this is the perception of the Third World by Western television audiences, where some categories of event are more frequently denoted in news and current affairs. Large-scale political violence and natural disasters are the predominant form of news image broadcast of Third World countries and developing countries such as China. The US and other Western nations predominantly appear in news as the active agenda-setters, while countries in the developing world are portrayed as passive sufferers of news events. These divisions are parallel to, and derive from, the division between the rich Western nations, which intervene in world affairs and control world institutions such as the World Bank or United Nations, versus the relatively impoverished and politically disempowered nations in the rest of the world. The academic study of news has focused especially on these questions of power, and how the ideologies of news reproduce relationships of dominance in both domestic and overseas news coverage.

## The public sphere

The cultural theorist Jürgen Habermas argued in favour of rationality and communication as means to improve society. Improved communication and rational debate about politics and society would enable people to liberate themselves from the apparently stifling bureaucracy of contemporary societies. This space of public debate is termed the public sphere (as opposed to the private sphere of home and family). In order to achieve this liberation and debate, access to the media and the free exchange of ideas in the media must be key priorities. The centralisation of ownership and control of the media, and ordinary people's lack of participation in them, are the main problems that he diagnoses: 'Insofar as mass media one-sidedly channel communication flows in a centralized network – from the center to the periphery or from above to below – they considerably strengthen the efficacy of social controls' (Habermas 1987: 390). In contrast to this, Habermas calls for individuals to take practical action to gain access to media and to use them for reasoned political debate.

For TV news to contribute to the formation of a public sphere, news must be available, accurate, balanced and representative of the events that could be the subjects of debate. There are some aspects of the contemporary (and former) presentation of television news that complicate its contribution to the public sphere. The specifics of the structure of news programmes are one of these aspects, and are discussed in the following section. But the organisation of news production and dissemination are also significant. Sources of television news are perceived as unequal by television viewers, with some regarded as more reliable than others, and news tends to flow around the globe from North to South and from West to East. Such a situation provides fuel for arguments that global television news exacerbates the separation between the West and other regions of the world where news seems to happen, and the insulation of television news from the lives of its viewers.

The relationship between place and television news is complex, and global TV news channels such as CNN and the global newsgathering enabled by satellite transmission make local and regional differences more, not less, important. Local news finds its identity alongside or by resisting the national and global news agenda, so that the dominance of global and national news becomes important to the production of local news. Local, in this connection, can also mean regional, in that television cultures cross national boundaries to include speakers of the same language or audiences that share similar cultural assumptions and ideologies (such as the British Asian or British Polish communities, who tune into trans-national news channels for news about their 'home' culture and people who share the same origins). In the global news landscape the concepts of society and nation are diminishing in usefulness. The concept of society as a unit bounded in time and space loses its force when, for example, live television news or sports coverage confuse time and space by broadcasting across time zones. Television also brings new ways of understanding space, such as the notion of a New World Order, for example, that change viewers' sense of their place in the world. Because television broadcasts such a range of images of culture, such as representations of youth and age, domesticity, work and gender, for example, global television provides the possibility of reflecting on local cultures. Global news provides resources for people to think about themselves and their social environment, in the same ways that local or national television does:

> An Egyptian immigrant in Britain, for example, might think of herself as a Glaswegian when she watches her local Scottish channel, a British resident when she switches over to the BBC, an Islamic Arab expatriate in Europe when she tunes in to the satellite service from the Middle East, and a world citizen when she channel surfs on to CNN.
>
> (Sinclair *et al.* 1999: 187)

Viewers negotiate their sense of place, time and community in relation to local, regional and global television cultures, by adopting or resisting ways of thinking and living that derive from television news and other TV genres.

Viewers who can afford access to numerous news sources (cable and satellite television channels, for example, but also internet news and email news services) will enjoy greater diversity and quantity of news, but will be further separated from the experience of news events than people who cannot access so much information. It has often been claimed that the world is not only divided into the rich and the poor, but increasingly into the information-rich and the information-poor. Television news producers gather and exchange news in a kind of news economy, producing a global news market that homogenises news inasmuch as it becomes a commodity for sale. News footage is offered to broadcasters by news agencies, and is accessed by satellite links. As well as using these mechanisms for exchanging news footage, news institutions have exchange agreements with institutions and broadcasters in other countries. The BBC, for example, has an exchange agreement with the ABC network in the US. Satellite technology enables the international news machine to operate twenty-four hours a day, sending both raw footage and complete news packages to national and regional clients. Because of the different languages used in different nations, news agencies mainly distribute images without commentary. This reinforces the perception that iconic visual images in news are in themselves objective, though clearly the activities of selection, editing and composition in news footage are as much a meaning-making process as the addition of voice-over commentaries for broadcast.

## News agendas

One of the most commonly used words to enter political discourse in recent years has been the term 'spin'. Spin has taken the place of censorship in democratic societies, as the predominant means of manipulating television news agendas, and either concealing possible news stories or bringing them to prominence. It used to be the case (in the Second World War, for example) that governments and official agencies would prohibit the reporting of some news events that, in unusual circumstances such as war, could threaten security or damage public morale. But now, rather

than prohibiting reporting, modern conflicts more often involve the chan-
nelling of information to the media by specially chosen spokespeople, for
example in the 1990s during the Kosovo conflict and in the Gulf War.

The acquisition of news is now carried out as much by news-gathering
from sources provided by the people and institutions that are reported on,
as by sending journalists to investigate issues. The discourse of news is
increasingly based on the editing, reworking and supplementation of
acquired footage and press briefings. In short, news often comes to the
news studio, rather than news teams going out to find it. In this situation,
it is especially easy for a news institution to become a victim of spin, or
to intentionally or unintentionally editorialise and comment, thus becoming
a producer of spin. But organisations that have a vested interest in providing information to publicise or support their cause can be very helpful,
for example charities may be willing to supply packs of information,
documents and spokespeople, and may be keen to contribute directly to
programmes by providing experts. Some charities, such as Greenpeace,
take camera operators with them on direct action activities, and are careful
to shoot footage that is of appropriate quality and sufficiently dramatic for
news programme packages. From their perspective, it is beneficial for
Greenpeace footage to be included in news programmes so that material
shot from Greenpeace activists' point of view becomes the illustrative
material in a news report. Clearly, the ulterior motives of research sources
and contributors need to be assessed carefully by news producers, and
occasionally television news organisations are subject to public criticism
for too easily accepting information and footage provided to them by a
participant in a news story.

## News structures

Television news consists of narrative reports, and can be analysed as narrative to discover how priorities and assumptions shared by news broadcasters form a code determining which reports have greatest significance
within the news bulletin. The reports with the highest news value appear
near the beginning of the bulletin (in the same way as the front pages of
newspapers present some stories as having the highest news value to
readers). The ranking of reports according to their news value shows how
the representation of reality offered by television news is not a denotation
of events, but a narrative mediated by the signs and codes of news

television. Binary oppositions, such as those between crime and law, Left-wing and Right-wing opinions, or home and abroad, are the basis for news narrative. Television news both shapes and reflects the dominant common sense assumptions about what is significant, since by definition what is deemed significant is what makes the news.

News narrative contributes to the process of constructing a common sense climate of opinion through which audiences perceive their reality. Therefore, television news shares the ideological function of naturalising the public arenas of politics, business and international affairs as newsworthy. News programmes seek to connote balance and objectivity by giving approximately equal time to conflicting parties and interested groups. But balance and objectivity are defined in relation to a common sense norm, a cultural construct, and will therefore shift according to the current balance of power. News narrative, despite its commitment to balance and objectivity, measures this balance and objectivity against the currently dominant ideologies in society, which occupy an apparently neutral position.

Television news deals with the potentially infinite meanings of events by narrating them in conventional subject-categories, like 'foreign news' or 'business news'. These divisions reflect the institutional divisions in news broadcasting organisations (Harrison 2000). Some news programmes title news stories with captions on the screen next to the news presenter, and these captions connote both the specificity of each news story, and the connection between a particular story and others in the same category. The effect of using this code is to restrict the narrative frameworks that are available for representing the story. Placing reports in coded categories restricts the viewer's capacity to make connections between one news report and another in a different category, or to bring an alternative narrative structure to bear.

Television news has to deal with events that are by definition new in each day's news, and to do this it has powerful codes for giving shape and meaning to news reports. Reports use four narrative functions (Hartley 1982: 118–19): *framing* is the activity of establishing the news topic, usually done by the mediating figure of the newsreader. For example, political news is usually coded as adversarial. Although mediators such as news presenters speak in a neutral register and establish themselves and the news broadcasting organisation as neutral too, the effect of this is to make the setting-up of the narrative code appear invisible to viewers: it seems to arise from the news itself rather than from how it is being presented.

*Focusing* refers to the opening out of the news report into further detail, conveyed by reporters and correspondents who speak for the news broadcasting institution. These institutional voices develop the narrative by providing background information, explaining what is at stake in the news event, and introducing comment and actuality footage that illustrates this. The interviews, film reports and comments by people involved in the news event are part of the function known as *realising*, since they ground the news story in evidence and personal commentary from interested individuals and groups. The availability of actuality footage gives important added value to news reports because it is crucial to the narrative function of realising the story. But although actuality footage might seem to be the dominant type of sign in television news programmes, its visual signs never appear without accompanying voice-over commentary. Realisation therefore tends to confirm the work of the news reporters' framing and focusing language. *Closing* refers to the way that a news report moves towards a condensed encapsulation of the report, likely to be repeated in the closing headlines of the news programme, that reinforces the editorial line decided on to structure the story. Closure might involve ignoring some of the points of view on the news event that have been represented in the report, or repeating key points already introduced by the frame or focus.

## News as an empty form

There is a paradox in the increasing quantity and speed of international television news. Television, with its focus on liveness, and the showing of actualities from distant places, draws on Western culture's belief in the power of photographic images to bear witness to real events so that seeing something happen on television news claims the immediacy and veracity of fact. But at the same time, the proliferation of representations of realities on television news distances what the viewer sees from his or her own physical everyday experience. Television always aims to contain and explain the real, especially through the form of narrative, and the desire to produce unmediated access to the real goes along with, but is contradicted by, the necessity to domesticate and contain the material. John Ellis (1999: 56) argued that television news

> has been driven by the demand that it should provide ever more instantaneous material, to the extent that flexible digital video formats plus

satellite technology are moving us towards an era of 'real-time' news in which we can see events more or less as they happen.

But these events are not presented in the raw, since they are always subject to a constructing interpretation. This mediation of news by the conventions and codes of news programme formats has led academic commentators to argue that the form of news takes precedence over its content: the medium becomes the message.

Main evening news bulletins are scheduled at fixed points, and their scheduling already connotes their importance. Their dramatic opening music calls the viewer's attention and the opening shot is normally a head-on address by the presenter to the viewer. News programmes are complex television texts, in which a large number of segments are linked together. There are likely to be sequences in which the news presenter is speaking directly to the viewer, sequences of news reportage, and dialogue between the presenter and experts in the studio or reporters live in a location where a news story is occurring. In addition, presentational techniques such as graphics, maps, statistics and diagrams will be used either alongside or independently of these forms of content. This level of complexity is managed by news production staff using the kinds of consistent structure and division of responsibilities described above, but because news is necessarily always new and yet news programmes are patterned in very consistent ways there are questions to ask about what viewers actually make of it and what impact it has.

At the time of the Gulf War in the early 1990s, the French cultural theorist Jean Baudrillard (1997) claimed that the almost non-stop news coverage of the war smothered the reality of the event, so that the war itself was in effect replaced by the television pictures that claimed to represent it. In 2001 another similar example happened when terrorists attacked targets in the US. Complex issues surrounding resistance to the power of the US in various regions, the several terrorist attacks taking place on 11 September, and questions about what the terrorists intended to achieve and what the proper response should be, were overwhelmed by a small number of brief and dramatic sequences of television pictures. A few seconds of footage of airliners crashing into the World Trade Center, a few seconds of the huge towers collapsing to the ground, and a few seconds of reaction to the event from shocked pedestrians in New York became the iconic TV images that represented this complex of issues and events, and were repeated innumerable times. Four airliners were hijacked at the same time, one crashing into the Pentagon, another crashing in Pennsylvania en route to another target, and two flown into the towers of the World Trade Center. The television coverage focused primarily on the World Trade Center events, partly because of the larger scale of casualties, but also because of the availability of several different points of view on the attack itself filmed by amateur camera users and the comparative ease of access to eyewitnesses, officials, government spokespeople and experts in the New York metropolitan area. News coverage quickly reduced to extracts of a few seconds duration showing the impacts of each airliner into the twin towers, brief soundbites from witnesses close to the scene, and a grainy still photograph of Osama bin Laden. Nevertheless, the days following the attacks were saturated with television coverage. CNN, for example, broadcast live to a worldwide audience of almost 1 billion, in ten languages including English, to 900 affiliated television stations, and British channels such as BBC News 24 and Sky News ran open-ended coverage.

As in the debates about the Gulf War, television provided the images that encapsulated a complex reality in a few seconds of coverage. The events seemed to be 'more real' because they were shown almost live around the world to millions of viewers, but were also 'less real' because the events were so quickly accommodated into the formats and routines of news broadcasting. Although channels began to cease open-ended coverage in the evening of the first day, news audiences remained high until the end of the week. The BBC adopted the strategy of simultaneous broadcast on its terrestrial BBC1 network and its digital channel BBC News 24. This strategy simplified the management of news broadcasting in a potentially chaotic situation, and also functioned as an advertisement for the recently launched BBC rolling news channel. ITN, by contrast, broadcast live news across five different networks: ITV, Channel 4, Channel 5, ITN News and Euronews. This enabled each network to maintain the well-known presenters associated with its programmes and provided different programming to viewers on each of the channels. There was some difference in approach between the BBC and ITN coverage. Although both news organisations often repeated video sequences showing the airliners crashing into the twin towers, BBC quickly introduced analysis and discussion into their coverage as well as live updates from reporters in the US. ITN, on the other hand, persisted with live footage (usually of presenters in New York and vox pop interviews) rather than analysis. All commercial breaks were dropped from the schedule during ITN news programmes.

While no one would deny that the events of 11 September happened, their reality was superseded by television news representations. Baudrillard argues that in fact we do not experience reality at all except in terms of the codes of television and other media. For example, family relationships are perceived in terms of the melodramatic narrative structures of soap opera and romance, and perceptions of law and order and crime are mediated through the codes of television police series. Baudrillard termed this state of affairs 'the hyperreal', in which the experience of reality has become indistinguishable from the television and media conventions that shape it. The process by which the hyperreal comes into being is referred to as simulation: the staging of events, feelings and relationships by means of the codes and conventions of television and media culture.

Western television sources based all of their coverage on a Western, and particularly American, point of view. It was very difficult for news broadcasters to provide actuality footage representing the point of view of anti-American individuals or institutions, particularly in Afghanistan (where the supposed organiser of the attacks, Osama bin Laden, was thought to be). Restrictions on Western television personnel there meant that on 11 September 2001 there were very few Western journalists in Afghanistan. There are very few satellite uplink points in Afghanistan and access to these is strictly controlled. But in any case Afghan government restrictions on Western journalists prevented them from filming in the country in the first place, so for a complex of reasons, explanation or justification of the attacks on the US could not be represented. The result was that poor-quality pictures of Osama bin Laden and a few seconds of controversial footage apparently showing Palestinians jubilantly celebrating the attacks on the US were the primary images representing alternatives to the vengeful and racist discourses emerging from the US in the aftermath of the attacks. CNN was exceptional in having a reporter in Kabul (the capital of Afghanistan) equipped with a satellite videophone. This technology allowed CNN reporter Nic Robertson to report live from Kabul by unfolding a satellite antenna, connecting the camera to the videophone, and transmitting live pictures. However, the videophone had to be smuggled across the Afghan border and used illegally for short periods in different locations.

The news coverage of 11 September 2001 is clearly an exceptional case, and some of the arguments made about it by academic theorists are deliberately provocative and extreme. But that day and the days that followed draw attention in a very striking way to the questions about structuring news programmes, using technology, and the political issues of access and agenda-setting faced by TV news staff and analysts of news.

## News audiences

It is likely that much of the dense content of TV news often passes the viewer by. Many viewers will find it very difficult to remember the news stories presented in a single broadcast, let alone the nuances of the different points of view and fragments of information in it. Instead, viewers will construct a sense of what is important, often based as much on their pre-existing knowledge of news stories, and on other information sources such as newspapers. Some of this cultural knowledge of news must be shared, since it enables news quizzes, for instance, like *Have I Got News for You*, to be both comprehensible and entertaining. But studies of audience response have tended to show that different audiences are diverse and specific in their response to news, and have capacities for active interpretation (for example, see Bruhn Jensen 1998 for an analysis comparing audiences in different nations).

In Britain, the long-established researchers The Glasgow Media Group studied the representation of Israeli and Palestinian Arab conflict in the Middle East and what viewers understood about it (Philo 2002). When the state of Israel was established in 1948, Palestinians living in the country were displaced from their land. In May 1948, a war between Israel and its Arab neighbours produced more refugees, many of whom moved to the Gaza Strip (then controlled by Egypt) and to the West Bank of the River Jordan (controlled by Jordan). In 1967, Israel was at war with its Arab neighbours again and occupied Gaza and the West Bank, bringing the Palestinian refugees there under its control. Eastern Jerusalem (formerly controlled by Jordan) was also occupied by Israel. To cement its control, Israel built settlements in the areas it had occupied. The settlements caused anger among the refugees because of the presence of Israeli citizens in former Arab territories, and also because their farming activities deprived Palestinian farmers of water. The subsequent violence in the Middle East consists of attempts by Israel to maintain its control over occupied territory, and attempts by Palestinians to resist the occupation and regain their land.

The Glasgow Media Group researched viewers' understanding of this conflict by undertaking a content analysis of television news stories on

BBC and ITN (counting how many mentions of the conflict there were, of what type, etc.). They also interviewed 12 sample groups of viewers, totalling 85 people, from a cross section of ages and social backgrounds. In addition they interviewed 300 young people aged between 17 and 22. Each person was asked what they had understood about the conflict from TV news. In the whole sample, 82 per cent named television news as their main source of information, and said that the main point in the coverage was the prevalence of conflict and violence. The news stories analysed related to the uprising by Palestinians beginning in September 2000 until the middle of October 2000. There were 89 bulletins broadcast, comprising 3,536 lines of transcribed text, of which only 17 lines explained the history of the conflict. The majority of the people surveyed did not understand who was occupying the occupied territories, or why. Among the sample of 300 young people, 71 per cent did not know that the Israelis were occupying the territory, and 11 per cent believed incorrectly that the Palestinians were occupying it and that the settlers there were Palestinian. Although many more Palestinians have been killed in the conflict than Israelis, only 30 per cent of the sample of young people recognised this.

Greg Philo (2002) of the Glasgow Media Group suggested that the reasons for this level of ignorance and misunderstanding were that journalists did not provide any explanation of the history of the conflict, or referred to it only by brief shorthand phrases that the viewers did not understand. TV news focused more on actuality coverage of violence happening than on explanations for violence. The content analysis revealed that Israelis spoke twice as much on television news as Palestinians, thus favouring the Israeli perception of events. The close relationships between British politicians and the US government led to TV interviewees favouring the pro-Israeli position adopted by the US, so this official position was reflected in television coverage.

It is too easy to simply blame TV news staff for the lack of real debate about social and political issues on British TV, and the appalling ignorance of British citizens about affairs in their own country and the wider world. News staff are under huge pressure to get news programmes made on time, and to compete with each other and with other media sources to break the news first and draw audiences. What everyone can expect though, is that the commitment to inform and explain that still underpins television in Britain will lead to greater diversity of news formats, channels of delivery and debates about what the function and effects of TV news can be.

## Profile | **Editor-in-chief**
David Mannion

**David Mannion is editor-in-chief of ITV News, with responsibility for national news programmes, the 27 regional newsrooms in England and Wales, and the ITV digital news channel (Brown 2004).**

He started work at the age of 17 for a news agency in Derby, then worked for local radio. In 1977 he joined ATV television, and then was appointed deputy news editor at ITN in 1979. In 1997 he was put in charge of the current affairs programme *Tonight with Trevor McDonald*. In his new post at ITV News he is in charge of about 1,300 journalists and technical staff. The main ITV News bulletin since October 2003 has been at 10.30 pm, after a troubled period beginning in September 2000 when the programme's schedule slot shifted around to different times.

> When news became a moveable feast, the audience began to disappear. 'News at When' was terrible, terrible. News at 10.30 is a blessing. We've done a lot of work on the audience. At 10.30 pm, it's slightly skewed towards men, slightly upmarket, older. We're adding sport every night, making it a slightly more upscale product, a bit more foreign news and business news.
>
> (quoted in Brown 2004: 2)

Under Mannion's control, the ITV news studio was revamped to include a huge video wall behind the presenters, on which a single large image or several separate images could be projected: 'We must just make sure we present news in the most visual way possible' (quoted in Brown 2004: 2). A related decision was to unify the visual style of ITV regional news programmes, to provide a common brand identity. Regional programmes are intended to become more news-led than magazine-style programmes fronted by friendly chatting presenter teams, and will focus more on issues affecting the majority of local people, such as transport or crime. Mannion's aim overall is to modernise ITV News and unify its style, so that it has strong recognition among the audience and a striking visual identity: 'With 24-hour news, news on mobile phones etc., news programmes are much more produced, built products. They have to be in order to attract and engage the audience' (quoted in Brown 2004: 2).

# Further reading

Alleyne, M., *News Revolution: Political and Economic Decisions about Global Information* (Basingstoke: Macmillan, 1997).

Baudrillard, J., 'The Reality Gulf', *The Guardian* 11 January 1991, reprinted in P. Brooker and W. Brooker (eds), *Postmodern After-Images: A Reader in Film, Television and Video* (London: Arnold, 1997), pp. 165–7.

Bignell, J., *'Television News'* in *Media Semiotics: An Introduction* (Manchester: Manchester University Press, 2002), pp. 105–30.

Bourdieu, P., *On Television and Journalism* (London: Pluto, 1998).

Boyd-Barrett, O. and T. Rantanen, *The Globalization of News* (London: Sage, 1998).

Brown, M., 'War of the News Walls', *The Guardian* media section, 26 January 2004, p. 2.

Bruhn Jensen, K. (ed.), *News of the World: World Cultures Look at Television News* (London: Routledge, 1998).

Dahlgren, P., *Television and the Public Sphere* (London: Sage, 1995).

Ellis, J., 'Television as Working Through', in J. Gripsrud (ed.), *Television and Common Knowledge* (London: Routledge, 1999), pp. 55–70.

Freedman, L. and E. Karsh, *The Gulf Conflict 1990–1991: Diplomacy and War in the New World Order* (London: Faber, 1993).

Gillespie, M., 'Ambivalent Positionings: The Gulf War', in P. Brooker and W. Brooker (eds), *Postmodern After-Images: A Reader in Film, Television and Video* (London: Arnold, 1997), pp. 172–81.

Habermas, J., *The Theory of Communicative Action*, vol. 2 *Lifeworld and System: A Critique of Functionalist Reason* (Cambridge: Polity, 1987).

Harrison, J., *Terrestrial Television News in Britain: The Culture of Production* (Manchester: Manchester University Press, 2000).

Hartley, J., *Understanding News* (London: Methuen, 1982).

MacGregor, B., *Live, Direct and Biased?: Making Television News in the Satellite Age* (London: HodderHeadline, 1997).

Norris, C., ' "Postscript": Baudrillard's Second Gulf War Article', in P. Brooker and W. Brooker (eds), *Postmodern After-Images: A Reader in Film, Television and Video* (London: Arnold, 1997), pp. 168–71.

Philo, G., 'Missing in Action', *The Guardian* Higher Education section 16 April 2002, pp. 10–11.

Sinclair, J., E. Jacka and S. Cunningham, 'New Patterns in Global Television', in P. Marris and S. Thornham (eds), *The Media Reader* (Edinburgh: Edinburgh University Press, 1999), pp. 170–90.

Sreberny-Mohammadi, A. with K. Nordenstreng, R. Stevenson and F. Ugboajah (eds), *Foreign News in the Media: International Reporting in 29 Countries* (Paris: UNESCO, 1985).

Stewart, I. and S. Carruthers (eds), *War, Culture and the Media: Representations of the Military in Twentieth-century Britain* (Trowbridge: Flicks Books, 1993).

Walker, I., 'Desert Stories or Faith in Facts?', in M. Lister (ed.), *The Photographic Image in Digital Culture* (London: Routledge, 1995), pp. 236–52.

# 15 Sport

## Introduction

The first and most obvious point to make about television coverage of sport is that watching television is relatively passive and private, while playing sport is both active and public. But this chapter stresses the ways that audiences for TV sport are encouraged to feel that they are part of the crowd of spectators present at most sports events, that they can take part in the expert evaluation of what the players do, and that they can share the feelings of achievement or disappointment that players experience. Television sports coverage focuses much more on the kinds of sport that viewers might already have experience of, whether as active players (in their youth at school or college, or as leisure activities) or as spectators. There is far more coverage of football and cricket, for example, than of sports that most people have never played or seen live, such as fencing or fives. An interesting exception to this general rule is the TV coverage of the Olympic Games. Here, the competition is between national teams, so television tends to cover events in which the domestic audience can be expected to be supporting British sportspeople. This occurs even when the British sportspeople who have some chance of doing well are taking part in sports that do not normally get much television coverage. So a strong British team in a horseriding event or a women's hockey competition at the Olympics might get much more attention at the Olympics than they would at other times.

The two main forces that draw television channels to cover sport are relevance to the audience's assumed knowledge and interests, and the possibilities for covering sport in an interesting way that exploits the possibilities of the television medium. A well-known example of this latter force is the success of television coverage of snooker. Before the widespread availability of colour TV, it was difficult to present snooker because the colours of the balls looked like relatively similar shades of grey. But once colour was introduced, BBC's snooker programme *Pot Black* gained large audiences and raised the profile of the game. Similarly, television sports coverage makes use of the potential to set up multi-camera outside broadcast (OB) for live presentation of football, cricket and other sports where multiple cameras can be positioned around the various sides of a playing area. The opportunities to shift quickly from camera to camera, and from long shot to close-up, deploy OB set-ups so that a coherent sense of space and drama can be introduced into the programme. It is a lot more difficult to exploit these possibilities for variety of shots in linear or small-scale sports like rowing or darts, though each of these sports do receive some coverage.

This chapter concentrates on the coverage of sporting performance itself, though sport on television also includes a much wider variety of programme types. In fact, there are different presentations of what seems the same kind of material. Clearly, football is most obviously covered by TV in the form of live or recorded screenings of matches. But football is also present in the form of programmes featuring discussion of football and interviews with players and other football personalities. The BBC game shows *A Question of Sport* and *They Think It's All Over* have a strong representation of football players, and mix information and discussion about football with light-hearted competition and banter. Representations of football and footballers also occur in commercials such as the Walkers Crisps ads featuring Gary Lineker, and fictional representations of matches and footballers' home lives are the premise for the ITV1 drama *Footballers' Wives*. As Britain's national game, it is not surprising that this particular sport crops up so widely across television genres and formats.

## Sport in the multichannel environment

In the digital television environment there are more broadcasting channels, and therefore smaller amounts of money per channel and per programme to spend because the audience sizes for particular programmes are correspondingly smaller than those of conventional terrestrial television. The costs of making programmes are therefore more difficult to recoup from advertisers, and need to be generated from the subscriptions paid by the viewers of interactive digital television channels, or from one-off payments made by viewers to see a particular programme. However, figures released by BARB in February 2002 reveal that 50 per cent of the UK television audience have access to multichannel television, and the growth in multichannel has been led by the availability of sport, especially football, offered more by Sky television than any other digital channel. Mark Sharman (2002: 8), director of broadcasting and production at BSkyB wrote: 'According to government figures, the total size of the television broadcasting industry was estimated to be around £6.7bn in 1999. This represented a growth of 50% since 1994/95 – much of it reflecting the growth in multi-channel.'

In May, 2002, British Sky Broadcasting (BSkyB) reported an annual increase in profits of 33 per cent, to £129 million. The channel had 6 million subscribers, paying an average of £341 per year. BSkyB is a verti-cally integrated company, owning the digital satellite platform on which its channels are broadcast. It also controls the technology used in set-top boxes to receive satellite programmes and sets the prices paid by rival channels to gain access to the digital platform through its subsidiary Sky Subscriber Services Ltd (SSS). The electronic programme guide that allows viewers to navigate between the channels broadcast by the Astra satellite system is also controlled by BSkyB, which charges £28,000 a year for a listing on the electronic programme guide. BSkyB is one of numerous television businesses controlled by the media entrepreneur Rupert Murdoch, whose media interests include film, television, newspa-pers, book publishing and magazines, and also financial stakes in major sports teams whose games are covered in the media. Since sport leads the growth in multichannel subscriptions, rivals have raised the profile of their sports coverage where they can in order to compete with each other. ITV competed by beginning screenings of Premiership football matches at 7.00 pm on Saturdays. The cost of buying rights to screen sport cost ITV £160 million in 2001, more than the £110 million that ITV spent on entertain-ment programmes. This shows the shared assumptions about the value of sport in contemporary British television.

The attraction of audiences by screening sport, especially football, has been enhanced by the introduction of interactive services accompanying the broadcast of matches. Around 40 per cent of the subscribers to the Sky Sports Active channel watch football games interactively. Digital technology allows them to select text information relevant to the game, and to choose the camera angle from which the game is presented on their television screen, for example. From the perspective of the television broadcaster, interactive television is a 'premium service' that viewers can be charged additional money to use. But because of the slow development of interactive television technology in Britain, for every new subscriber, some other subscribers discontinue their payment for these services. Digital television broadcasters aim to reduce this turnover in viewers, the 'churn rate', by finding new ways of enhancing television coverage with inter-active services. Eventually, it is hoped that television viewers will become so accustomed to these enriched television programmes that they will consider them essential, and the number of non-renewals of subscriptions will fall.

It has been difficult, however, to find ways of making money from digital television in Britain. New developments in technology of any kind are more likely to be adopted when they enhance a service that already exists, or offer services that are linked to an established brand or prop-erty. Sport, as a familiar programme genre that has obvious opportunities for interactive supporting services, has been a way into interactive tele-vision for many viewers. While interactive television is a decisive and important development in the screening of sport, viewers have always interacted with televised sport, and forms of presentation invite the viewer to become involved and to participate. For example, television coverage of sport routinely addresses the viewer as a witness watching the sport along with television commentators and spectators at the event. The spoken discourse of sports commentators also routinely invites viewers to make judgements about the performance of the sportspeople and to evaluate their success. The positioning of cameras in television coverage of sport provides a much closer view of the action than is normally available to spectators at the event itself, and cutting between camera shots allows the television viewer to identify with the efforts and emotions of the competi-tors. The production and editing of television sport is designed to promote viewer involvement and to stimulate viewers' interaction with the event as it is taking place.

A space is 'hollowed out' for the sports viewer to occupy, in which an active response and involvement is required. Strategies like these are intended to stimulate active viewing of television programmes, where viewers give their full attention to what they are seeing and hearing, and where there may be opportunities for action by the viewer. In an interac-tive sports schedule, there will also be space for advertising that can also exploit the potential for viewer response and activity. It is generally supposed by advertisers that the greater the attention given by television viewers to programmes, the more chance there is that viewers will also give their attention to advertisements. From an advertiser's point of view, of course, it is very important that viewers watch and remember the advertisements they have seen. Advertisements often include opportunities for viewer activity that may simply be invitations for the viewer to get a joke, solve the puzzle, or simply to figure out what product an advertisement is selling. Being intrigued by a visually interesting advertisement, and enjoying its wit, are in themselves kinds of activity that make the advertisement and its product more memorable. But pressing the red button on a remote control in sports programmes makes it more plausible that viewers might also use their remotes to access information about products advertised in the breaks between matches or at half-time.

## Just like being there

The inclusion of viewers in sports programmes takes place by several means. The most apparently straightforward sports coverage on television is the live broadcasting of a game such as a football match. The position laid out for the viewer is both to identify with any or all the players, but especially the audience at the game who are the viewer's representatives. Sports narrative is a series of confrontations between different discourses, each appealing to one of several kinds of authority and legitimacy. Television coverage of sport not only includes the relay of the game, where television is largely an instrument to bring the event to the viewer. It also includes introductory framing of an event by the studio presenter, and discussion among experts and former players at intervals during the coverage. But the person most recognised by viewers of sport is the commentator who puts the action into linguistic form, pointing out the high-points, moments of controversy or giving behind-the-scenes information about the players and teams. The role of the commentator is to arrange the different roles of spectator, evaluator and narrator into a single coherent discourse. Since the game unfolds linearly over time, the discourse is sequential, and has moments of greater or lesser intensity, breaks and climaxes, and will finally achieve a closing resolution. The commentator acts as a mediating narrator working on behalf of the audience and claiming to represent its varied and potentially incompatible concerns.

In the studio discussion that frequently accompanies television coverage of football, athletics or the Olympics, television formats are designed to replicate the conversations that viewers at home might have about the sporting performances they have seen. But this replication is far from neutral or 'realistic', since the television discussion format adapts it into a hierarchical and ordered form. The hierarchy is presided over by the host presenter, and usually includes professional experts such as former players, team managers and sports journalists. Occasionally, especially in late night programmes addressed to young adult sports fans, these experts may be supplemented by guest members of the public and a studio audience. It is obvious that the studio audience or a guest member of the public represents the audience of viewers, and stands in for them. But the more conventional arrangement of host and experts also plays a representative function for the audience at home. The role of the host is to mediate between the television viewer and the expertise of the invited guests, by representing the viewer's imagined questions and concerns. Television viewers, along with the expert guests, are invited to evaluate the behaviour and opinions of the sportspeople whose play or performance has been broadcast. In a manner similar to the analysis of television narrative presented in Chapter 11, the structure of the programme and its use of hosts and personalities are designed to encourage the viewer at home to feel included in an evaluation of the sporting action. Sport becomes dramatic, in the sense that high-points and processes of action can be identified, and heroes, villains and supporting characters can be praised or blamed for their contribution to the eventual outcome.

## Taking part

Television calls for viewers to take up membership of an imaginary community of viewers. This call to belong is parallel to the way in which the French philosopher Louis Althusser (1971) explained the concept of ideology. Ideology is a structure in which people are addressed as particular kinds of subject, and take up a position laid out for them by this call, along with the values inherent in the position to which they are called. People become individuals, subject to ideological values and constituted as subjects by ideology as the unique destination to which the call is addressed. Television coverage of sporting events has the ideological function of disciplining the range of ways that viewers are invited to interact with the coverage, drawing sport away from the undisciplined irrationality associated with 'hooliganism' and towards the expert evaluation by rational means that is associated with middle-class expertise and the exercise of knowledge. In sports television, for example, singing football songs and throwing cans of beer at the screen is not expected, whereas knowledgeable debate and respect for the rules and conduct of the game is expected. The use of slow-motion replays in sports programmes is a further means of presenting and encouraging this kind of rational and evaluative critique.

The ideology of sports coverage is therefore part of television's more generalised function of shaping the audience and the forms of response to television that it demands. Television sports coverage is constructed in order to invite the viewer's involvement through offering patterns of reaction to the sport directed by the commentator. Studio comment by invited sports experts (former players, managers, sports journalists, etc.) focuses on discourses of evaluation and prediction, and aims to invite the viewer to engage in speculation and judgement in a similar way. This imaginary dialogue between the viewer and the programme therefore lays out codes in which the viewer's response should take place.

This process of taking on a specific audience position is enhanced by possibilities for interaction with sports programmes. Some sports coverage, especially of football, invites direct forms of viewer interaction. This includes competitions to decide the 'goal of the month' or opportunities to win tickets to important matches. Sport is not the only television genre to feature opportunities for interaction: comedy programmes invite laughter, television commercials offer puzzles or jokes that the viewer is invited to figure out, and both commercials and programmes provide telephone numbers and websites that offer further information, special offers, or competitions. Television shopping channels are of course entirely predicated on this interaction, since the viewer is explicitly addressed as a potential buyer of the products shown on screen. Television institutions are concerned to provide a sense of activity and involvement for viewers, whether as part of the public service function to show and support initiatives in society, or as part of a commercial imperative to encourage consumption of products and services.

In relation to sport, these initiatives may occasionally have a purpose that seems to contradict the programme or channel's desire for audiences to watch more television. For example, the evaluation of skills in football coverage, or commentary on batting techniques in cricket coverage, implicitly suggest that viewers might wish to go out and play football or cricket themselves. Television is a domestic technology, embedded in the home, and it potentially competes for attention with other domestic activities and possibilities for leaving the home and engaging in sport. However, this can be understood in part as an outcome of the disciplining function discussed above, where the manner of participation in sport can be shaped along the lines of personal achievement and sportspersonship. It also responds to public service intentions to support the playing of sport as a healthy, community-forming and spiritually uplifting activity that contributes to the public sphere and the enhancement of social life.

## Profile | BBC head of sport
David Salmon

**David Salmon has been BBC head of sport since 2000. Before taking on this managerial role, he was Controller of BBC1 and had previously worked as director of programmes at Granada TV and head of factual programmes at Channel 4 (Kelso 2004).**

BBC has the rights to show highlights of Premiership football games until 2007, FA cup matches and England international games played at home until 2008, the European Cup football tournament in 2004 and the football World Cup in 2006. Under an agreement that guarantees terrestrial broadcasters access to sporting events that are deemed of national importance, BBC will also screen major championship competitions in rugby, tennis, golf and athletics. These include the Wimbledon tennis tournament, and the Olympics of 2004 and 2008. In 2004 however, BBC's position in relation to its competitors in sports coverage was weakened when it lost the rights to screen the Oxford and Cambridge boat race to ITV, having broadcast this event for 50 years. Although falling advertising revenues mean that commercial broadcasters are now less likely to be successful in wresting the expensive rights to major sports events from BBC, Salmon faces the task of maintaining the BBC's profile as a key provider of sporting coverage:

> Before my time, we lost the Premiership, formula one, cricket – and they were emblematic, iconic defeats. It was partly an adjustment from the analogue world and the three-channel world into the digital

multi-channel environment. Things were going to change, and they changed in a rough, unpredictable way.

(quoted in Kelso 2004: 3)

Salmon has a shrewd and expert understanding of the commercial and competitive pressures on TV sport, but holds to a quite traditional view of the significance of sports broadcasting. This derives from the public service commitment to bring a range of programming, both difficult and also popular and entertaining, to the widest possible audience:

Sport has a unique place in the cultural life of the nation, and it is right that the BBC reflects that. Events like Wimbledon and the Six Nations galvanise the passion of the UK. These are moments when the BBC can take something into an open, accessible public moment that millions enjoy.

(quoted in Kelso 2004: 3)

# Further reading

Althusser, L., 'Ideology and Ideological State Apparatuses: Notes Towards an Investigation', in *Lenin and Philosophy* (London: New Left Books, 1971), pp. 121–73.

Boyle, R. and R. Haynes, *Power Play: Sport, the Media and Popular Culture* (Harlow: Pearson, 2000).

Brookes, R., 'The FIFA World Cup', in G. Creeber (ed.), *Fifty Key Television Programmes* (London: Arnold, 2004), pp. 85–9.

Creeber, G. (ed.), *The Television Genre Book* (London: BFI, 2001).

Kelso, P., 'A Question of Sport', *The Guardian* media section, 8 March 2004, pp. 2–3.

Miller, T., G. Lawrence, J. McKay and D. Rowe (eds), *Globalization and Sport: Playing the World* (London: Sage, 2001).

Sharman, M., 'A Nation Tunes In', *The Guardian* media section, 18 February 2002, pp. 8–9.

Whannel, G., *Fields in Vision: Television Sport and Cultural Transformation* (London: Routledge, 1992).

# 16 Music video and postmodernism

## Introduction

Work on postmodernism in discussing television has been part of a shift from structure to agency. Structure refers to the institutions, networks of relationships and professional practices that condition the ways in which television is produced and broadcast. It includes theories of ideology and globalisation for example, which seek to explain audience responses and preferences, and also addresses the features of television programme texts, as the result of these structural conditions. Agency refers to a new value attributed to viewer choice, and the ways that audiences engage in negotiations with television texts and media structures in order to define themselves and empower themselves as individuals. Arguments about postmodernism address the political impact of the mass media.

The increased significance of the mass media is part of postmodernism and includes the liberating effects of the widespread distribution of information and ideas around the globe. On one hand, this provides unprecedented access to information, ideas and creative possibilities. On the other hand, it reduces the uniqueness of each individual and the specific cultures to which individuals belong, so that places and people become virtually the same and are all affected by the same assumptions, desires and fears presented by multinational commercial broadcasters. Music television seems to be a perfect example of postmodernism: the material it broadcasts appears to be shallow, based around commodity images with no 'message' except the injunction to buy, it broadcasts a flow of short videos producing an endless present or perpetual flow in which the day parts and fixed points of conventional terrestrial television schedules are largely absent. It was these characteristics that drew the attention of television theorists to the channel (and others that share similar features), and encouraged the American theorist E. Ann Kaplan (1987) to write the first major academic book that analysed the MTV channel as a postmodern form. The ideas about music video that Kaplan and other theorists put forward in the 1980s can be challenged however, both on the basis that they misunderstand some of the fundamental properties of music channels, and also that some of their wide-ranging theoretical ideas are problematic in themselves.

## The MTV aesthetic

Music television provides a 24-hour soundtrack to the lives of its viewers, in which the repeated sequences of video music work in combination with a restricted repertoire of imagery presenting the pop celebrities who make and appear in them. The celebrity pop performer on television is constructed out of a cluster of signs that can mutate and change according to context and over time, rather than being an 'objective' representation of a real personality who precedes the images seen on music TV. Kaplan (1987: 44) argued that this is a development that matches postmodern versions of identity:

> Perhaps most relevant to our discussion of the postmodernist devices in MTV videos generally is the blurring of distinctions between a 'subject' and an 'image'. What seems to be happening in the play with the image of the various kinds discussed is the reduction of the 'self' to an 'image' merely.

In other words, pop performers have their being in a world of images that are dissociated from an idea of their 'real' selves. It makes little sense to ask what Britney Spears is 'really like': she is known to her viewers and fans only through the cluster of images and meanings transmitted by the media. Madonna's manipulation of her persona is the most famous example of this, and more recently performers such as Kylie Minogue and Britney Spears have transformed their images from girlish innocence to more sexual personas. Celebrity pop performers' images change, producing changes in what they mean to their audiences, thus demonstrating that there is no stable self that holds their identities together coherently. While Kaplan was referring specifically to pop performers in making this point, she also wanted to argue that the same mutability of identity could be seen more generally in contemporary culture. Through fashion and consumer choices, everyone in developed Western cultures could define themselves through the images they project to others, marking a fundamental change in how ideas about the self and individual identity are produced and experienced. This kind of change is one of the features that leads cultural theorists to adopt the term postmodernism to label such a state of affairs.

Music television is a key part of a much wider culture of celebrity that involves the music industry, the internet, newspapers, magazines and radio. It is notable that the notion of an identity being constructed out of changeable appearances, changing fashions of self-presentation, and thinking of the self as an image put on display to other people, are all conventionally associated with femininity. The examples of celebrities changing their image given in the above paragraph were all women. When men change their image in the same way (as David Bowie has done, for example), this is regarded as the adoption by male performers of a feminine emphasis on style, fashion and narcissism. So, one of the consequences of the argument that postmodern culture is an image culture is that it is also a feminised culture.

As well as connecting music television to what she believed were dominant characteristics of celebrity culture and consumerism, Kaplan (1987: 44) used her analysis of MTV to make a claim that contemporary television, and culture in general, had developed into a new phase: 'Television in this way seems to be at the end of a whole series of changes begun at the turn of the century with the development of modern forms of advertising and the department store window.' Television is closely connected to consumer culture, the desire for commodities, virtual tourism and the representation of the exotic. Whereas shopping and experiencing the exotic used to take place outside the home (on tours and in shopping malls), these experiences can be indulged in at home, by watching television and interacting via a remote control. Leisure and consumption have always historically been associated with women, with femininity, and television too as the medium belonging in the home, in domestic space, has also been regarded as feminine. For Andreas Huyssen (1986), postmodernism's celebration of mass culture is a celebration of feminisation, and the aesthetic of music television has contributed to this. These ways of recognising the changing patterns of difference, especially gender difference, in music television performance, have enabled voices representing diverse audiences and identity groups to celebrate music television performance as a force for unsettling restrictive definitions of gender, race, age group and other ways of conceptualising identity. Music television and post-modern culture in general could be seen as a threat to patriarchy and the established masculine dominance over cultural life.

However, music television and other forms of postmodern TV not only draw on the resources of contemporary popular culture, but also on aesthetic forms that derive from the experimentation carried out by artists and film-makers in the Modernist period of the early twentieth century. Music video uses surprising montage combinations of images, often lacks conventional narrative progression, and uses colour, special effects and lighting differ-ently from other television programmes or mainstream cinema films. Many of these techniques derive from the experimental film forms developed in the early twentieth century by directors such as Sergei Eisenstein and Dziga-Vertov. Since MTV is clearly a mass audience television form, and television is itself part of mass media culture, the co-option of Modernist aesthetic forms represents the democratisation of what were once elite artistic techniques and ideas. Postmodernist theory values music television in part because it seems to undo the notion of culture as a hierarchy of taste, with an elite at the top and a mass popular audience at the bottom, and with distinct cultural forms offered respectively to the elite and the mass audience. Music television's mixing of Modernist experimental forms with commercial culture questions the hierarchies of taste and style in media dissemination and consumption that are associated with modernity.

For example, the ways that the MTV aesthetic has been explained here are not significantly different from how media theorists have discussed video art, made for gallery exhibition and not for broadcast, usually with an emphasis on experimental techniques and challenging ways of addressing the viewer. The American theorist Fredric Jameson (1987) uses the term 'video-text' to refer to commercial television and video art, and argues that video is postmodern. Video, 'closely related to the dominant computer and information technology of the late or third stage of capi-talism' (1987: 207) is 'a sign-flow which resists meaning, whose funda-mental inner logic is the exclusion of the emergence of themes as such in that sense, and which therefore systematically sets out to short circuit trad-itional interpretive temptations' (1987: 219). Because video enables the manipulation of time, cutting it up and slowing it down by using the capa-bilities of electronic technology, it can contrast with the ordered control of time, pacing and narrative, which television and film have customarily used. Jameson's conception of video and television is much closer to video art than to network television programmes and the aesthetic conventions and scheduling practices that they involve, but it is quite an effective description of how music television works.

Music video can therefore be paralleled with video art, at the same time as it belongs securely to mainstream commercial culture. Kaplan (1987: 47) refers to the makers of music video as 'artists', and explicitly regards their borrowing of ideas and forms from European and American art as well as popular commercial culture as a radical deconstruction of the boundaries between art and popular culture: 'video artists are often playing with standard high art and popular culture images in a self-conscious manner, creating a liberating sense by the very defiance of traditional boundaries.' Postmodernism involves mixing the hitherto experimental and innovative methods of the Modernists with commercially distributed mass commercial culture, and the theorist Andreas Huyssen wrote (1986: 57), 'it is by the distance we have travelled from this "great divide" between mass culture and modernism that we can measure our own cultural post-modernity'. In other words, postmodernism breaks down the division between culture for a small elite group and culture for a mass audience. Television has been a crucial contributor to this process, and MTV has been used as a key example in explaining and promoting this insight.

## Politics, gender and performance

The arguments about MTV in postmodern theory in the 1980s were also carried through in relation to the performances, especially MTV music video performances, of Madonna. Madonna offers radical challenges to conventional norms. She has challenged the representation of femininity by the repeated changes to her celebrity persona, suggesting a freedom of self-expression and pleasure for women. She has been critical of the Catholic Church, especially in its condemnation of sexual pleasure and homosexuality. She has confronted the limits of mass media representation, especially of sexuality, by producing pop videos and other commodities that have generated controversy and occasionally censorship because of their explicit sexual imagery and promotion of sexual pleasure for its own sake. Madonna's economic success on MTV, and the financial assistance for her career provided by her associations with major corporations can be seen as ways of using the capitalist media system against itself. Perhaps by drawing on the global media presence of MTV to get her messages across, and by drawing on connections with other globally recognised brands that keep her own celebrity image to the forefront, Madonna is able to disturb the very structures and ideologies that underlie contemporary television. The most interesting characteristic of postmodern theory, and of postmodern media culture, is the way in which contrasting ideas can be shown to be two sides of the same coin. The complexity and confusion that this produces in theories of television mirrors the complexity and confusion that postmodern theorists see around them in television itself.

Just as Madonna has been presented as an icon who can manipulate the creation of her own image by the media, and by MTV in particular, the play, reflexivity and multiple meanings identified in postmodern television texts are also available to audiences. As Robin Nelson (1997: 246) suggests: 'Postmodern texts might be summarily characterized by a formal openness, a strategic refusal to close down meaning. They create space for play between discourses allegedly empowering the reader to negotiate or construct her own meanings.' Television viewers construct sense from the diverse fragments of narrative, character, visual pleasure and intertextual reference that postmodern television offers. While there are moments of stability and involvement in television, the role of fragmentary signification, the withholding of resolution and the sense of being suspended in a perpetual middle is what makes the term postmodern useful for describing television now.

If television viewers construct sense out of the postmodern fragments that MTV and postmodern television in general offer to them, the fragmentation and multiplicity of the text must be reflected in the fragmentation and multiplicity of identity, inasmuch as television is one of the resources for constructing that identity. Identifying postmodern style and form leads to the argument that television is changing subjectivity. Theories of viewer positioning adapted from analyses of classical Hollywood cinema, such as those that Kaplan drew on in her work on MTV, would no longer be appropriate (as she argues herself) to MTV because the texts of music video are so different from those of cinema. The involving narratives with beginnings, middles and ends, and psychologically realistic characters in conventional cinema lay out a secure position for the spectator, and stabilise him or her in the identity of an audience member for the film in question. This kind of stable audience position seems inappropriate for the reflexive, intertextual and ironic processes of meaning in contemporary television and in music television especially. Features of television programmes match descriptions of identity as mobile, fluid and fragmentary, and this is one of the aspects of a political reading of music television.

If music television textuality both reflects and produces fluid and fragmentary identity, this can be seen as a resource for the reworking of the conceptual category of the individual subject in Western capitalist society. The ideological function of stabilised subjectivity is to hold the subject in a position in a social hierarchy and a gender role. If that stability is questioned, new configurations of social role and gender identity could be the result. Watching music television would then be a means to unsettle and advance the role of the individual subject in contemporary society. It is that possibility that has attracted television theorists to both studies of MTV and of postmodernism, since television culture of that kind matches the radical or even revolutionary politics of many theorists in the field.

The textual aspects of music television that this chapter has focused on so far are not the only resource for understanding it, however. The performers and videos featured on music television are surrounded by other kinds of text, in media other than television, that also refract and multiply their meanings. The meanings of celebrities depend not only on their construction and form within music television, but also the other discourses generated around them. The stories about pop stars in newspapers and magazines offer information and advertise performers and music commodities like CDs and videos in ways that support the personas established by the forms of the music videos themselves. The pop stars are represented as entirely familiar: articles and interviews profiling them presuppose familiarity with their identities, musical careers and influences, and major events in their lives. As a discourse that advertises both the star and his or her newest products, the underlying assumption in the codes of this discourse is the fascination with what products are about to become available for purchase. The popular press compare and test this discourse of commodification and advertising against reality, running articles on the 'real' lives of the celebrities, and on the differences between the marketing persona and the flaws, heartbreaks and scandals that they are involved in. The exaggerated coding of pop profiles and marketing images (their use of romantic or exotic biographical information, for instance) play against the down-to-earth and often sordid details of the performers' 'real' lives. So the viewer's pleasure in music television must therefore partly depend on his or her recognition of the mediation of the pop star persona by other television forms and other media discourses. The back and forth movement between the star as ideal and the star as a 'real' person in these discourses both maintains their separation from each other and shows how interdependent they are, testifying to the unstable border between the star as just another person on one hand, and the idealised performance or image on the other.

## Music TV and globalisation

Celebrity is the commodification of personality, and not only does music television further this process but it also advertises itself as a commodity that is purchased by multichannel audiences. In order to achieve this, a channel such as MTV needs to present its own personality attractively. This is achieved by simultaneously marketing MTV's global engagement with the global music and entertainment industry, and also by addressing local and regional audiences. In contemporary television culture there is no such thing as a common culture, a national culture, or an international culture. Instead there are numerous overlapping and competing cultures at local and regional levels, which co-exist with a multinational and global culture. MTV is programmed differently in each territory to which it is broadcast, though the formats remain largely the same and many of the products advertised on MTV are also global brands appearing in different languages and different territories. MTV is owned by an American media corporation. It can be argued that MTV is a vehicle for the global spread of American capitalist values, expressed through the international pop music market which sells products with no intrinsic value. In its early years, MTV advertising seemed to proclaim this in the slogan, 'One world, one image, one channel: MTV', which celebrated the erosion of local differences by the global channel. Connections between the MTV channel and global consumer culture could be seen in the deals made between pop stars and the soft drink industry, such as the association of Madonna and Michael Jackson with Pepsi Cola. Commercials featuring the performers and the soft drinks appeared on MTV, making a vicious circle of advertising that encompassed American performers, American television, American soft drinks and American record companies.

For these reasons, some cultures and nations have attempted to block the broadcasting of MTV within the regions they control. The processes of globalisation are open to regulation by individual nations, rather than being an autonomous and unstoppable process, and global markets are regulated by contracts and by international and national laws. But the world organisations that oversee international television agreements generally support the lowering of national restrictions and quotas, because they seek to create a global free market economy in communications. The World Trade Organisation, the International Monetary Fund, and regional agreements such as the North American Free Trade Agreement and the European Free Trade Association provide support for cross-border television exchanges that are based on the principles of unrestricted commercial exchange. The apparently free and uncontrollable television market is not a natural fact and depends on the taking of political decisions about deregulation and competition in television by nation-states and groupings of states. Countries and regional groupings tend both to deregulate and encourage globalisation, but also to introduce further regulation to protect their societies against it.

The case of MTV is therefore an interesting location to consider the analytical purchase of the media imperialism thesis, discussed by Herman and McChesney (1997), for example. The legacy of the media imperialism argument is that it is not American programmes or American television owners that perpetuate regressive kinds of television organisation. American programmes do not always dominate the schedules of countries with less developed television cultures, and even if they did, it is not proven that these programmes simply transmit American values to their audiences. Similarly, many American television producers are not owned solely or at all by American individuals or companies, and the ownership of television broadcasting institutions in other parts of the world is more likely to be through a combined deal between global media corporations and local or regional interests.

But the aspect of the media imperialism thesis that does remain valid is that the American system of television organisation has been successfully exported to very many of the world's national broadcasters. This trend tends to increase as deregulation and liberalisation of television markets advances with the collapse of rigid state broadcasting controls in former authoritarian societies. The financing of television by advertising, where audiences are targeted by particular programme types in order to deliver them to advertisers, is an American model that has become increasingly common. The American model of the competition between broadcasting channels affiliated to major network or cable and satellite providers is also adopted in nations that have their own indigenous television production bases.

# History and the MTV debate

The first academic writing on MTV was published in the late 1980s and early 1990s, and MTV has changed considerably since then. Rather than one channel, MTV is four channels (MTV itself which is a general pop music channel, MTV2 which plays more rock and alternatives to dance music, MTVHits which is a pop chart channel, and MTVBase which focuses on rap, rhythm-and-blues and soul), and in Britain there are three widely accessible music channels that compete with it. This raises an interesting theoretical question about how MTV could have been postmodern in the 1980s, but now may be a relic of a previous phase in television. If MTV is no longer postmodern in the sense that its aesthetic and organisation are not of the present, is postmodernism itself an historical phase that has now passed, or must MTV be re-categorised as modern rather than postmodern? How does postmodernism relate to the idea of history?

The French philosopher Jean-François Lyotard (1993: 44) argued that something is 'modern only if it is first postmodern'. He uses the term 'postmodern' as an adjective to describe cultural artefacts for which the criteria for aesthetic judgements about value and artistic success cannot be straightforwardly applied. This insight is clearly relevant to the debates about MTV discussed in this chapter (and also to other debates about television and value considered elsewhere in this book). For television theorists, analysis of MTV has led both to the condemnation of its aesthetic features as repetitive, manipulative and conventionalised, but also to the judgement that it represents a fluid, discontinuous and experimental representation of emotion, time and space that could provide a template for other innovative television forms. A further aspect of this problem of judgement is that the categorisation of the material is problematic, and therefore the critical approach that should be adopted to it is impossible to decide on. Kaplan, for example, drew on film theory to show how MTV refuses the conventions of point of view and identification that audiovisual sequences in cinema have used. On the other hand, Andrew Goodwin (1996) argued that this categorisation of MTV in relation to cinema was inappropriate, and that music video should be aligned with the aesthetic of the live pop performance or rock concert. Decisions about which category MTV video should be placed in determined the criteria of judgement brought to the problem by different analysts, and sometimes these criteria were incompatible.

It is this very incompatibility of criteria, and undecidability about value, that Lyotard cited as evidence that a cultural form is postmodern. What we think of as modern, as appropriate to our current state of culture, has to pass through this postmodern state of ambiguity and confusion. The condition of being postmodern is a state that can be recognised only after the event, once categories and criteria have been applied to MTV and it has become comprehensible by means of them. Once this has happened, the initial confusion about what MTV is can be resolved. But the resolution of ambiguity and the dispersal of the problem of judgement remove MTV from the category of the postmodern by definition. MTV is relegated to the epoch or style that preceded the postmodern, and that would therefore be called modern. But there was a time (probably the 1980s when the first attempts were made to categorise and evaluate MTV) when critical discourse could not gain a grip on the channel and its significance. MTV is modern, but that state of confusion in which it first appeared was a postmodern moment. This theoretically complex but very persuasive work on the definition of postmodernism has three main planks: first, that the term postmodern is retrospectively attributed. Second, the postmodern is a momentary condition that lasts for the short time in which new cultural forms are not yet assimilated into discourse and ideology. Finally, as a result of the first two arguments, the postmodern is not an epoch or period but is a characteristic of how cultural forms appear and are perceived. The positive contribution that postmodern forms such as MTV make to television culture is that they problematise categories and assumptions that are taken for granted in the perception and study of the medium. Once this radical postmodern moment has passed, and MTV can be explained, judged and categorised, its creative challenge and artistic interest reduce.

## Further reading

Barker, C., *Global Television: An Introduction* (Oxford: Blackwell, 1997).

Bignell, J., *Postmodern Media Culture* (Edinburgh: Edinburgh University Press, 2000).

Brooker, P. and W. Brooker (eds), *Postmodern After-Images: A Reader in Film, Television and Video* (London: Arnold, 1997).

Dowmunt, T. (ed.), *Channels of Resistance: Global Television and Local Empowerment* (London: BFI, 1993).

Goodwin, A., *Dancing in the Distraction Factory: Music, Television and Popular Culture* (London: Routledge, 1993).

Goodwin, A., 'MTV', in J. Corner and S. Harvey (eds), *Television Times: A Reader* (London: Arnold, 1996), pp. 75–87.

Herman, E. and R. McChesney, *The Global Media: The New Missionaries of Global Capitalism* (London: Cassell, 1997).

Huyssen, A., *After the Great Divide: Modernism, Mass Culture and Postmodernism* (London: Macmillan, 1986).

Jameson, F., 'Reading without Interpretation: Postmodernism and the Video-text', in D. Attridge and N. Fabb (eds), *The Linguistics of Writing: Arguments between Language and Literature* (Manchester: Manchester University Press, 1987), pp. 199–233.

Kaplan, E.A., *Rocking Around the Clock: Music Television, Postmodernism and Consumer Culture* (London: Methuen, 1987).

Kellner, D., *Media Culture: Cultural Studies, Identity and Politics Between the Modern and the Postmodern* (London: Routledge, 1995).

Lewis, L., *Gender Politics and MTV: Voicing the Difference* (Philadelphia: Temple University Press, 1990).

Lull, J. (ed.), *World Families Watch Television* (London: Sage, 1988).

Lyotard, J.-F., 'Answering the Question: What is Postmodernism?', in T. Docherty (ed.), *Postmodernism: A Reader* (Hemel Hempstead: Harvester Wheatsheaf, 1993), pp. 38–46.

Mundy, J., *Popular Music on Screen: From Hollywood Musical to Music Video* (Manchester: Manchester University Press, 1999).

Nelson, R., *TV Drama in Transition: Forms, Values and Cultural Change* (Basingstoke: Macmillan, 1997).

Woods, T., *Beginning Postmodernism* (Manchester: Manchester University Press, 1999).

Part IV

# Idea to image

# 17 Factual programming

## Background

Documentary is a wide ranging term that means different things to different programme makers. The term 'factual programming' is often used to cover all types of programming that are not scripted. Comedy, entertainment and drama are all scripted, and rarely come into the documentary category. However, there are documentary programmes that include elements of comedy and drama, and are certainly entertaining. The documentary should contain truthful reporting, be concerned with the truth and convey a truthful message. Documentaries have a reputation for being serious, reliable and objective in their reporting with a commitment to truthfulness.

The filmmaker John Grierson is generally considered to be the founding father of the British documentary film movement in the 1920s. He is credited with first using the word documentary to describe his factual film making. He described his approach to the films as 'the creative treatment of actuality' using 'fragments of reality'. Grierson realised that he would never be able to film 'reality', because the interpretation of the programme maker must always be taken into account. In the celebrated documentary film *Night Mail* about the mail trains that took the post overnight from London to Edinburgh, Grierson recreated scenes in the studio that he was not able to film on the train. He used some of the actual postmen speaking the natural dialogue they had used on the train while sorting the mail. While technically a re-enactment the authenticity of the material is not compromised.

Later Bill Nichols defined documentary as 'representing reality'. This is usually taken to mean that the act of representing the reality of a subject covers reporting, observing, investigating, interpreting and reflecting on that subject.

Documentary filmmakers sometimes have to direct contributors to go through movements and activities several times in order to get the required selection of shots. This is normal procedure, although many modern documentaries rely on the use of multiple hidden cameras, or unobtrusive, lightweight cameras with long recording times. The central truthful content of the documentary film need not be obscured by some elements of disguised fabrication.

The difficulty is that what appears to be 'real' and 'truthful' on television will differ from one viewer to the next. The viewer's interpretation of the programme is an integral part of the viewing experience. Broadcasters believe that modern viewers will accept a programme labelled documentary as a genuine attempt to reach a form of truth about a subject. But the area is still controversial.

In 2004 the American documentary film maker Michael Moore won cinema's greatest honour, the Palme d'Or, at the Cannes Film Festival for his film *Fahrenheit 9/11*. This was the first time the Cannes jury had awarded its prize to a documentary since Jacques Cousteau's *The Silent World* in 1956. Michael Moore in 2003 won Best Documentary Oscar, for his film *Bowling for Columbine*.

Many people feel that Moore is making interesting films, but that they are not documentaries. He uses the tools and forms of documentary, but manipulates his material to make convincing points. This means, argue his critics, that he is economical with the truth.

A truly objective form of documentary programme making is not possible. Documentary programme makers aim to achieve a version of reality that can illuminate a subject and appeal to a television audience.

## Documentary genres

Television companies like to split documentary programmes into genres according to content or style.

Lightweight and very small digital cameras, and the ability to record for long periods of time have revived the observational documentary. This is the type of programme that looks at how people live their everyday lives. It can be about life in an institution such as a hospital, ship or prison, or focused around people.

The approach is immortalised as 'fly on the wall'. Key programme makers such as Ken Loach and Roger Graef used this technique to observe the intimate lives of people in their own homes. This genre started with Paul Watson's intimate look at the lives of the Walton family in *The Family* (1973). Watson showed that to make strong programmes that were both illuminating and interesting the documentary director had to spend large amounts of time with the people involved. This type of documentary can still be provoking. The genre has mutated into the 'Reality TV' of *Big Brother*, which delivers higher ratings, but is not documentary at all in the Grierson sense.

## Docusoap

The idea of the observational TV programme with continuing story lines and based around interesting characters is not new. What is new about the docusoap is that it uses the techniques of drama, and the structure of the particularly televisual form of the soap opera, to provide narrative interest and excitement. The content and the characters are taken from events in everyday life.

A docusoap has an episodic structure with several interweaving plot lines each involving different characters. The genre has thrown up an unlikely collection of televisual characters. Maureen the terrible driver from *Driving School*, and Jeremy, the friendly fellow from *Airport.* Characters from docusoaps have become part of the minor celebrity circus that inhabits the hinterland of TV talk shows and game shows. Docusoap has had an effect in democratising television. Ordinary people at last have become central stage, and programmes about them deliver large audiences to the broadcasting companies.

User friendly digital cameras allow contributors to record their personal thoughts and intimate moments as video diaries at home or in a hotel room, without the intrusive presence of a film crew. Where the film crew is present they become a friend and confidante often featuring in the final cut.

## Documentary filmmakers

A documentary filmmaker such as Molly Dineen works on her own operating the camera and recording sound allowing unprecedented access to people's lives. This is especially effective in recording the daily life of a celebrity, such as ex-Spice girl Geri Halliwell (Ginger Spice). Called *GERI* this was a 90-minute documentary made in the three months after her departure from the Spice Girls. It was a memorable portrait of the predicament of the modern celebrity. It won the Indies Award nomination in 1999. Molly Dineen also won The Grierson Memorial Trust 2003 Trustees' Award for outstanding contribution to the art of documentary.

## The future of documentaries on television

The documentary continues to evolve. Vibrant filmmakers around the world are turning their cameras on a wide range of subjects. There is an unprecedented complicity between characters, the filmmaker and audience that is quite new in the history of documentary. The characters are encouraged to talk to camera, laugh at their mistakes and involve the viewer in the illusion of reality. Realism is no longer within the TV frame, but is seen to be a construct between the filmmaker, the subject and the audience.

The docusoap lost some of its appeal to channel schedulers in 2003 as it was perceived to have been overexploited. The genre has modified to take in more serious subjects, as well as getting on the life style programme wagon. The rash of relocation programmes from the BBC and Channel 4 in 2003/4 has brought back the presenter. The programmes still feature the lives of ordinary people, and draw their content and narrative structure from the events that shape their lives. But the presenter is now a helper and friend, who has to help realise the dreams of ordinary people. This is no *Jim'll fix it* type of programme where the TV company operate as a Deus ex machina giving a lucky viewer a great adventure.

These new docusoap style of programmes follow the lives of people as they move house, relocate their family and jobs abroad, or take on new work challenges. The logistics for the programme maker seem insurmountable. These programmes are successful, with good audiences, and there are successful publishing spin-offs.

This is a significant revolution in the way factual programming is perceived by broadcasters.

Alistair Fothergill, director of the remarkable and hugely successful *Blue Planet* series is confident that the explanatory style of documentary has a secure future. Some social documentary makers are more cautious, and even cynical about the future for the social documentary on British television. Paul Watson has become deeply cynical of the politics within institutionalised broadcasting. John Willis feels there is a uniformity, and 'formulaic quality about a great deal of especially British television that is devaluing the documentary. Now every documentary has to get the ratings and risk taking is being squeezed out'.

# Reality TV

Reality TV is a twenty-first-century genre of factual programming that is more entertainment than documentary, in spite of the title. The techniques and style employed purport to be documentary. In fact, the 'reality' is tightly controlled by the television company, and ferociously edited for maximum entertainment value.

The way the participants are presented does, in the better shows, allow for the unexpected elements of real life to shape the narrative. There are no script writers as such. Events happen in real time although we see the edited version. Reality TV programmes such as *Big Brother* are not obser-vational. The aim of the 50 or more cameras positioned around the set is to capture entertaining and interesting events in order to create a story line – the more shocking the better. The production team intercede at all points to control the narrative. The programmes are heavily edited to include spicy content. The contestants are chosen for the maximum potential to make interesting TV. The fact that they are called contestants instantly puts this genre in the game show category.

Nobody is fooled that these programmes are representing anything other than a manipulated reality. This does seem to interest larger audiences than the conventional documentary programme. Dedicated documentary makers are turning to the cinema, the internet and DVD distribution to attract attention and enthuse an audience. Television feeds on the success of these sometimes maverick filmmakers through chat shows and discus-sion programmes. Public service television can capture the Zeitgeist of the age, and play a central role in general education, by commissioning and broadcasting distinctive documentaries. Many people would argue that it is its job to do just that. The genre needs to keep a mass audience. To do this it must evolve and not be precious about its antecedents.

The success of Reality TV, and the newer forms of factual programmes including make-over shows and relocation programmes, has injected new vigour into the overall area of factual programme making. These pro-grammes may not educate in quite the way John Grierson envisaged, but they do provide a social snapshot of the times. Broadcast television has never had so many ordinary citizens as the main contributors to prime-time programming.

Television is becoming democratised by the documentary and not by the increasing nod to audience participation through emails and online, or telephone, voting. The viewer is both in the frame and in the armchair.

# Getting a programme on the air

## Treatment

A production starts with a 'treatment'. This is a succinct description of what the programme is trying to show, how it will be shown, and who it is aimed at. A TV treatment should be no longer than one page and include the vital statistics of the show. The audience needs to be defined – prime-time, children, daytime, early evening, late night. The presenter and/or any well-known contributors must be included, and the style of the show – studio, all location, video diary, or a genre. A budget suggested.

The treatment will be assessed by a commissioning editor or executive producer. If it is liked and thought suitable for the channel and the time slot the producer will be asked to attend a number of meetings. If all goes well the show will be commissioned and given a budget. It is relatively unusual for a one-off programme to be commissioned; the producermay go to an independent company who could take a bundle of similar programmes to a commissioning editor and offer a series of, say, science-based programmes to the channel.

## Production team

For an independent factual programme as in the example a team will be assembled by the producer. There is a researcher/PA, and an assistant producer who will also direct some of the programmes.

## Script

The next stage is to write a shooting script, or an expanded running order that will give some shape to each programme. Scripts for factual

## Example of a treatment

**Programme:** TO BE THE BEST

**Duration:** 1 × 25 minutes Independent production suitable for mid-evening on BBC2 or Channel 4

**Format:** Single camera shot on location on DV. Extensive postproduction.

**Audience:** Sports audience, but also of interest to a general audience interested in how the mind works, and people who take part in any sporting activity – from bowls to sand yachting, from football to lacrosse.

**Presenter:** Charismatic Olympic gold medallist in rowing for Great Britain.

**Aim:** The aim of the series is to explore in depth the mental, and psychological training systems used by top sports people. The advice, help and training methods used would be analysed and interpreted for armchair viewers.

**Resumé:** Top sportsmen and team coaches use sports psychologists, or employ a variety of mental techniques including meditation, visualisation and cognitive techniques to improve sporting performance. How do these techniques work, and do they work? The programme explains and explores with a light touch using new modern in-depth research from a leading UK university.

**Suggested elements:** The programme will interview a wide range of sports psychologists and other practitioners, and will test their theories. Top athletes, footballers, rugby players and cricketers have agreed to take part. A televisual young professor, who has tested many of these techniques, leads the university research team. She will present their research and explain their results.

Using some animation the programme will show how the mind works in relation to specific techniques.

Dynamic presenter, charismatic contributors and a firm public service remit within the field of sports science. A programme that will interest everyone who watched the Olympics, especially the rowing.

**Cost:** Average filming days for a 25-minute programme. Some animation. Average to low budget for a mid-evening programme.

programmes evolve throughout the production. What might start as a list of interviewees and locations will probably end up as a précis of the content of the interviews linked by pieces to camera, script for graphics and commentary. It is likely to be too long and will have to be adjusted for time in the edit.

## Recce

Recce comes from the French word reconnaissance and means a survey. This is the stage where you know what you want to film, and now need to finalise the locations or discover new relevant ones. The recce is linked to the research, and often done at the same time. Researchers carry their own portable digital cameras so that the pictures taken on location can be discussed in the production office. It depends on the type of production and the nature of the programme as to how much time and budget is spent on the recce. Filming a re-enactment of a battle in the Middle Ages for a historical programme at a castle clearly needs a precise and accurate recce. An interview in London may be able to be set up with just a phone call. Experienced producers never underestimate the value of a well-planned recce.

## Shooting

The structure of the programme is in place. The interviews and other activities to be filmed have been recced and set up for filming. The schedule is in place, and the film crew and artists booked. All you have to do is make sure you shoot enough exciting material to cover all elements of the story and make the editor happy.

Factual programmes are not known for large resources. As a researcher you are likely to have to go and interview a contributor. You may have a cameraman with you, or you may have to use a DV camera on your own. You are likely to set up the interview on the telephone, so make sure you have done some research first. Make sure you know what you want to get out of the interview. If the interviewee is an expert in medieval sword fighting, and you know nothing about it, then explain to your interviewee that you would like to have some background knowledge before you film the interview.

Ask on the phone about possible suitable locations. You will sort out the exact location where your interview will take place when you have

*Figure 17.1* Shooting an interview on DV

had a look round. Do this beforehand if you can. Choose a relaxing, quiet place. If it is interior then avoid busy wallpaper backgrounds, or pure white walls. Bookshelves are good, or an armchair with the background in subdued light. Do not film against a bright window unless you can light your subject (see Lighting).

Prepare what you are going to say, and do, on the day to relax and reassure your interviewee. People like to know what is going to happen, and what they should do. They want to know how long it will take, and sometimes even what sort of clothes they should wear. They want to know about the programme the interview will be part of, when it is scheduled for transmission, and on what channel.

The sort of person you want for your programme is very likely to be busy. Make sure you do not waste their time. Be organised and efficient. Do not be vague and unsure of how the equipment works. As soon as you have finished pack up and leave quickly.

It is most important to ask the interviewee to sign a release form – without this you cannot broadcast the interview.

Ask open questions. Ask one question at a time. You will usually want to cut out your questions, and just use the answers. Those answers need to be as comprehensive as possible. Open questions begin with who, what, when, where, why and how.

## Location filming

The research has been comprehensive, and the selected interviewees are ready to appear in your production. You have chosen contributors to offer balanced views. You have in mind some interesting and possibly quite dramatic locations. Above all you know how you are going to tell this story so that it will appeal to an audience. The exact details will be finalised in editing, but you have a very good idea of the linear narrative of your programme before you shoot your first interview.

The production team need to organise a schedule for each day of location filming.

1   Schedule for each day. What is going to happen, when and where. If you are employing a film crew or just a colleague then you must include a map of each location, and written directions of how to get there. Some smart production offices give grid references that can be input into a car satellite navigation system. Your presenter, maybe the contributor and your crew must know how to get to the location by the best possible route. Travelling takes time and time is money – your production money. You may have to stay overnight at the location. Put on the schedule the address, phone number and details of where the hotel/guest house is in relation to the filming location. Remember to put all your contact details on the schedule too, especially your mobile phone number and email.

2   Contact list of contributors, crew and production. This is an A4 sheet with the contact details of everyone involved in this shoot. This can

be handed out to all personnel – remember to keep secure as personal details should not fall into the wrong hands.

3   Release forms.

4   Clothing suitable for the occasion. There is a lot of standing around when you are filming, and it is important to keep warm. Old hands say keep your head warm at all times, and not too hot in the sun by wearing a hat, so that you can think clearly. Hence the ubiquitous use of US style caps. A cricket hat or cap works just as well and is cheaper. In the depths of winter wear heavy waterproof clothing that would be suitable for skiing. If you are filming in England you probably need a pair of wellies in the boot of the car.

5   Mini office. Most productions take a laptop to check emails and produce paperwork if necessary. We recommend for a longer shoot to take a portable printer to print updates to schedules, and scripts for the presenter.

6   For a fully digital set-up you may be able to download your rushes straight into your laptop so that you can see your rushes in the evening and do a rough edit.

7   Have a very clear idea of what you are filming and how you are going to film it. Do discuss this with other members of the team. You are all working toward the same end – an exciting production.

8   Do make notes of things to do at the editing stage. Do take still pictures if you think it will be useful for publicity or other reasons.

9   Do not overspend your budget. Television producers and directors are required to deliver within budget at all times, unlike film directors.

## Contributor's release form

All contributors who appear in any production that is going to be broadcast must sign a release form. It is always better to get the form signed by all contributors, even if you are not sure if everyone you film will appear in the final edited sequence. The contributor's release form covers all known rights in the universe. It is vital that you make sure you have all rights covered. Otherwise, when the broadcaster says that the interview is going on its website, you could find that the copyright for this interview to be exploited in this way, is not covered. The form also covers any subsequent uses of your programme for video/DVD or internet distribution, or any other exploitation yet to be discovered.

# CONTRIBUTOR'S RELEASE FORM

Programme Title . . . . . . . . . . . . . . . . . . . . . . . . . . . . . . . . . . . . . . . . .

Television Company . . . . . . . . . . . . . . . . . . . . . . . . . . . . . . . . . . . .

Address . . . . . . . . . . . . . . . . . . . . . . . . . . . . . . . . . . . . . . . . . . . . .

. . . . . . . . . . . . . . . . . . . . . . . . . . . . . . . . . . . . . . . . . . . . . . . . . .

Description of contribution (e.g. interview) . . . . . . . . . . . . . . . . . .

. . . . . . . . . . . . . . . . . . . . . . . . . . . . . . . . . . . . . . . . . . . . . . . . . .

Date of contribution . . . . . . . . . . . . . . . . . . . . . . . . . . . . . . . . . . .

Name of contributor . . . . . . . . . . . . . . . . . . . . . . . . . . . . . . . . . . .

Address . . . . . . . . . . . . . . . . . . . . . . . . . . . . . . . . . . . . . . . . . . . .

. . . . . . . . . . . . . . . . . . . . . . . . . . . . . . . . . . . . . . . . . . . . . . . . . .

Tel nos. (include mobile) . . . . . . . . . . . . . . . . . . . . . . . . . . . . . . .

In consideration of the above television company agreeing that I
contribute to and participate in the above television programme,
the nature of which has been fully explained to me, I hereby
consent to the use of my contribution in the above programme. I
agree that the copyright of this contribution shall be wholly vested
in the television company . . . . . . . . . . . . . . . . . . . . . . . . . . . . .

I agree to any future exploitation of this contribution by the
company in all media and formats throughout the universe.

Signed by contributor . . . . . . . . . . . . . . . . . . . . . . . . . . . . . . . . .

Date . . . . . . . . . . . . . . . . . . . . . . . . . . . . . . . . . . . . . . . . . . . . . .

Signed for the company . . . . . . . . . . . . . . . . . . . . . . . . . . . . . . .

Copy given to contributor.

## Filming in public places

The only time when you do not require people to sign a release form is when filming in public places. This applies only to non-speaking members of the public who are filmed in public places going about their rightful business. Public places mean streets and roads and shopping areas, and other areas owned by the community.

In private locations that admit members of the public such as swimming pools it is not necessary to ask everyone in the pool to sign a release form. You will need the permission of the owner of the pool or manager to agree filming and may have one area put aside for your use.

The rule is that people should be aware that you are filming. They have a right to know what you are filming, and what it is to be used for – news, documentary, entertainment programme or corporate video. They have a right to not take part if they so wish. Sometimes a judiciously placed notice giving this information can avoid any difficulties. If any people do not want to be seen in the film you are making, then they should be able to keep away from the area where filming is taking place.

In no circumstances should you tell anyone you can cut them out of the film in postproduction. You will forget who that person is and what he or she looked like. In the context of getting your programme made this will not seem important, but it could land you with a nasty letter, or even worse a law suit.

If you are filming with a celebrity, or any well-known personality, then you have the opposite problem of excluding the public from the filming area. This usually means employing security personnel, or cordoning off an area that you can use undisturbed.

Making a factual programme with children up to the age of 16 is more difficult than it used to be. You must ask parents for permission to film their children, and make sure the parents sign a release form. Identifiable children cannot be filmed in public places without parental consent. If the children have to miss any schooling to take part in the filming then a Local Authority consent form is required.

# Further reading

Lewis, I., *Guerrilla TV – Low Budget Programme Making* (Oxford: Focal Press, 2000).

Orlebar, J., *Digital Television Production – A Handbook* (London: Arnold, 2002).

# 18 Fictional television

## Scripting the idea

Television programmes of all types have their genesis on the page. The newest twist in the Reality television genre comes from a well-developed scenario on someone's computer. To create strong television programmes you need to be able to create strong scripts. Whatever theme you choose, you will need to develop the three crucial pillars of a good script: story (narrative), characters, location. This is particularly true of drama. Factual and documentary programmes also require at least a treatment on paper.

### Story

If you are going to write any sort of dramatic story you need to start with an idea. It can be helpful to think in terms of genre. Does your idea involve horror, science fiction, suspense, criminals, cowboys, romance, comedy, or teenagers? Maybe you are thinking along the lines of a kickboxing teenager who is involved with the supernatural. It may seem derivative of the *Buffy* series, but you could easily develop a particular take on this idea. French director Jean-Luc Godard famously said a film needs a beginning, middle and end, but not necessarily in that order. However, you would do well to stick to the normal sequence, as he did for his first films. This is the basis of all narrative, and the linear flow of a story acts as a formidable hook for a television drama.

## Character

Some ideas develop from interesting people you have met. You may have a character in mind who would be an effective secret agent, or the protagonist in a complex romance. John Cleese says he got his idea for the comedy series *Fawlty Towers* from observing hotel owners on childhood holidays in Torquay.

Ask a scriptwriter what he does all day. He or she is likely to say watching, and listening to people – in a café, in the pub, on a train, in a waiting room, or in a supermarket queue. Collecting snatches of potential dialogue, and observing potential characters. Your main characters need to be believable. The audience need to be able to believe in them as rounded individuals.

Start by writing a description of your main character. Begin with the physical – size, weight, colour of eyes and hair, size of shoes. Develop the character's likes and dislikes – likes swimming, playing the bass guitar, detective novels, riding a bicycle, Coldplay and The Darkness, scuba diving and Levi's jeans. Hates hamburgers, girls who smoke, peanut butter, Mondays, heights, and getting up in the morning. Some of these characteristics can be linked to the plot, but try to do it subtly. It is easier to develop an idea if you have at least one fully developed character. Imagine how your hero would behave in certain situations. Try putting him or her in a very cold place, or a restricted environment such as a prison cell. Work out how your character would respond to a dominating boss, intolerant manager, incredibly beautiful member of the opposite sex. Interview your character. Who might be out to destroy him or her and why?

## Location

Narrative ideas can often stem from a particular location. You might have visited a particularly engaging region, such as Cornwall. The dramatic seascapes and craggy coastline may have inspired you to write a story of smuggling, or witchcraft. An ancient stone circle may inspire you to write about a young girl who stumbles on a Celtic coin, and then digs up a hoard of silver. You may find a stylish penthouse apartment in Brighton is the ideal location to set your romantic drama about a dodgy art dealer who leaves his busy life in London to set up home with a new young artist.

Much of television drama aims to recreate a form of reality set in an urban location that the large audience in towns and cities can easily relate to. This is why you very rarely see science fiction on television, but you see a lot of police and hospital dramas. Soaps create their own sense of place, time and history around a tight specific location such as Albert Square. A drama can work well if it is located in an unusual setting that invites the audience to revel in its beauty, or be engrossed by its very strangeness.

You will need to be clear in your mind where your story is going to be set. Choose a location that you know. It is useful if you can get there easily. For a short you may choose somewhere intimate – a narrow boat on a canal, a dockside or an interior. There are some definite advantages in setting your story at one flexible location. 'Whodunit' murder stories are often set in a country house. It makes the drama more intense and claustrophobic. Select an exciting and relevant location that is realistically within reach.

You now need to go into development. This is a state of mind much favoured by Hollywood scriptwriters, where very little appears to get done. But ideas are cooking, characters are being fleshed out, locations are being thoroughly visualised. The creative juices are being stirred, and eventually a script unfolds as if by magic – that is the theory anyway. It always involves a lot of very hard writing and rewriting.

## The short

Writing, shooting, casting and directing a television drama can be very expensive in terms of time and resources. Even with an inexpensive digital camera the pictures may look good, but what about the sound? You need at least one professional microphone, and a set of film lights, such as a red head kit.

We suggest that you start with a 10-minute drama. This is an acceptable length for a 'short'. There are recognisable TV slots for this genre. It is affordable to produce. It is straightforward to write. You have enough time to develop one or two characters often in one main location. There is no need for complex subplots.

Writing for television is about entertainment. This does not mean that you cannot include serious themes, and complex issues and ideas. It is important to want to convey something of value when you write a short. You may want to say something about the ecology of the planet. You may want to show the intelligent, or spooky, side to a stereotypical character such as an asylum seeker or homeless person. You may want to show the comedy in the life of a professional dog walker. However strongly you feel, your message must be conveyed through the development of character and plot. No audience wants a sermon.

## The protagonist

The central character is usually the protagonist of the story. Your protagonist must have clear motivation to achieve his or her aim in the film. Motivation arises from inner character, and experiences in the central character's past, called 'back story'.

The protagonist is the driver of the action. Audiences like to feel sympathetic to the protagonist, and like to feel that there has been some development in his or her life. Some action movies just show the main character achieving a particular aspiration. All right if you have a big budget for action special effects, but not much good as a scenario for a short.

Make your choice. Create a protagonist who can achieve a goal, or go through a transformation of personality as well as getting the girl, or the diamonds. Make your protagonist go through psychological or supernatural hoops. You may not want to write another *Erin Brockovich*. But there is something universally appealing in the poor, rejected protagonist who overcomes insurmountable odds to achieve a worthwhile goal. Movies where protagonists do not achieve their goals by the end of the film have a habit of leaving the audience feeling depressed and downhearted. This may not be the best way to end your first television short.

## The adversary

In a typical dramatic scenario the protagonist will have an adversary. This is a character who has the job of making it as difficult, and often as dangerous, as possible for the protagonist to achieve his or her goal. In an action film, such as a James Bond movie, there will always be a recognisable, often stereotyped, bad guy. Bad guys often represent a variety of distasteful, or downright anti-human, traits but this need not be immediately apparent. A successful adversary is often a wolf in sheep's clothing. Looking cool, acting normally, but all the time being from the Norman Bates charm school of psychopaths. Try to match the cunning of your adversary to the skills and talents of your protagonist.

# The treatment

A television company or broadcasting executive will need to see a treatment of your idea, before commissioning it or putting any money into further development. This is a detailed outline of your idea. A drama does not have the same treatment as a factual programme. It tells the story, describes the locations and the characters. It shows clearly the structure of events. It will definitely show the beginning, middle and end of the story. This is the basic three-act structure. Above all the treatment must show the structure of the film – what happens when and why. A well-structured film is often a good film. Check for yourself by looking at the structures of universally acclaimed films such as *The Godfather*, *The Usual Suspects* or *Titanic*. Your treatment should not be a long document. Just one page, or at the most two. This is quite adequate for a TV short. A longer drama will have a more detailed treatment showing all the twists and turns of the plot, and giving full characterisation.

It is a good idea to include in the treatment a page of dialogue to show that you can write dialogue, and that you know the professional way to set out a script.

# Script layout

Writing a script for television is an exciting and exacting process with basic rules and conventions. The basic standards for setting out a TV drama come from Hollywood. The good thing about this format is that one page equals one minute of final screen time. This is most helpful in calculating the length of scenes and how long your piece will run on the screen. A 30-minute television script is 30 pages or about 6,000 words.

A television script has a new scene for each new location. Each scene has three important parts:

- a heading and a scene number;
- a description of the scene;
- dialogue.

## Heading and scene number

The heading informs the reader of the scene number, and details of where the scene is set. Use capitals. EXTERIOR or INTERIOR; DAY or NIGHT. Also put the location in capitals on the same line.

```
(Scene)  10.  EXTERIOR.  NIGHT.  GRAVEYARD.  REMOTE
CHURCH.
```

You need to be consistent with what you call your locations. It is either a flat or an apartment, but not both. The names of places should be consistent.

## Setting: a description of the scene

The setting of the scene is always written in the present tense. The description is written across the whole page under the heading and single-spaced.

You should aim to describe in as few words as possible anything that is relevant to the action or the plot. Do not describe details of the set, or what the characters are wearing, unless it is absolutely relevant to the action. If a character is wearing a coat to conceal a gun, then that is relevant. On a character's first appearance describe salient aspects of the character's psychological and physical make-up. This is more about motivation and potential psychological development than what the actor will eventually look like.

```
WILLIAM WELTHAM is young, dishevelled and cool. He
works in a dead end office job. Sings and plays
guitar at night in a local pub, under a pseudonym.
Thinks he should be famous, but is not at all
sure he is ready for a fat recording contract.
Ambition is not his second name. Sensitive, and
caring, he likes children. Hates commitment.
Desperately needs someone to take him on and bring
out his true self. Lives alone. Likes listening to
digital radio. Collects unusual clocks.
```

## Setting out a page of dialogue

- Name each character in capital letters, in the middle of the page.

- Use a left margin of about 1.5 inches.

- Put instructions for the actor in brackets at the place where they should happen in the script. (Pulls gun out of glove box in car.)

- Put page numbers in the upper-right corner of the page.

- Set up a template for your script.

Television producers and commissioning editors want to know if you can write realistic and sharp dialogue, and if you can structure a story. They also want to be sure that you can write a script. Here is an example of how a TV drama script should look.

# Example of a drama script

A television script has a standard format. Script formats are derived from a strict Hollywood convention for movie and television scripts.

Hollywood scripts always use Courier 12 font. Page numbering is top right. No page numbering on page one. Use double spacing between each character's dialogue. It helps to set up a template for a script on your computer. Professional script writing software is available, but expensive and not really necessary. Do not put in 'stage' directions unless they are crucial to the plot. Do not put in camera angles, or director's notes. That is for later. This is a script, not a shooting document. See pp. 194–8 for an example (not to scale).

# Structure and sequence

## The opening

Whatever length of film you intend to make, you need a strong opening. This is part of the first act – the beginning. If you do not hook your audience in the first few minutes, you will find it much harder to keep them glued to the screen throughout. It is often a good idea to write the opening last. Television dramas do not require the sort of dramatic action packed sequence that denotes Hollywood movies. Setting up the character is more important. This is small screen drama viewed at home. The audience will be looking for interesting, believable characters. In your opening set up the character – age, job, clothes, mannerisms, and put them in a visual setting that gives the viewer an instant understanding of the type of drama that could unfold. A windswept tower block with broken windows, stark grey sky and poorly dressed young people is going to be about poverty, crime and maybe redemption. You can show this in the first minute or so of your drama. Contrast that with a shot of Canary Wharf in the city, smart suited young businessmen talking on their mobiles while walking purposefully to work. You have the opening of a drama about two brothers – one successful and working in derivatives in the city, the other down on his luck and selling drugs on a Glasgow housing estate. Intrigue the audience as to how this can unfold. It need not be stereotypical. The younger brother could be an undercover police officer staking out a potential cover for al Qaeda terrorists. TV drama works well when the plot stems from the motivation of the characters. In your opening sequence try to place your main characters in an environment that suits them and that has several plot possibilities. Successful TV dramas have been located in institutions such as hospitals and schools, but also in a village, small town or recognisable city such as Liverpool or Glasgow. American director Robert Altman has one of the most well worked out openings in his film *The Player*. The beautifully composed opening sequence is one very long shot that sets up the story, introduces the main characters and contains the vital clue to the ending.

You might have a good idea for the opening, but get your story worked out first, and then create an impressive opening scene.

## Getting the story right

Work out the structure of the story. This includes everything that happens to make the plot work. The plot is the important events that make up the story. The plot stems from the main characters, and what motivates them to achieve their aims. Write down what your main character wants, and how he or she is going to attain it. Then write down how your main character develops because of the experiences he or she is going to go through in the film. First of all you can do this in chart form just suggesting the relevant action with one or two words – High school kid – Freshers Ball – CIA – Betrayal – Loss of friend – Determination for survival – New

PILTDOWN  MAN

by

Angelo  Rabelroll

Farlee  Avenue
Angmering
Sussex  UK

Scene 1

FADE IN:

EXT. DAY. CAFÉ BY THE SEA.

SEA WASH on a pebble beach. Sunny.

Wind is flapping the flags. Seagulls overhead. Two
men are sitting at a café table. On the table is
a SKULL loosely wrapped in a Burberry scarf.

BAILEY is in his early twenties. Studying
anthropology he is animated, intense and excited.

STEPHEN is an osteopath in his mid-twenties.
Successful, well dressed, single.

                    BAILEY
          It's got to be the one. Nothing else has
          this scar feature or . . .

                    STEPHEN
          How on earth do you know? Why would it
          be here anyway?

                    BAILEY
          When they buried it at Piltdown they
          didn't think it was good enough. But
          it's better. It's the real thing.

                    STEPHEN
          I'm not certain. We would look complete
          idiots. What if they took DNA and found
          it was from the twenties. You prove it is
          prehistoric. You can't. You've been
          duped.

3

                    BAILEY
        I've done some forensic stuff. It stands
        up. And I've done some reading. Piltdown
        was a centre of power.


                    Scene 2

EXT. THE PROMENADE. DAY
CLAIRE is roller blading along the sea front with
her dog on a lead. Tall, athletic early twenties.
Ambitious. Freelance journalist.
CLAIRE arrives at the café table with a rush. She
almost falls into STEPHEN's coffee.

                    CLAIRE
        So that's where my scarf is. I've been
        looking for that all day — you stole it.


She picks up the scarf. The skull skids across the
table and falls off.
BAILEY dives for it. He catches it as it slides
off the table. He almost falls over. The dog
barks.

                    CLAIRE
        What the hell is that?. . . Yuck! That's
        gross.
        Are you into devil worship?

4

STEPHEN

Don't invoke ancient spirits

CLAIRE

What's so cool about this relic? It's
grotesque — you can't fool me that's
Neanderthal man.

BAILEY

That's a million dollars — that's what
that is. And you nearly lost the lot.


Scene 3


EXTERIOR. NIGHT. WOODED AREA. AN OLD QUARRY.
BAILEY is working with a futuristic detector
device. There is a bleeping. He gets out a large
digger tool and prises something out of the rock
crevice.
STEPHEN is crouched over scientific instruments.
Bailey uncovers a medallion-like object.

BAILEY

Check this out Steve. It's got ferrous.
It's also got a sort of bronze . . . It's
prehistoric all right.

CLAIRE

We must have evidence or the paper won't
print the story. Wow! The instruments are
going crazy.

The Instruments are seen to be complex, linked
to a laptop. The screen shows animated graphs
and scientific displays. They jump about in a
frenzy.

                    STEPHEN
          Now Claire do you believe in the power
          of the ancients . . . this was a burial
          site. There must have been burial rites.

                    BAILEY
          She still thinks it's superstitious
          rubbish. She's hung up on being an
          investigative journalist. If you can't
          interview it, it's not real.

                    CLAIRE
          Yea OK something's got to be here.
          I'll believe it when I see . . .


Suddenly the instruments flash. The laptop crashes.
There is a mysterious cracking noise from the
rock face. The rocks roar and split open. A black
void appears with something dark moving inside.

                    BAILEY
          They're back. They want the skull.

acceptance by father. This gives you the rudiments of the story, but very little detail of how the plot will develop. You now need to work out what will happen, and in what order it will happen. This is structure, or plot.

## Writing plot

This is a simple scenario.

Twenty-something, career driven single parent runs a successful fashion business. Father of her little girl is an alcoholic. Disillusioned with men she is sent on holiday by her exasperated business partner. Scuba diving in the Red Sea she nearly drowns, rescued by a mysterious handsome stranger. She has to reassess her life. Rejects him and goes for someone she knows who offers security. But he is struggling with his sexual identity. After a series of accidents and trials eventually realises the handsome stranger is the one.

The tease is that you think she would fall in love with the handsome man who rescues her. She perversely decides to go for the sardonic, gentle child minder who looks after her daughter, but who is having a crisis about being gay. The intrigue is in how her rescuer eventually ends up with the right girl. This is where the details of the plot are crucial.

OK, so you have seen it all before in Hollywood films. Making this simple scenario work for TV calls for a closer look at the details of the scenario, as it would affect a real person. A real person could not afford the lavish life style that all Hollywood characters seem to follow. She has her two children to think of. Many viewers would empathise with this situation. The character is a mother who is resentful that she has to care for two children with only basic maintenance from the father. This has been her first holiday for over five years. This is a not uncommon scenario.

Your job is to make the plot fit a believable situation but be exciting enough to hook the viewer. A typical TV drama would go for realism all the way through, and then create a strong ending effecting closure with a most unrealistic event or twist in the plot. This can work and give an emotional climax. Sometimes though it is better to work out for yourself how this might end in a way that is more likely to happen in real life.

As a short film this could all take place in the choice location of a Red Sea resort such as Sharm El Sheikh.

## Pace

You will need to vary the pace of the action. The action can move between the highs of activity and danger, and quieter periods of self exploration and revelation through intimate dialogue. In the best scripts the climax grows organically out of the elements of the story. Periods of action can alternate with moments of reflection or character building dialogue.

There are devices you can use.

### Foreshadowing

Foreshadowing gives the audience subtle clues as to what might happen later, or how a character might develop. It sets up possibilities that can be developed later. A cleverly developed scene can plant an unconscious awareness in the viewer of what might happen. You don't want to be too obvious and give too many hints and clues, but foreshadowing can lead to a more satisfying story.

### Treatment of time

Everything the viewer sees apparently happens in present time. This does not stop you from jumping backwards and forward in time. Soaps and serials almost never do this as they want the viewer to be present in a continuing saga of nowness. We accept, for example, the convention that time is compressed in *Friends* to give the impression of an almost timeless day-to-day existence.

A good drama can exploit time to great effect interlacing the past with the present and even foretelling the future. In fact, you can create any time period you wish – past, present or future – but it all will appear to be happening now.

You decide on what timespan would work best for your film. To create a claustrophobic, intense atmosphere where the characters are under pressure, set your film in a tight timespan. Perhaps just 24 hours. Richard Curtis in his films – e.g. *Love Actually* – always includes Christmas Eve. This is a good day of the year for something dramatic and life enhancing to happen.

Think carefully about the time span of the drama. How long will it take for your main character to fulfil his/her goal? Squeezing the action into a short timespan can make a big difference to the pace and feel of the drama.

### Back story

Hollywood writers are very keen on back story. This is the unseen part of a character's past life, occasionally alluded to in the text. You may know a lot about your main character, but the viewer knows nothing. The back story illuminates the reasons for the protagonist wanting his or her goal, whether it is for ultimate power, or love, or just greed. Back story may mean dropping into the script factual details about the past. This may be details of where a character was born and grew up. It often works better if you can suggest a more psychological back story, such as an inability to relate to the opposite sex owing to some trauma in childhood. A believable, contemporary TV character will suggest back story just by the way he or she talks – Geordie accent means grew up in Newcastle – and the way the actor plays the part. Sometimes it is useful to have a charcter who has no discernable back story. Think of the Clint Eastwood character in the Sergio Leone films. He comes from nowhere and goes back to nowhere. This can make for powerful drama.

A character's actions, appearance and what he or she says should suggest indirectly what has happened in the past, and what the effect has been. It is important to show how a character changes in the face of adversity or conflict. People can reveal their true nature through their conflicts. Drama thrives on conflict. The choices your characters make help them to evolve and become believable, rounded, human beings.

*Flashback* is the classic way of revealing back story. Use sparingly as it can hold up the action. On television it can be done using short black and white scenes that resemble grainy documentary, or home video shots. This can heighten the sense of realism. Dialogue is an effective way to fill in back story. TV drama is more wordy than a movie. The small screen favours the close-up, and its use to reveal intimate details. Sometimes simple jump cuts offering scenes from the past can effectively fill in back story. We often feel TV drama writers, or producers, are too cautious of using filmic time shift devices. The audience is sophisticated and can easily cope with instant changes of time as the *Buffy* series has shown.

## Storyboard

The important word is *story* not *board*. A storyboard is a very good way to work out the visual structure of your drama. You do not have to be good at drawing to make a useful storyboard. Use stick men and simple cartoon-like designs to show how your plot develops. When you reach the production stage a storyboard is a tool to help all the other members of the production work on what the director wants to see on the screen. The director creates the storyboard as he or she is very much in charge of turning the script into a visual experience. As a writer you can provide visual clout to your ideas with a simple storyboard (see pp. 204–5).

The storyboard should show:

- Cuts, wipes, dissolves and other visual effects that are required for the plot.
- The period of the action. Is the film set in the past or future?
- The approach to the film language such as suggested camera angles but only if they are necessary to the plot or characterisation.

It is not necessary to storyboard every single moment of the film, just the significant action.

Once you have got your ideas into storyboard form, you need to make sure everything will work together and there are no nasty holes in the plot. The director will do a storyboard for the whole drama. It may be reworked many times before it is actually used on the set. This final storyboard will be the one the cast and crew use to help them create the drama.

## Budget

Television always has tight budgets. If you really want to write drama for television your first attempts should not need vast resources to be made. It may be better to avoid science fiction, exotic locations and a large cast. Large crowd scenes are expensive. Leave the expensive war dramas, period action scenes to the movies and concentrate on writing tight psychological dramas. Often intimate naturalistic stories set in an everyday situation can be effective and look good on television. Television is referred to as an intimate medium. This can lead to a more fulfilling experience for the audience.

Of course you need action. Work out clever ways of letting the audience imagine the scenes that cannot be filmed for budget reasons. You do not need to actually see a car accident. The plot will almost certainly rely on the outcome of the accident rather than the details of how it happened. Modern digital cameras make some effects quite easy to film. For example, you can hire an underwater blimp (waterproof cover) for a small DVC camera for under £50 a day. This will allow you to film underwater in a shallow sea, or swimming pool where the water is clear. This sequence can then be cut into a scene where someone falls into a lake. The background and cloudy water effects can be added during the edit.

## Further reading

Hart, C., *Television Programme Making* (Oxford: Focal Press, 1999).

Lewis, I., *Guerrilla TV – Low Budget Programme Making* (Oxford: Focal Press, 2000).

Orlebar, J., *Digital Television Production – A Handbook* (London: Arnold, 2002).

Orlebar, J., *Practical Media Dictionary* (London: Arnold, 2003).

*Figure 18.1* Example of a storyboard

PAGE TWO

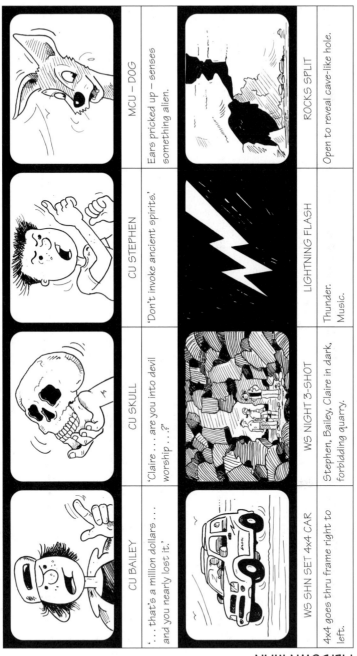

PILTDOWN MAN

| CU BAILEY | CU SKULL | CU STEPHEN | MCU – DOG |
|---|---|---|---|
| '. . . that's a million dollars . . . and you nearly lost it.' | 'Claire . . . are you into devil worship . . .?' | 'Don't invoke ancient spirits.' | Ears pricked up – senses something alien. |
| WS SHN SET 4x4 CAR | WS NIGHT 3-SHOT | LIGHTNING FLASH | ROCKS SPLIT |
| 4x4 goes thru frame right to left. | Stephen, Bailey, Claire in dark, forbidding quarry. | Thunder. Music. | Open to reveal cave-like hole. |

# 19 Practical programme making

.......................................................................................................

## Camera

.........................

The acquisition of moving pictures and sound for television is now almost entirely digital. A camera will record in a digital domain, and this digital information will be stored on a variety of tape formats, or on hard disc. The popular DV format is ideal for television production, especially in its superior quality format of DVCAM. Good quality productions use Sony Digital Betacam, affectionately known as Digibeta.

A further development of digital video is to record directly onto a hard disc. The hard disc format offers greater flexibility as rushes can be downloaded directly into a computer. This is the way the industry is moving. The BBC has pledged to be in a tapeless environment by 2010.

A typical hard disc drive (HDD) recorder records a digital signal on to a user removable standard 2.5 inch compact hard disc drive. Usually there is a choice of either a 40 Gb or 80 Gb hard drive giving either three or six hours of digital recording time. Some hard drives can be pre-configured by the cameraman to record in the file format of the editing system that the production team are using. If the material is to be edited on AVID then the hard disc is configured to the particular AVID software. The disc can be removed and connected directly into that system.

To take steady, well framed pictures a camera needs a good quality tripod. You will also need spare batteries for the camcorder, and a charger to keep them topped up ready for use. Digital tape comes in a variety of durations depending on the tape format. Always take more tape than you think you will need. All you need now is a good quality microphone. Do not rely on the mic built into your camera. The sound may sound all right

*Figure 19.1* Portable digital sound kit

in your earphones, but when you get back and play it on a decent audio system in editing, you will realise how muffled and distant those interviews are. You may put a lot of effort into the pictures but the sound is equally important, and equally difficult to get just right.

## Sound

Recording good quality sound on location is often more difficult than recording pictures. Low-budget productions can spend a lot of time working on the pictures for a production, and put less energy into making sure the location sound is of sufficiently high quality. A simple interview can be recorded by a cameraman with a lapel mic. For anything more complicated a sound recordist should be employed. The sound recordist will have a portable sound mixer, and a variety of microphones that are selected to suit the situation. If more than one mic is used the inputs can be mixed to obtain a good balance between several voices, or background sound effects or music. For television production stereo sound is recorded directly onto digital videotape, or hard disc with the pictures. For some drama productions very high quality sound is recorded onto DAT tape, or the new generation of hard disc sound recorders.

A variety of microphones are used according to the situation. Factual programmes and news typically employ a rifle mic such as a Sennheiser. This is a directional mic. It is pointed at the sound source, such as a person's mouth, and picks up clear, high quality sound with little unwanted background noise. A rifle mic is very sensitive to handling and wind noise. It can be protected by mounting the mic in a cradle inside a hairy wind-shield to stop the wind creating bumps and crackles as it passes across the sensitive areas of the mic. The mic inside its windshield can be attached to a pole – known as a fish pole – and held above an interviewee's head, and therefore out of shot. Many news and current affairs crews use this as their standard mic.

Personal, or lapel mics are also used, especially for interviews. The mic is clipped onto an interviewee's shirt collar, and can be plugged straight into the camera. Radio mics are also popular. A radio mic is similar to a personal mic, but instead of a cable has a small transmitter pack that is hidden in a back pocket, or attached to a belt. The camera can be fitted with a small receiver that picks up the sound from the radio mic.

The sound recordist will have receivers for radio mics that are plugged into his or her portable sound mixer.

The first aim of good location sound recording is to ensure that all voices are 'on mic'. The voice is clearly audible, has a full frequency range and is not distorted in any way, and there are no overlaps. Overlaps are where voices overlap each other and so make editing difficult. Interviewers' questions must not overlap answers. In a dialogue between two characters the speech from each character must be recorded cleanly, with no overlap from the other speaker. This is not so easy in many situations such as a love scene. The art of filmmaking is to do any over-lapping dialogue, required by the script or the director, in the edit and not on the set. This allows complete control in postproduction.

## Location lighting

Lighting is an essential part of TV craft. A well-lit subject enhances the viewing experience. Most importantly it helps the viewer decode the information provided in the programme. Modern digital cameras can shoot in low ambient light situations, which for some documentary loca-tions is suitable and relevant. Often, though, people look flat and two-dimensional. This does not encourage the eye to dwell on a person or interpret what they are saying. The viewer is literally not getting the full picture.

Specialist lighting for television is more an art than a science. A gifted and experienced lighting cameraman or DOP can command high rates of pay because he or she can transform a scene with the strategic placement of a few film lights.

To create the most effective television pictures it is essential to know about the qualities of light:

- Light has intensity or brightness. The automatic exposure system in a camcorder will react to this quality by changing the aperture (iris). The brighter the light the smaller the aperture.

- Light can be hard, giving shadows, or soft. Generally television prefers soft or diffuse lighting.

- Light creates contrast. This is the relative brightness of the lightest and darkest areas in the frame.

- The direction the light is coming from affects how the subject looks.

- The quality of the light itself is affected by its colour temperature or colour quality.

- The most effective way to create good lighting for television is to use soft, diffuse powerful lamps which are carefully positioned for maximum effect.

Lighting cameraman Jonathan Harrison (*Broadcast* May 2004) puts it this way: 'Lighting cameramen should try to diminish the depth of field and create layers using light and props, and the considered positioning of your subject. The key is to make your audience focus on the subject of importance in the frame.' For any drama scene he is a great believer in the importance of a recce and in planning ahead. 'Look at the available light sources within the space you'll be filming, and enhance accordingly. Think about your background and perspective and what you'll focus on. Decide in advance on camera positions and what lights you'll use.'

## Film lighting kit

A basic film lighting kit is three or four red heads that fit snugly with their stands into a suitcase-type box for portability. A red head is

*Figure 19.2* Red head television light with barn doors

an 800 watt tungsten lamp which is mounted on an adjustable stand. It can be used in a 'flood' position to light a wide area, or in a 'spot' position to focus the light on a smaller area. This is a powerful light and it gets very hot – always use heat-resistant gloves when adjusting the head. Each light comes with barn doors – four metal flaps that are attached to the front of the light, and control the spillage of light into unwanted areas.

There are many types of film lights available, from a small 'dink' to a huge several kilowatt 'brute' for large film sets.

A standard light that has been used for many years is a blonde. This is an adjustable 2 kilowatt lamp that makes a very good key light for most occasions. It is, however, a heavy lamp that takes a lot of power. With a lightweight digital camera you also want compact lamps. A manufacturer that has won an academy award for technical achievement is Kino Flo. Their equivalent of a blonde is a Diva-lite 400, which is small and very efficient.

If you have to hire a light we would suggest a Dedolight kit. This is a modern light that stays sharp and even across the spread of the beam. It works well with a video camera and is compact, practical, powerful, easy to mount and move, and uses less energy than conventional lights.

*Figure 19.3* 'Dedolight' location lighting

# Three-point lighting

The basic lighting plot for a person, or people, in a particular location is the three-point lighting plan. This makes it the ideal way to light an interview or a dialogue scene with two actors in drama. It can be set up quickly and uses only three lamps. Three-point lighting is so called because it uses three lights from three different points to illuminate a subject:

- the key light;
- the fill light;
- the back light.

## The key light

The key is the main light to illuminate the face and body of the subject. It is placed in front of the subject, but offset and slightly raised. Looking at people in everyday life we see them lit from above by the sun, or in an office by ghastly overhead strip lights, or from the side by light from a window. At home we are more used to seeing our family lit by table lights, sometimes in a pool of light from just one light source in a room.

Three-point lighting is a way of making a subject look as though he or she is lit naturally, in a way that suits the surroundings. Lighting that is seen to be coming principally from the side and is slightly raised typically offers the best and most natural look for an interview. Imagine that you are going to film and light one person who is sitting in an armchair in a domestic room, and looking towards the camera.

1   The key light is set up at an angle to the camera. It should shine into the eyes of the subject, and should be raised above the eyeline. The subject will not want to be dazzled. Make sure the key light is not too high, or there will be dark shadows under the eyes. Now check for highlights and hot spots on the subject. You may need to use some scrim (French tissue paper) to tone down the brightness of the light. Use pegs or clips to stretch scrim over the film lamp to create a softer light. If there are a few hot spots on the face, the best way to deal with them is to use a dab of make-up powder to stop the shine. Overlit subjects do not look as though they are in a naturalistic setting.

2    You can adjust the intensity of the light using the spot/flood adjustment at the back. Remember you are lighting for the camera, so keep looking through the viewfinder to check how the subject looks.

3    Restrict any spillage from the light by using the barn doors.

4    Digital video cameras are very sensitive to light, and work well in low light conditions. Don't flood the set with unnecessary light. Make sure you can see all the features of the subject's face.

## The fill light

The aim of the fill light is to 'fill in' the darker areas that the key has not reached and to reduce contrast.

The fill light is placed on the other side of the camera to the key, and is as close to the camera as possible. The fill light is a soft, diffused light with an intensity that is typically about half that of the key light. By putting scrim over a lamp you are effectively increasing the size of the light source and creating a softer light. Always check it looks right through the viewfinder. If it appears to be too bright, reduce the intensity of the light by moving it further away from the subject.

You are aiming to model the face of your subject in the armchair – this means show the features of nose, eyes and mouth in a flattering way.

Make sure the fill light does not show up more of the subject's face than the key light. This will not give good modelling of the face.

## The back light

The main purpose of the back light is to create depth and solidity to the appearance of the subject(s) and to give a lighting contrast between foreground and background. This gives a 3D effect, and depth to your picture.

In practice this means illuminating the back of the subject. This gives a 'glow' or highlight to the hair of the subject, and creates a pleasing effect.

The intensity of the back light varies according to the subject. A woman with long black hair needs more light, and a bald man needs less.

The back light is most effective if placed exactly behind the subject. This may not be possible on location, so a compromise is necessary and it is positioned to one side.

The back light should come from the opposite side to the key light. You can always make the light softer with scrim or a diffuser.

Check through the viewfinder that the back light is actually creating the effect you are looking for. Ask a helper to 'flash' it – turn it on and off – to see what effect it has. Move the position of the light to create greater depth, and try seeing the difference between 'flood' and 'spot'. You will need the barn doors to restrict the light source.

## Reflector

A reflector is one of the most useful pieces of equipment you can have in your lighting kit. It is used to reflect light from the sun or a light source onto your subject.

It can be a large piece of white polystyrene, which has to be held with a clip in a lamp stand. It is better to buy a fold-up type reflector that has a white or silver surface on one side, and a gold surface on the other. The reflector can be used to direct sunlight, or artificial light, onto the subject's face giving the face a natural lift.

There are a few things to remember when you are lighting a scene. Most people look better on video with some extra lighting. Mixing natural daylight and tungsten lamps is fine providing that you use a blue gel on the film light. This changes the colour temperature of the artificial light to approximately that of daylight. Remember to do a white balance on your camera after you have lit the scene.

Avoid filming someone against a white wall or window. The strong daylight outside the window will make your subject look dark. An experienced lighting cameraman will be able to balance the interior scene with the exterior daylight, but it is not the thing to do on your first shoot. If you are plugging your film lights into a domestic power supply use an RCD (Residual Current Detector), and check that the supply can take the wattage of your lights. Keep film lights away from anything that can catch fire, such as curtains. Turn them off between takes to preserve the life of the bulbs and reduce the amount of heat on the set.

## Camera set-up

• Set up the camera on the tripod with the lens at the eye level of the contributor.

• Put a chair next to the camera. As the interviewer you will sit in that chair.

- Make sure you sit with your head at the same level as the camera lens.
- Attach the tie mic to the contributor.
- Tell the contributor to look just at you, and not at the camera.
- Check that camera and mic are working by recording a few minutes of the contributor talking. The classic way to do this is to ask the contributor what he or she had for breakfast that morning. This allows you to set a sound level.
- Identify the contributor by name, and for greater accuracy give the date, while the tape is running. This gives the editor a sound ident for the interview.
- Use three shot sizes for a standard interview. If you have a camera operator ask him or her to change shot size after each question. This will give you more flexibility in editing. Standard interview shot sizes are: mid shot (MS), mid close-up (MCU) and close-up (CU). If you are on your own start with an MCU and change the shot size after every two or three questions.

## Cutaways

Think about what pictures you are likely to need in editing to paste over some of the words of the contributor. These are called cutaways, because you cut away from the frame showing the interviewee, to something else that is relevant to what he or she is talking about. When you edit the sound you will cut out repetitions and keep the core answers. If you do not use cutaways and just edit the picture, it will appear to jump. This is called a jump cut and it comes as a visual interruption of the flow of the inter-view. Cutaways allow smooth transitions through the interview, and allow editing of unwanted words and phrases.

Cutaways enhance the visual aspects of the interview, and visually explain elements of what the contributor has said. Your editor does not want just a talking head. You will always need many more cutaways than you think. Shoot everything that is remotely relevant. Remember to shoot a selection of wide shots and close-ups.

It is useful, too, to have a variety of pictures of the contributor that can be used to introduce him or her, or as cutaways. These are known as walking shots. This is because you film the contributor walking into their house, or outside in the garden, or just along the street. Again, make sure you have a selection of shot sizes.

# Visual grammar

### Shot, reverse shot

This is the basic sequence in classical continuity narrative construction. For example, shots of two characters engaged in dialogue will favour first one and then the other. The camera will frame on one person facing camera right and on the other facing camera left. Camera right and left means from the camera's point of view (POV).

When these shots are edited together it appears that the two characters are interacting. The audience read the alternation as a link between the two people, even if they were not actually together when the shots were filmed.

There are important things to consider when setting up this structure. First, the eyelines of the two characters must match. If one character is standing up then the other character's eyeline has to be looking upwards towards the standing character. Their eyes should engage with each other, or appear to do so. Also the shot size should match, so that each character's shot is the same as the other. A change of shot size should be motivated by the dialogue in a drama, or what is said in an interview.

### Crossing the line

This is a phrase you will hear quite often, especially on a television drama set. It refers to an imaginary line that can be drawn between the eyelines of two interacting characters. That line is crossed by moving the camera to the wrong side of one of the characters. What happens is that, for example, the person facing right suddenly faces left, and so does not appear to be looking at or interacting with the other person. The audience will sense discontinuity. Crossing the line while filming, say, a rugby match can have the team that was playing from left to right suddenly playing from right to left. The line is also called the 180-degree rule.

If the line is crossed then a cutaway can bridge the gap. Another way is to have a shot in which a camera movement allows the audience to observe the participants in the scene changing position in relation to each other.

With so much steadicam filming, camera movements are often fluid and undefined. The editor has to choose which sections of the shots will cut together in a way that the audience will understand.

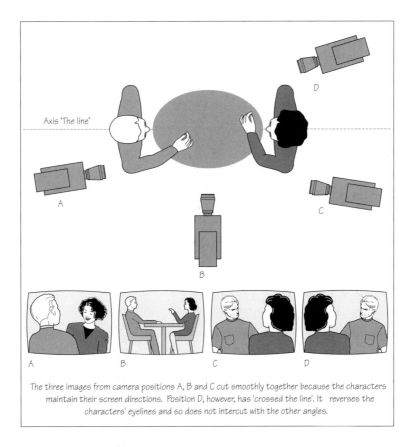

The three images from camera positions A, B and C cut smoothly together because the characters maintain their screen directions. Position D, however, has 'crossed the line'. It reverses the characters' eyelines and so does not intercut with the other angles.

*Figure 19.4* Crossing the line

Similarly, if several shots show a character travelling, say walking down a street, the character must consistently enter camera right and exit camera left, or there will be the impression of reverse or random movement.

## Postproduction

The producer and director will work out a paper edit of each sequence. They might make a rough edit on their computer. Particular attention will be paid to getting the best out of the interviews. It greatly helps to have transcripts of the interviews. The editor will work on a full rough cut and then discuss this with the production team and then create a fine cut. Music will be added, the sound mix balanced in a sound dub. Finally, the programme will be transferred onto the transmission format of the broadcasting company. (See page 244.)

## Further reading

Millerson, G., *Television Production*, 13th edn (Oxford: Focal Press, 1999).

Orlebar, J., *Digital Television Production – A Handbook* (London: Arnold, 2002).

# 20 Television framing and shot size

..........................................................................................

There are so many TV channels and so much material produced for twenty-first-century audiences, it is tempting to film every interview in the same way – with a hand-held camera that rarely stays still. Some aspirational TV programmes, particularly for young people, are so concerned about the attention span of their viewers that they define content by style. The interviewing style revels in a postmodern approach of non-traditional shot sizes and camera angles. The out of focus shot, the constantly moving camera, the canted angle, the extreme close-up, the crash zoom, are the overused visual vocabulary of the ultra cool programme. Where there is little substance, a lot of style keeps the eye on the screen. For a programme offering real substance the more traditional use of the camera allows the content to reach the viewer.

A well edited television programme will subtly use shot size and framing to tell the story, illuminate the characters' feelings, refresh the action and develop the tension of the narrative. This should happen without the viewer being aware of anything but the framed reality of the drama. The way the shot is framed affects our perception of the person being interviewed or the character in the serial. Shot size and lens selection can make the subject look dominating, powerful, or defeated and downtrodden. It can also make the subject look interesting, involving, and the sort of person the viewer would like to talk to, confide in and can relate to.

A selection of shot sizes has developed that fit the TV frame naturally. These standard shot sizes help the viewer deconstruct the image. Used sympathetically they do not come between the viewer and the message. Shot size is more than punctuation. It indicates emotion, content, and point of view.

There are standard shot sizes that are conventionally used in all forms of television programme making. These sizes fit the TV frame naturally – both 4:3 and 16:9 widescreen – and can be edited together to make visual sense of the content.

Shot sizes are labelled according to how a person is seen in the frame, when looking through the viewfinder of a camera. The camera is placed on a tripod, and the lens is set up at the level of the eyeline of the subject. In television, shot sizes are known by their abbreviations.

**VBCU – very big close-up or ECU extreme close-up**  Fills the screen with just part of the face of a person. This can be the mouth, or one eye, or both eyes in a typical Sergio Leone shot.

**BCU – big close-up**  The face fills the frame, cutting off some of the forehead or part of the chin, or both. This shot aims to capture depth of feeling and the subject's inner emotional state. Often used when a person is recounting a tragic or important event that has had a profound effect on his or her life.

**CU – close-up**  The person's face with the bottom of the frame along the line of the shoulders, just below the knot of a tie.

**MCU – medium close-up**  The most common shot in factual television and news programmes. Shows a person's head and shoulders but not the waist. The bottom of the frame runs along the top of the pocket on a man's shirt.

**MS – medium shot or mid shot**  Shows the top half of a person's body. Cuts off at the waist for a person who is standing up or sitting down. Typical shot for a news reader at a desk.

**MLS – medium long shot**  Typically used for a person standing up. The bottom of the frame is around the knees.

**LS – long shot**  Shows a person in full length, including the feet.

**VLS – very long shot**  Shows the person or people quite small in the frame, with more dominance given to their relationship with the setting.

**ELS – extreme long shot**   A very long and wide shot usually of a place but can contain presenters, taken from a long distance away, often from a helicopter or crane. Typically used as an establishing shot, or to note an extreme change in location. Used more in fictional programmes.

**WS – wide shot**   A wide angle of the subject clearly showing the context of a scene and the setting.

Shots are also described by the number of people they contain. Two people in the frame is a 'two shot'. Three people in the frame is a 'three shot', and so on.

Movement of the camera alters a shot. The camera can move closer or further away from the subject. The camera may be on tracks or on a wheeled pedestal or a dolly. A camera can move sideways while keeping the subject in shot. This is a crab shot. Moving a camera from left to right or vice versa is a pan; best only used for landscape shots, or where there is a definite beginning point and ending point.

Moving the camera lens but keeping the camera in the same position – on a tripod, for example – is a 'zoom in' or 'zoom out'.

*Figure 20.1* Two shot in Frascati, Italy

*Figure 20.2* (a) BCU – big close up; (b) LS – long shot

# Bluescreen

Many factual programmes have a variety of contributors talking about a number of different topics. It can make better television to have control over the visual backgrounds to the interviews. You may have a wildlife expert talking about elephants in India. It can be effective to show elephants as a moving image behind the contributor. Some shows like to have a constantly moving background behind their studio presenters and location contributors. This electronic technique allows one image to be overlaid over part of another image. In TV this technique is known as chromakey, or bluescreen.

An interview can be filmed against a large, carefully lit blue sheet, or screen, that can be erected on location, or set up in a studio. Many TV studios have a blue curtain specifically for chromakey work. This blue background is then replaced in postproduction with other moving images relevant to the programme. The very successful BBC factual series *Walking with Dinosaurs* employed this technique (and computer-generated images (CGI)) extensively.

Bluescreen is used extensively in drama productions and particularly films. With this technique actors can walk around futuristic sets, or surf on giant virtual waves without leaving the studio. CGI can be integrated with live action as in the *Lord Of The Rings* films to create startling effects and impressive images. With bluescreen, you do not have to send your reporter to New York to do a story on the hip-hop clubs. You can put her in a small studio specially designed for the purpose with all blue floor and walls. Modern sophisticated bluescreen studios allow the director to cut between close-ups and long shots. Carefully selected pictures that have already been shot in New York will replace the blue areas. The reporter will appear actually to be there, in the heart of the city. She can even walk around the streets and sit down on a bench in Central Park. Hollywood films tend to use green screens, allegedly because so many of the actors will be wearing blue jeans. This technique uses the chosen colour of blue or green to act as a key for another set of pictures. An actor wearing blue jeans may find his legs dissolve into a scene from somewhere else.

# Framing

Most TV production uses the standard shot sizes when framing a scene. However, the increasing use of steadicam and a natural tendency to break out of the conventions can lead to imaginative framing. There are some basic rules that viewers subconsciously use to deconstruct a scene. Framing makes a great difference to the meaning of a shot. The viewer will be able to see who is dominant in a scene by the way the director sets up and frames each shot. Where characters are placed in the frame is crucial to their relationship to each other. A character who is dominant in the frame will be camera right, and showing a full face, or more of the face, than the other character who is less dominant. As the relationship changes in the scene so the other character will become larger in the frame, and/or move to the right side of the frame. This can be done by various means:

- editing – cut to the reverse shot at a different angle;
- the character physically moves round the other character to a dominant position;
- the camera tracks round to put the dominant character in the most dominant position in the frame;
- the camera zooms in to a CU of the dominant character (rather too crude for most directors).

Framing is an important element in the way realism is assessed by the viewer. The director wants the viewer to see a coherent complex of visual signals. These will assist the viewer in interpreting not only the plot and characters but the many other elements that make up a complex narrative. These range from the period that the story is set in to the psychological persona of the characters. This is known as *mise-en-scène*. (See page 228.)

## Camera angle

Shots are also described by the position of the camera in relation to normal eye level. If the camera is positioned at eye level the person in the frame is looking directly at the audience. Low-angle or high-angle shots each create a specific effect. With the camera placed lower than the eyeline the effect is to give the impression of the character being dominant and powerful. This is deployed most successfully by Leni Riefenstahl in her 1935 film *Triumph of the Will* showing the power of Hitler at the Nuremberg rally.

If the camera is placed high above the eyeline and looks down on the character the viewer senses an increased sense of vulnerability in the

## Example 20.1

A young woman confronts her boss at work over fraud and corruption in the company. The framing will tell the viewer a lot about what is going on which will be reinforced by the dialogue.

The scene begins with the young woman walking into a long room. The boss is seated at a large, imposing desk at the end of the room. As she walks towards him in a long shot the audience senses her insecurity and lack of power.

When she reaches the desk she starts to confront him. The framing needs to show that she has some power, but is not yet dominating the boss.

A low-angle two shot from behind shows her back view just dominating the right half of the frame, with the seated boss in the left of the frame. We see his face and not hers so she is still in a subordinate position.

The boss starts to assert some authority and gets up in the shot. He is larger in the frame, and the woman appears to be losing the argument. She opens a folder puts onto the desk a sequence of photographs of the boss with a girl in a nightclub. The camera shows close-ups of the photographs, and then cuts to a close-up of the woman. She is now fully in control. The next shot is a two shot with the man sitting down at the desk and the woman, her face to camera, delivers a line of dialogue, turns round and leaves the room. The last shot is a mirror image of the first. She is walking back down the room towards the camera. The camera sees her face and body getting larger within the frame and the boss looking smaller at the desk. She has made her point.

character. To get the camera really low down a special 'baby legs' tripod is used.

A director will use the camera angle to suggest a variety of emotions. The canted, or angled camera, in Hollywood *film noir* of the 1930s and 1940s suggested to the viewer that the character in this particular scene was not to be trusted, or that something untoward or even evil was happening. In Dennis Potter's TV series *The Singing Detective* an author lies in a hospital bed with his consciousness slipping in and out of the thriller he is writing. This mental transition is effected visually by the camera rotating slowly in vision. The close-up of Philip Marlowe, the patient, becomes a heavily canted angle close-up, leading the viewer to realise that in his mind he is now Philip Marlowe the detective writer. The picture then cuts to the time and period of the thriller.

Other shots labelled by the position of the camera include the top shot. The camera is placed high on a crane to look down on the action in a drama. A top shot can be from a remote camera attached to a blimp in the sky to give a very high-angle shot of a cricket match. As cameras have become smaller, so they can be fixed almost anywhere. A top shot from a camera fixed overhead in the ceiling adds visual variety to a sequence and may suggest a slightly voyeuristic viewpoint. A top shot can be startling or extremely dramatic. Attached to the top of the mast of a yacht in a storm it can give a view of the boat below that can almost induce nausea.

## Camera movement

Camera movement is a creative tool used in many television programmes. There are two sorts. There is the movement of a static camera known as a tilt up or down, or the horizontal movement of the camera known as a pan. The whip (very fast) pan has become overused in factual television as a tool to increase the pace of a sequence and apparently hold the viewer's attention. It often ends up annoying the viewer and punctuating the smooth flow of the show.

The second form of camera movement is a track, or a dolly, in or out. It can also be a crab, which is a movement sideways, common in music programmes. The whole camera moves, usually in or out or around the subject. A tracking shot that moves in to a subject maintains the relationship of the subject to the background. In a zoom in shot where only the lens is turned, the background changes and goes out of focus making the subject appear to come towards the viewer. A camera track in allows the viewer to approach the subject and maintain the same relationship with it. A camera track can alter the point of view of the viewer as the camera can reflect the dialogue and change in dominance within a scene.

Camera movement should always be for a purpose suggested by the content or information within a scene, or activity. This is known as a motivated camera move as it follows an action or is prompted by an event within the scene.

Examples:

- a pan will follow a presenter as she walks across the set to another contributor;
- a track will follow two characters as they walk along a path chatting together;
- a track round two seated characters starts on a two shot to show how the meeting is balanced. The camera moves round to a single shot showing that this character has now become the dominant force in the scene or the instigator of the next action.

To effect a tracking shot the camera needs to be mounted on a dolly, or a crane, or in a TV studio on a pedestal. A dolly is any suitable wheeled mounting for a camera. A crane is a counterweighted, long metal arm with a flexible camera mounting that can be raised and moved either by hand or remotely. Jimmy Jib is the popular name for a camera crane with a multidirectional camera. An operator at ground level using a small monitor and joystick controls the camera remotely.

The most popular mounting for modern TV productions is now the steadicam. This is a TV camera mounting system where the camera is attached to the operator with a harness. This allows the operator to move or run with camera and shoot the scene with virtually no camera shake or sideways movement. The operator frames the scene using a small monitor located at waist level. The steadicam offers great flexibility, is able to film on any surface that the operator can walk on and is able to offer superb camera angles from the actor's point of view. Traditionally this shot was accomplished by a hand-held camera giving a hand-held wobbly effect noticeable in documentaries, where it has the cachet of suggesting authenticity.

## *Mise-en-scène*

*Mise-en-scène* literally means put on the stage, or in the scene. It applies to any sort of programme because all television is a construct, but it is mainly useful in analysing fictional television. *Mise-en-scène* is more than just the physical objects in the scene. It includes the camera angle and any camera movement, the framing, the shot size and the mood of the lighting, the careful placing of the actors, and the make up and costume.

When analysing *mise-en-scène* take a sequence from a programme, or a scene from a drama, and look at these components:

**The setting**    Is it a set, or is the action filmed on location – how can you tell, and why is it important? Is it a realistic or naturalistic set? Work out the period of the action, and the clues that have been deliberately placed to remind you of the period. What objects are in vision to authenticate the period e.g. the saloon bar in a western, or Albert Square in *EastEnders*? Some props carry forward the narrative e.g. a knife or a gun. Decide what they are doing in the scene, and what narrative device was used to get them there. The setting may be bland, or in soft focus to place the emphasis on the characters. The director may decide that there should be no extra information in this scene other than close-ups of the characters. This is common in soaps and serials. One of the advantages of these genres is that there is a pool of common knowledge shared by the regular audience. Everyone knows the look and feel of the Queen Vic in *EastEnders* or the police station in *The Bill*. The set will be dressed to look different to emphasise a story line. It can be something simple like Christmas or the tragic death of a character.

**Characters**    Costume and make up are important in defining character and, to some extent, genre. Comedy uses visual clues to emphasise character. Fictional television uses costume and make up to signal a range of emotions and traits including a character's mood, time of life, job, ambitions, anxieties, state of mind and social status. The art of make up for television is often to make the face as naturalistic as possible under the set lights. All presenters and many guests require some form of make up to appear to look perfectly natural in a television studio. This is due to the harsh nature of the lighting, and the way many talk shows want a cheery, sunny visual feel to their shows, which involves high levels of overhead lighting.

For a period drama set in a particular epoch the make up artist will have done extensive research studying photographs and paintings of the time to get the make up to look authentic. Costume and make up often play the most important part in the *mise-en-scène* of any period piece, sometimes hiding the lack of an authentic location.

**Lighting**   In a two-dimensional medium such as television, lighting is most important as it helps create a three-dimensional image that is most convincing to the viewer. Conventional analysis of film lighting is to differentiate between hard and soft lighting. Television lighting directors are versed in these techniques, but also invent new ones. Hard light is associated with well-defined shadows, and is particularly obvious in *film noir* movies, or classics like *The Third Man.* Soft light is diffuse and has few shadows and works very well for video cameras. Most TV studio shows use large soft lights to illuminate the set without casting any shadows. Television is beamed into the audience's sitting room and most of the time works hard as an entertainment medium not to upset the viewer. Soft lighting helps to create a friendly visual environment, although this can often be spoiled by ghastly studio sets.

On location and in a drama, lighting has much more to do. Look for the source of the key light. A scene can appear to be illuminated by just one light source from a window, or perhaps a candle. Is this actually the case or are there other hidden sources of light? There almost certainly will be. Faces usually need separate illumination to make them stand out from the background set. The three-point lighting plot (see the previous chapter on practical programme making) is most commonly used as the basis to light a fictional scene. A well-lit interview will use three light sources to create a visually satisfying three-dimensional image of the interviewee. A DOP may use many more lights of different sizes and power to create a particular feeling or atmosphere for a scene. Genre can be defined by the way the set is lit. The under lighting of a character's face, swirling mist and a 'moody' set have become key indicators of the horror genre.

**Acting**   Everyone feels they can comment on acting in a film or a television programme. The popular criterion for 'good' acting is naturalism. Some of the best-loved actors on television are often anything but naturalistic – for example David Jason in *Only Fools and Horses*. Comedy allows the outrageous as we laugh at exaggerated human traits or foibles – think of John Cleese as Basil Fawlty.

Acting is the hardest element to analyse in a programme. Look for facial expression, movement, gesture, and use of the voice. Casting directors for television soaps and serials look for the actor who as him- or herself naturally looks and speaks like the scripted character. Television is a realistic medium. Television acting is not at all like acting on the stage where command of the body and voice is essential. The ability to project character, deliver a meaningful performance and have screen presence are most important for major television dramas.

Run of the mill television fiction can be accused of relying on the same faces delivering the same type of role. Commissioning editors are reluctant to take risks and prefer a well-known television face that can fit any part to a new name who might be exciting but not perhaps to everyone's taste.

Some areas to analyse in TV acting go outside the frame. Discussion of television *mise-en-scène* can include other televisual elements. Television tends not to isolate an acting performance as a film does. The viewer brings to each scene visual luggage from the rest of his or her recent television experience. The worry is that this visual luggage can mean that viewers and broadcasting companies see acting talent as set in stone and eschew the new generation of actors that is always coming up. A film director will spend months looking for a new fresh face; this is unusual in standard television fiction.

**Postproduction**    The way the pictures are edited together, the choice of music, the selection of background sound, and the mix and balance of the sound all contribute to the *mise-en-scène*. Modern postproduction can completely change the original filmed sequence. Digital effects and animation can be added, the picture colourised or the colour drained from it, the motion slowed or speeded up, unsightly buildings from the location shoot can disappear.

Some TV material is shot against a bluescreen so that extra pictures can be added in post. This is costly and time consuming, but not nearly as expensive as it used to be. Many special effects are designed to be unobtrusive, or invisible. *Mise-en-scène* analysis attempts to see what has been the effect of postproduction on the meaning and interpretation of the scene or sequence.

# Further reading

Millerson, G., *Television Production*, 13th edn (Oxford: Focal Press, 1999).

Orlebar, J., *Digital Television Production – A Handbook* (London: Arnold, 2002).

# 21 Television studio

The television studio is an important part of the TV production process. A TV studio is expensive to run, but it accomplishes a number of objectives in one place and at one time. The essence of a TV studio is that it is a multicamera environment capable of creating whole programmes in the one space. Television studios vary in size, availability and complexity of electronic equipment, and what they are capable of doing. Some are able to host a studio audience while others are compact and designed for news bulletins, or sports broadcasts.

A TV studio is a sound-proofed area with a flat floor, and a high ceiling where lights can be attached to a grid. There are no exterior windows but interior triple glazed glass panels that look into the control gallery and sound suite. In a large organisation such as the BBC some studios have a visitors' area that looks down through glass panels onto the studio floor. In other words this is a vast open space with enormous TV potential.

In the early days of television broadcasting nearly all programmes originated in a TV studio. The studio was television. You could broadcast films as a film or do an outside broadcast. The idea of television was to transmit pictures and sound from a highly controlled live studio to the audience at home. The modern TV studio is now just one element in a vast production process that includes video, hard disc, film, graphics, satellite links, videophone reports, outside broadcasts and the TV studio. At one point in the 1990s as video camcorders became inexpensive and reliable some large broadcasting companies thought they could dispense with their studio facilities. Studio production is now back in business, although as a leaner and more flexible option for producers.

*Figure 21.1* Television studio – student production

The sort of programmes that are made successfully and reasonably economically in a TV studio vary from chat shows like *Parkinson*, to light entertainment shows such as *Blind Date* and the Lottery shows. In the 1980s there were still some drama productions working in a TV studio although often not using the full potential of a multicamera set up. A film studio is quite different from a TV studio. A film studio, such as the ones at Ealing in west London, is a vast sound-proofed space that has to be filled with everything – set, lights, camera and sound kit as well as actors and crew.

A TV studio comes equipped with a minimum of four or five cameras, a sound boom, a sound mixing desk and a vision control gallery for mixing all the video inputs. Even the smallest studios have a vision mixing desk and a sound mixing desk. It is cabled up for a computerised lighting rig, sound cables and vision cables. There is nearby storage for scenery. There are nearby rooms for make up, and a green room for contributors to sit in while waiting to take part in a show. Some studios are capable of going directly on air; all have facilities for recording the output of the studio onto high-end digital videotape machines, or hard disc. A TV studio has links to videotape input machines (VT), telecine (transfer of film to video), and sophisticated graphics. In a nutshell a TV studio offers the space and all the technical facilities to make broadcast-standard television programmes under one roof, and this is its attraction to programme makers.

# Studio personnel

## On the studio floor

**Floor manager**   Responsible for everything that happens on the studio floor. He or she is an important member of the studio crew who is responsible for safe and efficient working on the floor. This includes the entire performance area and the audience seating (if appropriate), and camera movement areas. The floor manager has two-way communication with the studio gallery, and relays directions from the director to the presenter and other contributors, who are not able to hear talkback from the gallery. He or she is helped by an AFM.

**Assistant floor manager** (AFM)   He or she works to the floor manager, and wears headphones to be able to hear talkback from the control gallery. The AFM has a variety of duties including collecting guests and actors from dressing rooms and the green room.

**Floor assistant**   Helps AFM and the floor manager. This is a good first job as the floor assistant does anything he or she is asked to do, especially greeting guests and contributors in reception and taking them down to the green room. He or she gets artists to the right place at the right time.

**Camera supervisor**   Experienced cameraman in charge of all the camera crew, who typically operates camera 1. He or she advises on difficult shots and camera angles.

**Camera operators**   Part of the camera crew. He or she operates a camera on a pedestal, hand-held, or mounted on a crane, and is in constant touch with the director via headphones.

**Assistant camera operator**   Works with camera operators, and holds and carries cables.

**Boom operator**   Operates the sound boom. This is part of the sound equipment and the boom operator holds a microphone at the end of a telescopic tube to swing above the cameras, getting the microphone as close as possible to the talent. The boom is used less than it used to be, as lapel mics are more flexible.

**Autocue/portaprompt operator**   Operates the prompting equipment that displays the script on a screen in front of the camera. He or she can control the speed, movement and size of the script, slowing down or speeding up according to how the presenter reads.

**Set designer**   Creates and draws up the complex scale plans of the set. This is built and then put in place on the studio day under the supervision of the set designer.

**Make up**   Supervises the make up of the presenters and contributors.

**Costume**   Costume designer can select the wardrobe for presenters and supervise the style and design of costume for any actors or contributors.

**Stage hands**   Moves scenery and makes final adjustments to the set.

*Figure 21.2* Studio camera operator

## In the control gallery

The main feature of the control gallery is the very large bank of television monitors arranged across a long wall. In front of this is the vision mixing desk that controls all these vision inputs. Audio is controlled in an adjacent gallery, or sound suite. The lighting gallery and technical control are nearby.

**Director**    Responsible for the artistic interpretation of the show. He or she calls the shots and generates the energy and drive for the whole studio day. The director writes the studio camera script, and works with the production team to make the best use of the studio.

**Production assistant**    Sits next to the director in the gallery. He or she works on the timing of the show, and keeps continuity notes. This role involves assisting the director in all administrative details leading up to the studio day: booking contributors, checking copyright on music and setting up contracts. It is a busy job.

**Vision mixer**    Operates the vision mixing desk, or panel, cuts, mixes, wipes from one visual source to another. The vision mixer works closely with the director, needs a good sense of timing and rhythm, and an ability to work in a sometimes stressful environment. On a large show he or she will work with another vision mixer who sets up and controls the digital video effects (DVE).

**Technical manager**    Overseas all the technical facilities of the studio. This ranges from VT inputs and recording, to phone lines and OB sources.

**Lighting director**    Devises the lighting plot for the show in consultation with the director, and set designer. He or she supervises a number of lighting personnel who set up, move and control the many light sources needed on a studio show.

**Vision supervisor** (racks)    Supervises the colour balance and exposure of the cameras, and balances the cameras to give a uniform picture from each camera and other incoming vision sources.

**Sound supervisor**   Mixes and monitors the sound from the studio. He or she has one or more sound assistants to operate tape or CD players or telephone sources, and set up microphones.

**Sound assistant**   Assists sound supervisor in sound suite and on studio floor.

# The studio day

A regular live studio programme such as *Blue Peter* needs a crew of about 30 to get it on the air. The day starts early in the morning for the set designer and the stage hands who have to wheel the set into place and secure it in the specified position. This has been marked on a grid floor plan. Just because it is a regular programme does not mean that the set is exactly the same each time. Depending on the items in the programme and the guests, the set will be adapted. If an elephant is going to be part of the show – it has happened – then arrangements are made to create an area that would suit an elephant. The lighting designer then has to rearrange all the overhead lights for that particular set on that particular day. This is all done before 9.00 am.

Traditionally a studio day begins on the dot at 10.00 am with a camera rehearsal. This is where the director does a 'stagger through' – so called because it is a stop-start procedure – going through each sequence of the script. Each shot may need some explanation for the cameras, and all the other technical elements in the show such as explaining last minute changes, or tricky moves or visual effects. For a regular show the camera operators and other studio personnel will know what to expect and how things will run. After the stagger through there will be a full rehearsal with the presenters but not the guests. This is to check the lines of the presenter and that autocue can be easily read. The director will go over all the moves each presenter has to make and explain where the guests will sit, and which cameras will get that shot of the elephant.

It will probably be time for lunch after the rehearsal. All these people need feeding. The show may not go out until fairly late in the evening, or there might be an evening recording with a studio audience. A studio day is rarely less than 10 hours and can be much longer. Because a studio show is multicamera the aim is to produce as complete a programme as possible that needs very little editing or that can transmit live. This leaves no room for mistakes and retakes as on a feature film. The performances, the technical arrangements, and the length of the show have to be absolutely spot on. In practice nearly all shows, other than live shows, are pre-recorded. The programme is edited for time, and to tie together the number of different sections that may be recorded out of sequence. Conventional high-end video editing in a final editing facility is expensive, so as much as possible is compiled and completed in the studio.

## Running order

A studio script has its genesis in the running order. This is created by the producer working with the director, and is the order in which the various items that make up the programme are to appear. This is the start of the studio process. For a magazine programme video items will have been shot and other material gathered. A presenter will almost certainly be on board and the production team will have ideas for studio items and guests for the show. Magazine programmes are particularly suited to studio shows because all the items can come together and be smoothed into one flowing programme on the studio day. The producer and an assistant producer will be working on booking guests, selecting music, finalising filmed items and the linking script for the presenter. They will try to get a balance of items, with a large important piece that carries some dramatic televisual clout as the last item. Graphics will have to be ordered from the graphic designer. Possibly archive footage will be required to illustrate an interview. This needs researching and dubbing to video, and the copyright cleared. Props have to be selected and sometimes made specially for the programme. There are the logistics of getting the presenters and the guests to the TV studio and home again – normally another job for the PA. When the running order is finalised it will need to be agreed by an executive producer. There may be budget implications of certain apparently expensive items. The producer has to make sure that the show does not overspend. If the show has a celebrity guest that could require extra planning. They may only be able to be at the studio for a very short time. He or she will want to know in advance what questions are going to be asked. The contract could pose problems. Normally a contract expert will draw up watertight contracts for guests on broadcast programmes with a scale of appropriate fees. Above all, the production team will want to make the show interesting, entertaining and relevant to the target audience. They will make sure they are very well prepared with an excellent studio script.

## The studio script

The studio script is the bible of the studio day. This is a meticulously prepared schedule and script that includes everything that is going to happen on the day. Because so many people work in a TV studio everyone needs to know exactly what is happening when and where. For example, when is the first rehearsal and who are the guests and what dressing rooms are they in? The floor manager and his AFMs need to know who needs to be where and at what time. Anyone working on the studio floor will at some time during the day need to look at the floor plan. The central section is the actual camera script itself. This is a shot by shot break down of the whole show. It has all the visual and aural information that make up the particular show, including sound cues, dialogue, camera angles and shot sizes.

Each shot is numbered on the left. The number of the camera taking that shot is above the line and next to that is a letter that denotes the camera position on the floor plan. Under the line is the shot size – MS or MCU and the name of the person who is in the shot – presenter or guest. On the right of the page is the dialogue and the line indicates the cut point, which may be at the beginning of a line or at any point that the director thinks is relevant and adds to the visual narrative. There will be other directions on the script for the cameras such as PAN TO 2 SHOT, or for the vision mixer such as WIPE or MIX. The person playing in the videotape will have notes such as Stand by VT. Full details of each insert are given including the tape number, the in words or first frames, and the out words or end visual sequence. Most importantly there is the duration of the insert. The PA will be constantly timing each section of the show, and adding them together to give an overall timing, so that at any point the director knows how much time there is left or, very occasionally, if the show is short. The script will indicate where any music that is to be played into the programme starts and stops. If the show has live music like *Top of the Pops* then the lyrics of the song will be printed, and the time signature of the music shown. The PA will count each bar of the song so that the vision mixer can cut on the beat.

The script is a lengthy document that has been carefully put together over the preceding weeks by the production team. It can still only be an anticipated version of how the studio day will run. Everyone marks up their own copy of the script according to their role in the programme. The director, PA and vision mixer mark up in pencil as they know there are likely to be many small changes as the day goes on. A well run studio day is an efficient and compelling way to get a programme on the air. It is immediate and can cover many different elements. Performers will rise to the occasion or respond to a live audience. Everyone will strive to perfect their particular contribution and work to a thoroughly professional standard. There is a lot of professional pride at stake in creating a satisfying studio show.

Many universities and colleges have a fully operational TV studio. It may not have the very latest electronic effects, but it will provide an excellent training ground to work with TV studio equipment, and learn how to put together a studio show. You may be surprised at the professional looking show you can produce in a studio session. Try putting a student band in there to record live, or mime to a CD. Then have a presenter interview the band members. Put the whole show together in the TV studio, and show it on a monitor in the students union as part of a student-run TV magazine programme.

# Definitions

**DVE**    Digital video effects. These are visual effects such as spinning the picture or superimposing one picture over another, that are created by the vision mixing desk in the gallery.

**Camera card**    Each studio camera has a number. The PA will print a card for each camera that lists all that camera's shots and moves.

**Chromakey**    Electronic effect that overlays one picture on sections of another picture. Widely used in television for a variety of effects from putting a presenter apparently in another city or landscape to creating sci-fi backgrounds and effects e.g. *Doctor Who*. The colour (chroma) blue in the picture is used to key (be replaced by) other images. Some TV studios have a large blue curtain that can be pulled across the back of the set so that a presenter can stand against a blue background that can be replaced via chromakey. The vision mixing desk has a button that sets up the chromakey effect.

**Floor plan**    A diagrammatic map of the TV studio floor superimposed on a grid reference system that shows the exact positioning of the scenery, relevant large props, studio cameras, microphone boom, and other important items as well as entrances and exits.

**Foldback**    Sound played through a speaker situated on the TV studio floor, or in a radio or sound studio, so that artists or audience can hear the studio sound or sound that has been pre-recorded or originated else-where. It is particularly useful for a singer miming to a recording as the recording can be heard from studio speakers, but the singer can still sing into a live mic.

**Graphics**    Generic term that describes any lettering or other artwork created for the television show, e.g. the cast list, names of contributors or title sequence to a programme.

**Name super**    Means name superimposition. This is the standard way to name a contributor to a TV studio show. It appears in the lower third of the screen and is superimposed over the image of the person. Created by a caption generator such as ASTON.

**Pedestal**    A wheeled mounting for a studio camera that allows the camera to go up and down as well as move sideways and backwards and forwards. It has a small black and white monitor as a view finder and headphone links to the gallery.

**T/K or Telecine**    Electronic equipment that scans 16 mm or 35 mm film and allows it to be videotaped or stored digitally.

## Studio directing

Some of the terms you will hear a director using in the gallery:

**Cut**    This asks the vision mixer in a TV studio gallery to make a sudden, clean transition from one picture to another. This is not the same as on a film set, or video location shoot where **cut** means stop the action. It never means this in a TV studio. To stop all the action on the studio floor the director's command to the floor manager is **hold it**.

**Cut to three**   This asks the vision mixer to cut to camera 3.

**Mix**   This asks the vision mixer to make a gradual transitional from one image to another, known on film or in editing as a dissolve.

**Wipe**   This asks the vision mixer to make an electronic video transition where the incoming picture wipes away the picture already on the screen. There are a large variety of wipes with names that reflect what they look like, e.g. clock wipe that wipes in the next picture on the screen like a fast clock hand.

**Super**   This asks the vision mixer to introduce a new image, usually a graphic such as the name of the studio guest, and overlay it onto the existing picture, which is likely to be a shot of the guest.

**Fade up**   This asks the vision mixer to slowly fade in the picture from a blank screen, or as an extra visual source that might be superimposed onto the existing picture.

**Fade to black**   Fades the picture to a black screen to indicate the end of the show or the end of a sequence. Typically this is the last action on completion of the show. Also used is **fade sound and vision**.

**Lose**   This command from the director can be either to the vision mixer or to the floor manager. To the vision mixer it means take out a super-imposed picture such as a caption. To the floor manager it means take away some object from the set that is no longer needed, or is in the way.

**Take out**   Asks the vision mixer to take out a caption, electronic effect, or other superimposition.

**Run VT**   Asks the video tape operator to play the insert tape. This has been set up at a starting point agreed during rehearsal.

**Go sound**   The command to run a CD or any other sound source from the sound gallery during the programme is **go sound** or **go** and the name of the source, e.g. CD.

**Cue Anna**   Asks the floor manager to make a sign to the artist Anna to start speaking.

**Wind up**   Asks the floor manager to make the wind up sign to the current speaker, meaning it is time to come to the end of your piece. This instruction is particularly used during studio interviews.

# 22 Postproduction

ostproduction happens after the production phase where you have acquired all the moving images and much of the sound you need to make a programme. The process of postproduction is everything that you need to do to finish the programme and make it ready for transmission. The technical aspects of this process are now digital. It can be a costly and complex process using sophisticated high-end editing facilities, computer-generated animation (CGA) and digital imaging, or it can be done on your computer at home. Postproduction for television takes place at both ends of the spectrum. The other aspect of postproduction deals with finalising the paperwork, checking copyright and contracts, and marketing the programme. It may have a broadcast slot on a main channel but look at how busy those schedules are. To make your programme stand out and be noticed often requires a clever marketing strategy.

## Editing

All programmes, except live broadcasts, are edited. Editing is digital on computer typically using AVID or Apple's Final Cut Pro editing systems. The director works with an experienced editor to arrange the pictures and sound in the best way to tell the story. Most television programmes are shot with a ratio of at least 10 to 1. Ten minutes of video material will yield one minute of edited programme. In a large television production company a 30-minute factual programme will take a few weeks to edit. Drama could take longer. Then it will be approved by the producer, the executive producer and maybe the channel controller. A freelance director, working on DV with a small production company, may edit a similar 30-minute programme at home, using an effective but relatively inexpensive editing software such as Adobe Premiere. The result is the same. The programme can be fully edited for content with effects, mixes, wipes and dissolves all in place. A factual programme could be ready for transmission needing only a minimum of finishing.

Nearly all programmes for broadcasting on terrestrial channels go through a finishing process. This is a digital process to refine the edited programme. It involves colour correction and grading, adding effects, tidying up any images that may not look right or have unwanted content, and making a broadcast format master recording of the programme. The sound is remixed and balanced in a sound dub. This process used to be known as the online edit, where the original pictures and sound were conformed from an offline version of the programme. The increased power of computing systems and improved software means desktop editing is now online, manipulating the actual images and adding real-time effects. Sound, too, can be mixed in the edit.

The aim of postproduction is to produce a programme that meets the highest technical standards, is complete with all graphics, title and end credit sequences, and conforms to the format, style and reputation of the broadcaster. Some satellite channels will not require the postproduction resources of a prime-time ITV or Channel 4 programme with millions of viewers. Lower budget and news channels can transmit programmes directly from the desktop edit.

## Digital editing

The DV format has established itself as a popular and cheap digital shooting and editing format for television. Many colleges and universities have DV cameras and DV editing systems such as Adobe Premiere. The industry uses AVID Xpress Pro or Final Cut Pro. You shoot the material on a DV camera and bring the camera to your PC and then transfer the images and sound directly into your hard drive. This needs to have a large amount of storage space. DV format uses a standard compression ratio of 5:1. Five minutes of pictures require at least 1 GB of hard disc space. DV files are large, and need a fast interface to transfer from the video camera to a PC. This is done with a FireWire (developed by Apple) and with the international standard IEEE 1394. Since FireWire remains an Apple trademark, many other companies use the IEEE 1394 label. Sony refers to it as 'i.LINK'. DV is carried by FireWire in its compressed digital state. Copies made in this manner ought, in theory, to be exact clones of the original. However, while the copying process has effective error masking, it doesn't employ any error correction technology, and there can occasionally be drop out problems. This technology has only become ubiquitous since early 2000. The PC industry has worked closely with companies such as Sony, to incorporate IEEE 1394 into PCs. This means the communication, control and interchange of digital, audio and video data is available to everyone with a modern, large-capacity computer.

One aspect of DV editing that can be annoying is audio drift. This has dogged DV editing systems since they first appeared. Minute variations in data rate and the logistics of synchronising a video card and a sound card cause some audio tracks in AVI files to drift out of sync. Better quality video capture cards circumvent this problem by incorporating their own sound recording hardware and by using their own playback software rather than using a standard component, such as video for Windows. Microsoft says its ActiveMovie API will eliminate audio drift problems.

The advent of the DV format means that quality is no longer the preserve of the professional. Home DV video cameras are used by broadcasters and have their place in factual and entertainment programming. The hugely costly star vehicle entertainment shows, and quality broadcast drama will continue to use high-end technology, such as digital Betacam or HD formats. Some directors prefer to shoot flagship drama in 35 mm film with a more extensive postproduction process, although it is likely to be edited on an AVID system.

## Editing techniques

The art of storytelling for television relies on a good story, and a strong, effective story telling technique. The story has to be in the right order and it has to be told with an assured delivery, varying the pace and rhythm. There need to be light and shade, with climaxes and quiet periods. These are the skills needed for video editing. Many television programmes are formed and fashioned in the postproduction process. Good editing can make everything in the production look better, but it cannot rescue a bad script or disguise terrible camerawork. There is very little you can do with off-mic, badly recorded sound – except record it again. So do not rely on postproduction to sort out all the problems that occur on a shoot. It can do a great deal technically such as flip pictures, reconstruct sequences, create slow motion and even change a grey sky to a blue one. Sequences without those vital close-ups cannot be miraculously saved in postproduction. It can't tell a story if there is not one there to tell.

## Visual grammar

For a smooth flow that does not jolt the audience out of the illusion of continuity, certain conventions are followed. These are devices by which the actual space that exists between each shot is smoothed out in the finished programme. The illusion of continuity is maintained first of all in production. Visual detail must be consistent. This is of paramount importance in drama, where all the professionals involved share the task of checking continuity. Make up, costume and props are helped by the continuity PA who takes polaroid or digital pictures of each set-up. Each day the set is checked against a video of how it looked in the last shot. Objects must not disappear from a mantelpiece, and turn up on a nearby table. Clothing, make up, hairstyle and the hand that carries the bag or gun have to be consistent, or the viewer will notice that something is wrong. Any suggestion of discontinuity destroys the flow of the narrative, steers the viewer away from the characters and provokes feelings of unease.

Visual grammar is also concerned with movement. A hand gesture begun in a wide shot has to be seen as the same movement when the editor cuts to the close-up. Imagine two characters running after each other in a chase scene. If they leave the shot running, then the next shot should not show them walking along slowly. An entrance through a door should not show the doorknob being turned in both the interior and the exterior shots. The editor cuts the shots to show continuity of action, period, place and space and to compress time. An action that takes place in real time takes much longer than we tolerate in a drama or a factual programme. The editor can use the audience's understanding of visual conventions to move the action along, or it can be subverted. Jean Luc Godard uses jump cuts for political and cultural reasons in his films, for example *Weekend*. He wants the audience to notice the jump cut and be reminded that they are watching a film. He wants them to be aware of the illusion of cinema, and in a sense the political trick that they have consented to, in order to question the form and content of cinema itself.

# Shot, reverse shot

The basic sequence in classical continuity narrative construction is the shot, reverse shot technique. For example, shots of two characters engaged in dialogue will favour first one and then the other. The camera will frame the first character – a man – facing right of frame. This means that from the camera's POV he is looking to the right of the frame. The other character – a woman – will be framed from the camera's POV, looking to the left of the frame. Edited together the audience will think that the two characters are facing each other. In a drama the whole scene will be shot once with the camera framing the man facing to the right, and then again with the camera framing the woman facing to the left. Both characters will repeat their dialogue even when the camera is on the other character. The director has to make sure that the eyelines of the two characters match. If their eyes do not appear to engage with each other the audience will be disorientated. The editor can cut at any point from one shot to the other, depending on what is said and how it affects each character. This sequence is the basis for every film and TV drama, and is especially evident in soaps. A clever use of variety of shot sizes adds to the drama, and the audience's understanding of the relationship between the characters.

In factual programmes the technique is also employed even though the two characters are now an interviewer and a contributor, and may not be in the same room. It is used to carry out a standard interview or juxtapose opposing views. In most filmed interview situations the interviewer is asking the questions out of shot. After the interview the contributor may leave the location. The cameraman then films the interviewer asking the 'reverse questions', making sure that he or she is facing the opposite way to the contributor, and that the eyelines match. The illusion is preserved in that the questions appear to be being asked at the same time as the contributor is answering them. The reverse questions and pictures of the interviewer nodding help greatly with the editing. The editor can cut out parts of the interview, and insert a noddy of the interviewer to cover the cut. This is not considered dishonest, or to undermine the veracity of the interview. Journalistic ethics and broadcasting compliance do not allow for a change of meaning to be exploited by this technique. It is a technique to help the viewer stay with the programme. Some programme makers (especially in the 1980s) tried to do away with this illusion, and make the cut in an interview more obvious, either with a little dissolve or a straight jump cut. This can be a useful tool in certain cases where authenticity and credibility are

*Figure 22.1* Shot, reverse shot

at stake, but it can also look too contrived and get in the way of what the contributor is saying.

A postmodern audience accepts many of the subversions of the conventional such as the jump cut, the use of multiscreen effects, the exaggerated compression of time and slow motion. A visual trick observable in many documentaries is the speeding up of part of a sequence or long shot. A group of young clubbers may be hurrying along the street to their club destination. The camera pans them across a road at which point the editor speeds up the movement in vision so that the clubbers reach the entrance to the club very quickly. The movement then slows down to normal speed. This completely undermines the conventional continuity, but is acceptable as a postmodern stylistic embellishment that appeals to viewers brought up on the discontinuous visual world of music videos. Digital non-linear editing has opened up to the home editor many of the effects, visual tricks and picture manipulation that was previously only available in the cinema, or by hiring extremely expensive high-end digital technology in a facility house. Whether this leads to more audience involvement with programmes, or more incisive documentaries, or richer story telling is up for debate. What is certain is that televisual forms, styles and conventions will evolve as the technology develops, and as producers and editors look for more ways to grab an audience.

## The postproduction process

This is the sequence of events for a factual programme. It is very similar for a drama.

1  View rushes.

2  Log rushes. For any programme, or even a short insert item, it is worth making a record on paper of everything that you have filmed. Logging means writing down the 'in' timecode and 'out' timecode of all useable material, and briefly commenting on the shot, e.g. WS river. Speedboat comes in left. 22″ (22 sec).

3  Send cassette/CD of audio of long interviews to be transcribed. This will give you the interviews in a written form. Most people find it easier and more accurate to edit long interviews on paper than directly on the screen. Short interviews are straightforward to edit on the screen.

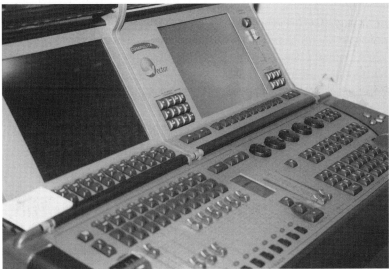

*Figure 22.2* (a) Digital non-linear video editing on 'Adobe Premiere'; (b) Portable digital video editing equipment

4  The paper edit. The paper edit is the cutting order for your programme. This is the sequence of shots and the edited extracts from the interviews in the order that you think will make most sense, and give a shape and structure to your programme. This will not be the final order for all the sequences. The paper edit is a structured starting point that can be cut together for the first assembly. It should be too long. This is normal.

5  Mark up the transcripts. This is where you will be very pleased that you have written transcripts of all those long interviews that were done months ago. Mark in highlighter pen, and with an identifying number, each block of words that you want to use from each interview. You can cut and paste them into the paper edit, but make sure you retain a copy of the full transcript. It is impossible to find short extracts without referring to the full transcript.

6  First assembly. Follow the cutting order created at the paper edit and assemble all the shots and sound together. At this stage do not worry about jump cuts, poor sound or anything technical – just get the story together with a beginning, middle and end.

7  Rough cut. If the assembly shows a clear structure, and contains all the relevant material, it is now time to make a rough cut. This should be within a few minutes of the final duration, have a definite structure and include the cutaways. Irrelevant material should all go at the rough cut stage. Be ruthless and only keep what is essential to drive forward the story.

8  Write an early version of the commentary. Most factual programmes need commentary of some sort. There will be sections of the programme where interesting and hopefully relevant shots need an explanation, or an introduction to a new contributor. The rule of thumb is that three words of commentary equal one second of programme time – 30 words needs 10 seconds of pictures – quite a lot.

9  Second rough cut or first fine cut. Add the commentary. Select and add the music. Trim the programme to be within 30 seconds of the final duration. Check the sound overlaps, cutaways and any tight edits. Add archive material and rough version of graphics.

10 Fine cut. Trim to exact programme duration. Add final graphics, mixes, effects and opening titles, and credits. Track lay sound for the

sound dub. If necessary and the budget allows, take your fine cut to a facilities house for finishing.

11   Enjoy the BAFTA.

## Postproduction postscript

Postproduction is a major cost in time and resources for any production. The major resource is the time required to edit the programme and then finish it. The editing process is time consuming. It takes thinking time, and editing skill, to get the most expressive combination of pictures and sound to tell the story in a way that will satisfy an audience. You will need to show a rough cut of the programme to a senior person such as an executive producer. Changes will be suggested. After the fine cut has been agreed then the programme has to be finished. This will involve a sound dub to smooth out the sound and add music if required. The final process is to create a master tape for transmission. This can include adding graphics, a title sequence and channel logos and copyright as required by the broadcaster. A short sequence of evocative images that could work as a trailer can be put onto another tape for publicity. But here is a health warning – postproduction always takes longer and costs more than you expect. Always allow twice as much time as you first think you will need. Allow time for other people to make changes. Broadcasting companies are apt to make last-minute changes in schedule and programme duration. Leave plenty of time before your delivery date. Above all, start postproduction as early as you possibly can. With a laptop it is possible to rough edit the rushes as soon as you have shot them – what a good idea!

## Further reading

Amyes, T., *Audio Postproduction in Video and Film* (Oxford: Focal Press, 1999).

McGrath, D., *Editing & Post-Production* (Screencraft series) (Oxford: Focal Press, 2001).

# 23 Television compliance

.........................................................

Broadcast television programmes are subject to a number of laws and operational guidelines. It is important to know something about these laws and guidelines before embarking on making a programme of any type. Commercial programme makers for commercial TV operate within guidelines and regulations laid down by Ofcom. Regulations for programmes of all genres, including the stricter codes of conduct for screening commercials, are available from Ofcom. Programme makers for the BBC follow the Producers' Guidelines laid down by the governors of the BBC, and available on the BBC website www.bbc.co.uk. Both sets of regulations and codes of conduct cover very similar areas. Programme makers working for commercial and public service television companies need to be aware of the main areas where the law affects television programmes.

## Taste and decency standards

.........................................................

Taste is subjective, and will change according to the time and what is fashionable. It can vary from place to place and from one part of society to another. It is very difficult to define; as a programme maker it is something that becomes part of your make up. Always be aware of your audience, whether they are children or adults, and when are they viewing – prime-time, afternoon, late night or minority?

Decency is more general. It spans cultures and generations. It is concerned with respect for the traditions, background and rituals of all people and their beliefs. Television standards tend to blend taste and decency. There are programmes that transgress the majority view on taste, and cause offence to many people at the time e.g. Monty Python's film *Life Of Brian*. When it first came out this film was considered by many people to be offensive and blasphemous. Taste changes. A decade later this film was broadcast on BBC2 with little comment.

Offence against decency is usually more serious. An offence against decency implies the concept of actual damage and offence to a member of the audience. Regulators will only condone such breaches if they feel the subject matter justifies it and is in the public interest. But the problem is tricky. Who actually defines standards? Ofcom is charged with maintaining standards of taste and decency across all television.

Laws prescribe the limits within which broadcasters can operate. Regulation, known as compliance, keeps the advertisers, broadcasters and makers of commercials in check against offending the public, and making spurious claims in advertisements.

The BBC is required in its Charter not to broadcast programmes that 'include anything which offends against good taste or decency or is likely to encourage or incite crime or lead to disorder, or be offensive to public feeling' (BBC Guidelines). This is a delicate area as people of different ages, convictions and cultures may have sharply differing expectations of what a television service should be able to show, especially in terms of bad language, sex and violence.

Recent UK research suggests that while people have become more relaxed about the portrayal of sex on television, they remain concerned about the depiction of violence. The use of strong language affects some audiences more than others, and can be a particular source of offence on the internet. Parents with children are naturally concerned about what appears on television. Most people expect to be given clear signals if they are about to see controversial material or hear strong language. What is acceptable in the cinema, on DVD, or in computer programs and on the internet will not necessarily be appropriate for television, or for a broadcaster's online service. In this area of taste and decency the cornerstone of British policy is the 9.00 pm watershed. All the major broadcasters have signed up to this policy. Before this time all programmes on domestic channels should be suitable for a general audience including children. The earlier in the evening a programme is placed, the more suitable it is likely to be for children to watch. The watershed reminds broadcasters that particular care should be taken over inclusion of explicit scenes of sex and violence, and the use of strong language. The watershed period runs from 9.00 pm until 5.30 am the following morning.

Ofcom's guidelines for the broadcast of bad language, violence or sexual material in post-watershed programming are open to some interpretation. There are no outright bans, but decisions on breaches of the guidelines are dependent on many factors. For example, there are guidelines, but no fixed rules, for the treatment of extreme sadistic and sexual violence. This is an area that programme makers clearly need to think very carefully about before including such scenes in their programmes. In fact, the legislation on the portrayal of the occult and paranormal on television is probably stricter than that governing violence. Taking all these guidelines into consideration, it appears that there is no fixed idea of what is within the bounds of taste and decency – it is a subjective matter that can vary from programme to programme depending on the content, intended audience, and time of broadcast.

## Sex and violence

Any twenty-first-century viewer will have noted that there are many opportunities to discuss sexual behaviour and view sexuality on television. Viewers have become more liberal in their acceptance of sexually explicit material post-watershed. There is still control over the use of some sexual language on television, and the showing of explicit sexual activity. All cases have to be referred to an executive producer, and sometimes the channel controller. Sensitive handling of the material can prevent causing widespread offence. The context of the scene, the intention of the production, and the expectations of the audience have to be taken into consideration when planning the use of sexually explicit material.

Research shows that violence on television can upset many people and, in excess, it can be accused of desensitising viewers. Audiences are concerned about the portrayal of violence they perceive as realistic, or shot in a way that appears to be close to their own experiences. Violent scenes before the watershed are not acceptable. Consideration is given to the time of day when any violent sequences are shown. Trailers of violent programmes or movies with violent scenes shown before 9.00 pm should not include unsuitable material. Programme makers should consider the impact on the viewer of any violence in a programme. Over familiarisation with controversial scenes in an editing suite can lead to the programme makers losing sight of the impact the material will have on the audience on first viewing. The basic rule is to make sure the violent incident is appropriate within its context.

In news and current affairs, audiences are more likely to accept disturbing material so long as it has a clear moral context, and is recognised as being true to life. Programme makers often have to make decisions about the portrayal of violence in drama and factual programmes. It is best to seek advice at the script stage, and definitely before filming begins. If contributors use bad language, or refer to sexually explicit activities, make sure they understand that this part of their contribution may not be broadcastable. Scenes of domestic and sexual violence, especially where women and children are portrayed as victims, attempted suicide, and any scene that may give the impression of approving of violence should be approached with extreme caution.

# Bad language

The use of bad language on television used to generate the most letters and telephone complaints. In recent years viewers appear to be less concerned about bad language than they used to be. Audiences are most likely to complain if they are taken by surprise by the use of swearwords, or if the use of bad language feels gratuitous, or is used in a programme contrary to the expectations of the viewers of that programme. Bad language on *Animal Hospital* would not be tolerated, but on a late night chat show it would be acceptable. Terms of racist abuse are considered to be offensive by all sections of the audience, and must be avoided at all times. Abusive names relating to disabilities are not acceptable. Before including any bad language, and this primarily means the use of the 'f word', in your drama or factual programme always check with a higher authority.

All complaints and comments about taste and decency on all domestic television channels go to Ofcom. Of all the complaints upheld by Ofcom since its augmentation, most dealt with unsuitable behaviour broadcast before the watershed. Complaints received about adult-oriented programmes tended not to be upheld or were resolved, especially where the broadcaster in question had taken steps to deal with the problem promptly. This suggests that Ofcom's role in the future may develop into an advisory panel rather than a regulatory one. Over the years public opinions and thresholds of acceptability have changed. The various broadcasting regulatory bodies are now rolled together in Ofcom. Ofcom keeps abreast of developments through consumer research, which feeds into their decisions. In a multichannel environment, and with broadcasting linked so securely with the internet, it may be that consumers might prefer broadcasters to be self-regulatory like newspapers, who have no regulatory body.

# Television and the law

Certain areas of broadcasting are regulated by the law.

## Privacy

Programme makers need to respect the privacy of individuals at all times. The only justification for bringing someone's private life into the public domain is that there is a wider public interest. Traditionally in English law, there has been no right to privacy. However, there has been a clutch of court cases where famous people have won over privacy issues. Catherine Zeta-Jones and Michael Douglas sued and won against *Hello!* magazine for publishing unauthorised photos taken at their wedding. Supermodel Naomi Campbell won a privacy case against the *Mirror* newspaper, which had made public her battle against drug addiction. These cases were argued under the European Convention of Human Rights which came into force in October 2000. Article 8, section 1, of the convention states: 'Everyone has the right to respect his private and family life, his home and his correspondence.' This can cause legal difficulties as it appears to sit awkwardly with article 10 which enshrines the right to freedom of expression.

In the UK, programme makers may film anyone in a 'public situation', such as walking in the street, or in a public shopping area. Even a quiet beach can be considered a public place, and this is where the paparazzi take shots of famous people sunbathing. Some well-known people are questioning this intrusion on their privacy. Newsreader Anna Ford was dismayed when first the Press Complaints Commission then the High Court refused to agree that paparazzo pictures taken of her on holiday breached her privacy. It was ruled that a publicly accessible beach in Majorca in August was not a place where she could reasonably have expected privacy.

In Naomi Campbell's case, the newspaper broke the law by publishing the times and nature of her medical treatment. Keeping medical data private is the right of any individual. So although there is no law of privacy in the UK individuals may be able to use the law of confidentiality to protect their privacy. In terms of making television programmes this could raise some difficult issues in some circumstances. In all cases of using photographs, correspondence or diaries, permission from the owner should be sought. In cases where this would put the programme in jeopardy, legal advice should be obtained to see if there is a justification that the material is in the public interest.

## Programme research

In the post-Hutton report climate it is essential that programme researchers keep clear records of conversations, and the sources of their information. Any programme dealing with controversial public policy, or matters of political or industrial controversy must be fair, accurate and maintain an impartial respect for truth. The programme should ensure that the views of all contributors are not misrepresented. The watchwords are fairness and integrity.

The BBC is paying particular importance to accuracy. It is warning journalists not to rely on memory, but refer back to their notes, or preferably to record all interviews on tape. The Producers' Guidelines say:

> With serious and major allegations, a full and accurate note of conversations is an essential element in the BBC being confident about the broadcast. If notes give rise to any doubts whatsoever about what was said, then the journalist must check their accuracy with the source before broadcast. In any event, the editor as publisher should be satisfied as to the fullness and accuracy of the note.

Any researcher on any programme should follow these guidelines. A large, hard-backed book with details of all phone calls, with times and contact details, and notes on relevant conversations, is a good way to keep accurate research notes. Some editors of factual programmes insist on seeing all research notes before any filming.

## Copyright

Studying television or working in television you need to know about copyright. Television programme making is about bringing together ideas and creative people and their work. Much of this work, such as music and scripts, and the actual television programme itself, is protected from unlawful copying by copyright. Copyright goes back a long way. Writer Jonathan Swift got the first Copyright Act passed in 1709 with published books protected for 21 years. Copyright is an intellectual property right. It is a way of protecting the tangible result of creative work – such as music or writing – from being used by someone else for their gain. Copyright exists throughout the world. National laws cover different countries. The principles remain broadly the same. Always check before using copyright material. The 1988 Copyright, Designs and Patents Act covers copyright of all types, including intellectual property. The Copyright and Related Rights Regulations amended this in 2003. These amendments, which update the Act for the digital age, came into force on 31 October 2003.

Ideas cannot be copyrighted, but the expression of an idea in a tangible form can be. This includes your own creative work. Copyright protects you from the piracy and copying of your original work. It could be a script, a film, a play or a TV programme format, or an original musical work such as a pop song. The most obvious use of copyrighted material on television is the use of commercial music from a CD, or when you copy music onto any format, tape, minidisk or MP3. In the UK, programme makers need to know about the 1988 Copyright, Designs & Patents Act. The aim of this Act is to protect the tangible result of creative work from unfair exploitation. These are what are covered by the act:

### Original literary, dramatic and musical works

Not just books, plays, film scripts and magazines, but programme schedules, opinion polls and airline timetables. TV signature tunes and 30-second radio ads are covered by the Act. Today literary, artistic, musical and dramatic works are protected for 70 years from 31 December of the year in which the author died. Using extracts from books and publications in television programmes for review purposes is usually acceptable, if the publication is fully referenced. Readings from novels, or adaptations of any published work must be cleared for copyright. Even an extract from Shakespeare will come from a published edition. You may not have to pay the author but you will have to pay the publisher. If in doubt, always check.

### Original artistic works

All works of art such as paintings, drawings, art videos, maps, photographs and plans are covered by the Act, and protected for 70 years. Do not assume that because the artist has been dead a long time you can use the reproduction of Van Gogh's sunflowers for your gardening programme.

The colour photograph of the painting is almost certainly covered by copyright. Museums and galleries jealously guard their copyrighted reproductions, but may be open to negotiation.

### Sound recordings

The 1988 Act was brought up to date and amended in 2003. One of the amendments is that all sound recordings are copyrighted for 50 years from the end of the calendar year in which the recording is made. This mainly refers to music copyright. Music copyright is complicated because any or all of the people involved in producing a CD have rights – composer, lyricist, instrumentalists, singers, the record company, the arranger and the publisher of the music. Working in television or on a student video, you are bound to get involved with music clearance.

### Commercial recordings

All commercial recordings whatever format they are on – CD, MP3, DVD, vinyl, tape or hard disc, are subject to a copyright payment when they are copied. Putting music on your video is copying. Its use will need to be cleared for broadcast, and rights will need to be paid for. You will see a warning written on commercial CDs: unauthorised public performance, broadcasting and copying of this compact disc is prohibited.

### Composed music

A programme maker may ask a composer to write music for a forthcoming broadcast production. This music will be composed, performed and recorded exclusively for your production. This can be music recorded 'live', or created electronically on computer, or a mix of both. This is known as specially commissioned music and the production usually buy out all broadcasting rights to the music. This can be expensive but allows the programme to be exploited in all markets including the internet, satellite and cable.

### Production music

This is music that has been commissioned, composed, performed and recorded especially for television and audio productions such as advertisements, broadcast programmes, film and video productions. It is available from company libraries, who are very willing to send copies of any CD from their catalogue. The value of production music is that there are no pre-clearance formalities. All you have to do is buy a licence from the

Mechanical Copyright Protection Society (MCPS) that covers all the rights required to include that work in your production. All the rights belonging to each recording have been 'bought out' by the company. This music can be cleared for world transmission, and paid for at a reasonable, set rate by obtaining a licence from MCPS. To find production companies look in The Knowledge on the website: www.theknowledge.com. MCPS can supply a full list of over 60 specialist libraries: tel. 020 7306 4500; fax: 020 7306 4380.

There are three basic sets of rights in commercial sound recordings: the rights in the musical work, the rights in the recording of that work onto CD, and the rights to broadcast it. The first rights are to the musical work itself. This is known as 'the song'. The rights to the mechanical copying of the musical work are obtained from MCPS, or the copyright owner. The second rights are to the sound recording made by the record company. To copy that sound recording the rights are most often obtained from the record company, or through one of the copyright societies – Phonographic Performance Ltd or Video Performance Ltd or British Phonographic Institute. You will also need to make sure that the right to broadcast your chosen commercial recording has been cleared through the Performing Rights Society (PRS). All broadcasters have an agreement with, and pay fees to, PRS to broadcast commercial music. You will need to log all music details found on the record label in order to clear these rights, and ensure royalties are paid.

**Student work and educational use**

For students there is a special exemption on the copying of commercial discs. For projects where copyright discs are copied on a student video as part of an educational course, and used within an educational establishment, such as a college or university, no copyright payment or clearance is required. The video must not be used outside the educational establishment. This concession does require you to log all music details.

**Copyright on the spoken word**

This covers all broadcasts such as Sky News, and a non-broadcast interview. If you record an interview with a politician, the politician owns the copyright in the words. The broadcasting organisation owns the copyright in the recording that you make while working for that broadcaster. The broadcasting company can use the recording in the way agreed, but the speaker has some defence against the words being used in a different context, or being deliberately distorted. Once an interview is freely given, the interviewee cannot change their mind and say it cannot be transmitted. A refusal to be interviewed can be broadcast, as the Act cannot be used as a form of censorship of free speech.

### Feature films

There is copyright on all films. Copyright is 70 years from the death of the last survivor out of the principal director, the screenplay author, author of the dialogue or the composer of the specially written music. Extracts released by the film distributor can usually only be broadcast in the week of release, but always check with the distributor. Using extracts from movies is possible but must always be negotiated. The exact use of the extract and the context will be closely examined. A documentary on disco could negotiate for a clip from *Saturday Night Fever* arguing that the film had an inspiring effect on the disco movement. It is likely to be expensive to get copyright clearance to use extracts from Hollywood films.

### Copyright on the internet

Contrary to what many people think, much of the original work on the internet is copyright. Look for the copyright logo on a website. It is hard to enforce copyright on much internet material. It is best not to assume you can copy any creative material and broadcast it, especially visual material such as pictures. Systems will evolve to police copyright on the internet. Fortunately a lot of material is deliberately copyright free.

## Defamation

The one area of law that most affects broadcasting organisations and programme makers is defamation, and particularly the law of libel. The simplest definition of libel is telling lies about someone. The libel laws in the UK protect the individual through the Defamation Act of 1996. Lord Justice Beldam defined this as: 'The (right to) protection against attacks on reputation and honour is as important in a democratic society as the right to freedom of the press' (*Kiam* v *Neil* 1996).

It is important to know just what committing libel means, because it is possible to libel individuals, groups or organisations. To commit libel a broadcaster would have to broadcast something that is defamatory. The courts normally apply these criteria to test whether a statement is defamatory:

- Does it expose a person to hatred, ridicule or contempt?
- Does it injure the person in his or her profession or trade?
- Does it cause a person to be shunned or avoided?
- Does it reduce a person in the eyes of right-thinking people?

Only one of these criteria has to be violated for there to be grounds for a case. The broadcasting company as the publisher of the television programme is responsible for making sure that a libel does not occur. The broadcaster is responsible if a libel is committed by a guest on a TV programme. An individual who sues a broadcasting organisation for libel has to prove three things in court: that the alleged libel is defamatory, that it relates to that person, and has been broadcast to a third party. Secondary libel can occur when a broadcaster repeats a libel that has been made elsewhere, in a newspaper for example.

There are three principal defences against libel that the lawyer for a broadcaster could use:

- *Justification.* This is the ability to prove that the facts as given in the programme are true, and that the broadcast material is telling the truth.
- *Fair Comment.* This is where the broadcast material was made as a fair comment on a matter of public interest. The criteria are that the comment is fair, accurate and based on fact, without malice and of public concern.
- *Privilege.* Privilege refers to statements in broadcasts of court proceedings, or of parliamentary proceedings or other public meetings. The reports of these proceedings must be fair and accurate, and contemporaneous. In qualified privilege the reports must not be motivated by malice. The defence of privilege acknowledges that occasionally it is necessary for a person to freely speak their mind, even if when doing so he or she falsely damages another person's reputation.

## Contempt of court

All types of television programmes can be involved at some time with court cases. This means that you will need to know about the law of contempt (Contempt of Court Act 1981). The law of contempt aims to uphold the integrity of the legal process. A broadcaster risks contempt of court by broadcasting an interview, or any material that may influence the jury and prejudice a fair trial, or make a statement that risks impeding or prejudicing the course of justice.

When a suspect is arrested and charged with committing a crime, or when a summons is issued in a civil case, the case becomes 'active'. This means there are restrictions on what a broadcaster can do. The 'active' period ends once sentence has been passed in criminal cases, and on judgment in civil cases. If you are hoping to interview people in a court case, or report on proceedings, follow these guidelines:

- Do not broadcast pictures, or comment, that could influence people involved in the case – witnesses, jurors, lawyers. Details of evidence could fall into this category.

- Do not broadcast anything that could prejudice the case.

- Do not broadcast interviews with witnesses or have dealings with them that could prejudice the case, before the case is over.

- Never speak to a juror about the case at any time, even after the case is over.

- Do not speculate about the outcome of a case, or comment on the outcome of a case due for retrial.

- Do not go against the court's wishes, or report what a judge has said must not be reported.

Contempt of court is a very serious offence. Dangers arise when the case comes to court and material is discussed on air that might be considered background material. Newspapers are most likely to be involved in this type of background piece, but a broadcasting organisation must not repeat material likely to prejudice the case.

One of the most high profile cases was the collapse of the trial of two Leeds United footballers in 2002. The *Sunday Mirror* was fined £75,000 for contempt by publishing an interview with the victim's father who said his son was the victim of a racial attack. The trial judge had said in court that there was no evidence of a racial motive. The interview was published while the jury was still considering its verdict. Because of the contempt of court the trial was abandoned, and a retrial ordered, at a total cost of over 2 million pounds. Inaccurate court reporting can lead to contempt proceedings. The BBC was fined £5,000 in 1992 for making an inaccurate report of a trial in progress. 'It was held that the report contained errors which had created a substantial risk of serious prejudice since it was foreseeable that publication would delay and obstruct the course of justice' (Welsh and Greenwood 2003).

As a broadcaster or journalist, you have rights to be able to report court cases that do not have reporting restrictions. You have the right to report a 'fair-and-accurate' account of court proceedings. Reporting restrictions are lifted when a case reaches a conclusion. This is when the defendant is: acquitted or sentenced; freed without charge; is unfit to plead; an arrest warrant has expired; the case is discontinued. However, if there is to be a retrial as in the two Leeds United footballers' case, care must be taken that the retrial will not be prejudiced. Most television programmes are pre-recorded. A possibly contentious programme can be shown to a lawyer who can advise on contempt and other legal issues. There are real dangers in live talk shows, or discussion programmes, where issues of the day are aired. This is where careful briefing and some knowledge of contempt law is essential.

# Further reading

Welsh, T., and W. Greenwood, *McNae's Essential Law for Journalists* (London: LexisNexis, 2003).

# Part V

# **Future shock**

# 24 Overview

## Introduction

This chapter presents an overview of where we think television is heading, and where new studies of television might lead. We have structured this chapter by including brief comments on the institutions and economic structures of television, especially in Britain, the impact of new technologies for producing and watching television, the current trends in television forms, genres and formats, and the ways that audiences are changing in their habits of viewing and their expectations of television as a medium. In each of these sections, we not only discuss the possible evolution of television but also provide some critical commentary on these trajectories in the immediate future. In our view, people engaged in studies of television and in the making of television professionally, should develop a knowledgeable, critical and responsible attitude to change in order to take an active part in it.

The expansion of the teaching of television has led to a proliferation of books that pass on the techniques and skills of making television, and many books that discuss and summarise existing research. Because graduates from university degree programmes in Television and Media Studies now make up a significant proportion of the body of younger television industry professionals, there are opportunities for academic studies of television to grow by making further connections with the television industry. The heritage in the 1960s and 1970s of television academics making distinctions between progressive or conservative programmes, and the highly theoretical arguments about form and meaning, meant that theories of television had little effect on writers and production staff in the business of making television.

However, some academic research into audiences has been funded by television companies and regulatory bodies, and it seems possible that academic concern with the aesthetic, historical and evaluative criticism that characterises work in the humanities disciplines may also have an impact on production, a move that this book aims to encourage. As the funding of the BBC, and debate and discussion about public service television in Britain continue, the questions about the role of television in society will also draw academics working on television into more public forms of debate.

## The future of the BBC

The availability of cable and satellite in developed countries such as Britain has the effect of diminishing audiences for the terrestrial channels as hundreds of channels split up the audience. Falling audiences for non-commercial network terrestrial television channels like the BBC's pose a threat to their funding, since they cannot expect viewers to pay television licence fees if they are rarely watching BBC programmes. But to try to grab audiences back by imitating the programme formats and audience address of commercial television causes another problem, since duplicating the output of their rivals means BBC has no claim to being an essential alternative. In February 2002, BBC launched its two new digital channels for children: CBBC and CBeebies are respectively for 6–13-year-olds and for pre-school children. There are 14 other channels competing for the child audience. BBC Four, an arts and culture channel, was launched later in the same year, and BBC3 began with programmes mainly for young adults. The question of the BBC's competition with other channels remains a hot issue, as the BBC has built on its well-known brand, with its values of 'quality' and trustworthiness, to introduce channels that rival the companies currently dominating the new multichannel landscape.

Public service is an attitude and not a genre of programme, so people working in television and those doing critical work in Television Studies should defend the claims both of high-budget and aesthetically demanding work, but also the range of popular formats and genres, such as quiz shows, sitcom and soap opera that fulfil the public service remit of offering diverse kinds of form, topic, and mode of audience engagement. The future of PSB, and in particular the BBC, cannot be extricated from the issue of funding. The licence fee that supports the BBC is currently under review.

Alternative methods have been suggested (see Part I) but it is likely that the licence fee will continue as the main source of PSB funding. The BBC may have to share this funding with the other PSB providers, ITV1, Channel 4, S4C and Five. The BBC's Charter is up for renewal in 2006. In 2004 Tessa Jowell, Secretary of State for Culture, Media and Sport, invited comments on a set of questions about the BBC and its future. The Government published a Green Paper setting out its thinking on the BBC's future, and will later publish a White Paper with final recommendations. The BBC set out its case on its website, and it has identified what it calls 'public value' as the cornerstone of its case for the renewal of its Charter:

> Public value should not be seen as a broad justification for what the BBC does but as a practical test that can be applied by the BBC itself, by its Governors and by the public, to decide what it should do – and how well it does it.
>
> (BBC 2004 Building public value)

Ofcom, the regulator for the UK communications industries, conducted a 12-month review of public service television broadcasting with detailed analysis of the UK public service television broadcasters. Its report will feed into the Government's review of the BBC's Charter.

Ofcom's report recommends that the licence fee should stay in its present form:

> To maintain its role at the heart of broadcasting in the digital age, the BBC should be properly funded. For the period of the next Charter, a TV licence fee model should continue to fund the BBC; the BBC should not carry advertising, nor should existing services become subscription-funded.

The report seeks to improve the provision of PSB in the UK:

> Our ambition is for an enduring and pluralist system of PSB for the digital age, with a variety of providers. It should supply content which contributes to PSB purposes and characteristics, which has reach and impact, which makes full use of new technologies and distribution systems, but which is value for money and which would not be provided in sufficient quantity by the market.
>
> (Ofcom review of public service television broadcasting
> – phase two, Sept 2004)

One of its more bizarre suggestions was to suggest a new PSB channel to act as competition to the BBC, and to be run by extra funding from a 'topped up' licence fee. The government is not predisposed to raising extra revenue from the licence fee, and this idea is unlikely to be popular.

From a political perspective, it is inevitable that the government will seek in the new Charter to change some aspects of how the BBC is governed. Ofcom has come down firmly in favour of severing the link between the Governors of the BBC and their regulatory role. The Ofcom report is unequivocal: 'clarifying the separate roles of governance and regulation of the BBC should be a central objective of the Charter review process.' There is little doubt that Ofcom would like to see the regulation of the BBC put under its wing. It already regulates taste and decency over all television broadcasting.

## Global television

Even in the global television economy of import and export of programmes and programme formats, television still has a largely national character. Television in the developed world is still largely organised on national lines, but television exports internationally from West to East and North to South and have been hotly debated. Any discussion of the future of television needs to take account of the social and political significance of how trans-national and national cultures of broadcasting work in relation to each other. Globalisation can refer to the phenomenon whereby some programmes or genres of television have spread across different nations and cultures, so that the television schedules of different countries can seem surprisingly familiar. One way of explaining this is to use the concept of media imperialism, in which it is argued that 'world patterns of communication flow, both in density and in direction, mirror the system of domination in the economic and political order' (Sinclair et al. 1999: 173). A second meaning of globalisation is to refer to the power of corporations that are relatively independent of nation-states, and that broadcast by satellite into several countries or regions. Third, globalisation describes the common culture that can result from the circulation of the same media products across diverse markets, and the consequent similarities between the consumers of products distributed in this way: the global audiences.

Britain is relatively unusual in global terms because its major broadcasting organisations mainly show programmes made in Britain. Britain also does relatively well in gaining export revenue from overseas sale of programmes. For example, the BBC nature documentary series *The Living Planet* has been sold to 82 countries, while the children's programme *Teletubbies* has been sold to Estonia, Portugal, Israel, the US, Australia and New Zealand. Nevertheless, American television far exceeds British television or television from any other European country in export revenue and coverage. The countries with the highest proportion of domestically produced television are the US, Britain, Brazil and Japan, followed by Canada and Australia which use imports to top up domestic production. Most of the nations of South America, Africa and Asia have small television industries and insufficient revenue to make many programmes. They use imports to fill 50 per cent or more of their schedules. The national television networks of Brazil and Mexico have the funding and facilities to make many of their own programmes, but for broadcasters in the developing world it is much cheaper to buy imported programming than to make their own. Older US television series can be acquired for just a few hundred dollars, as part of a package of programmes. Production costs have already been covered by screening these programmes in the American market, making them almost cost-free profits for their distributors. The higher production values and aura of sophistication of imported Western television in underdeveloped nations means that sectors of the television audience that are attractive to advertisers may be more likely to watch them. This marginalises the importing nation's domestic television culture, reducing its profitability, and also fills prime-time slots with Western programmes in which commercials advertising Western products often appear. Thus an ideology of consumerism and the reinforcement of Western values may result.

The sale of programme formats is similar to the business of selling complete programmes to other national broadcasters, and involves the sale of a programme idea and its narrative structure, character relationships and setting, often including the scripts for batches of episodes. So rather than buying tapes of the original programme itself, overseas broadcasters acquire the template, which enables them to remake it using their own facilities, performers, native language and locations.

But formats that gained large audiences in one country do not always succeed in another. The US sitcom *The Golden Girls* was tried in Britain (on ITV), using scripts from the US version with small adjustments for British viewers. The idea of remaking the programme must have seemed attractive to producers, since the US version had been a staple part of

Channel 4's prime-time sitcom offering. Although the cast of the remake included well-known British comedy actresses the programme was a commercial and critical failure and was cancelled after six weeks. *Married for Life* was a British version of the US sitcom *Married . . . with Children*, which ran for over 200 episodes in America (and was also broadcast by ITV in Britain), but the British ITV version ran for only one series. Some television companies specialise in the development and sale of formats: Action Time specialises in quiz formats, and has sold them widely in Britain and abroad. The Dutch company Endemol developed *Big Brother*, and its vast audiences in Holland were often paralleled when it was subsequently sold around the world.

Technologies such as satellite broadcasting allow global audiences access to television news and actuality footage, providing new openness and democratic access to information. On the other hand, criteria of news values determining global importance are exercised in choosing what to broadcast as global news, and the events chosen necessarily acquire global significance. Global news may produce monopoly control of information by a few broadcasters who impose Western news values across the world, and agenda-setting by news editors becomes more significant, since the audience may need increased guidance and support in understanding news about foreign events. News formats become simpler and regularised (reports are short, story structures are simple), and the conventions in news formats tend to predominate over the information they communicate. Furthermore, although global news (and other television forms) enables its audience to witness distant events, these services' images of the apparently comfortable Western lives and abundance consumer goods in both news stories and advertising may have negative effects. For Chris Barker (1997: 230),

> television on a global scale has the capacity to contribute to democracy (via the principles of diversity and solidarity) through its range of representations, genres, arguments and information. However, the vision of television as a diverse and plural public sphere is seriously compromised by its almost complete penetration by the interest-based massages and images of consumerism.

The international flow of television and its disruption of local cultures can be regarded as politically progressive, though the immediate impact of television has often been to intensify conflicts. The selection of news

*Figure 24.1* Modern production technology – 'steadicam' with HD widescreen camera

stories on national television networks around the world, and the structure and form of news broadcasting there, are influenced by CNN, BBC World and other global news providers because their news values affect national broadcasters.

However, the meanings of television programmes are understood in relation to the cultural environment and expectations of viewers, and are not just hypodermically injected into them. Audience research by Tamar Liebes and Elihu Katz (1990) found that viewers of the 1980s' American soap opera *Dallas* in different national cultures understood it in very different ways. They chose to study *Dallas* because it had been widely exported and was being used as the main example of a supposed trend towards global homogeneity in television, dominated by American dramas. But perhaps surprisingly, *Dallas*'s representation of the 'American dream' of financial success and personal happiness was understood in very different ways by different groups of viewers. Jewish members of a kibbutz in Israel saw its characters' unhappy lives as proof that money does not bring contentment. By contrast, members of a North African cooperative thought it proved how money rescues people from everyday problems. Russian Jews who had recently arrived in Israel from a Communist system believed *Dallas* was a subtle critique of capitalism that unconsciously exposed its contradictions.

Despite the often fatalistic and despairing commentaries on globalisation that have been widely disseminated by journalists and pundits, and in academic debate, it is not a natural and unstoppable process. Global television corporations can be restrained by national or local regulation, so political decisions that are open to democratic participation can require these corporations to operate differently in different places. Global distribution networks may transmit the same television programme to large audiences and in many regional markets, but the ways in which a programme is received (by whom, how, and the significance of receiving global television in a particular society) will be different in different contexts. John Sinclair and his fellow authors (Sinclair *et al.* 1999: 176) explain that:

> Although US programmes might lead the world in their transportability across cultural boundaries, and even manage to dominate schedules on some channels in particular countries, they are rarely the most popular programmes where viewers have a reasonable menu of locally produced programmes to choose from.

Globalisation theory not only addresses homogenising processes, but also processes of differentiation. Globalisation theory also brings together economic, institutional, textual and reception approaches in a way that is useful and not as common in other aspects of the study of television. Transnational flows of television seem set to continue, and these debates about the significance and effects of globalisation will become increasingly important.

## Beyond postmodernism?

Inasmuch as globalisation is part of postmodernist theory, it deals with the trends in television that connect populations, regions and nations together in parallel with the increased interconnectedness that characterises the present and the likely future of global civilisations. The two questions about the future that arise from this are whether postmodernism has now become the common present and future culture of the New World Order, and what the political and social consequences of this would be. Since 'post' means after, postmodernism has to be thought of as a stage or moment in time that follows another moment previous to it. For television, using the term postmodern means having to establish what 'modern' television is. Modern means what is characteristic of the present. But as culture moves on, the distinction between what was modern and what is happening in the present tends to break down. New experiences lead commentators to describe their own time as modern, assigning what had been called modern before to the pre-modern.

So paradoxically the postmodern could be characterised by a return to features that are thought of as pre-modern. If postmodernism reacts against the modern, one way of establishing a difference from the modern would be to go back to pre-modern features of culture and recycle them. These past elements lose their historical place and significance, and, some theorists of the postmodern claim that postmodernism erases history, and produces the sense of a perpetual present. The French philosopher Jean-François Lyotard, in *The Postmodern Condition* (1979) argued that postmodernism entails a loss of confidence in theories of historical progress and belief in the future, such as Marx's theory that history moves by dialectical struggles between the world-views of different social classes and that it is inevitable that the working class will eventually triumph over the bourgeoisie, or the liberal theory that humankind evolves towards ever greater understanding between peoples and the betterment of lives through technology and democracy. These and other large-scale 'grand narratives' of emancipation and progress have lost their legitimacy and purchase.

However, this attitude to progress is highly Euro- or US-centric. If modernity consists of the period of industrialism and mass culture, surpassed by postmodernism's post-industrial cultural landscape and fragmentation of mass audiences into niche audiences, it is much easier to find evidence for these shifts in the European nations and the US where industrial and mass culture first took root. It is much harder to explain postmodernism in terms of these shifts in parts of the world (like the African nations, or South America) where industrial and cultural development has not taken place in this staged way. These now post-colonial societies have very mixed cultures in which there are both highly developed media cultures but also deeply traditional and rural cultures at the same time. The theories of fragmented subjectivity, changed senses of space, time and identity, which can work quite well as explanations of how Western culture has changed, fit much less comfortably onto societies where inequalities in access to media, culture and wealth are much more marked. Theories of postmodernism tend to assume that it is a global phenomenon, though it is easy to find examples of nations that are still struggling to become modern industrial mass societies.

Equally, within Western television cultures, there are still significant struggles by under-represented groups to enter the television industry and to find representations of themselves on television that seem fair and accurate. Postmodernist theory understands identity as fragmented and temporary, built out of the images and experiences of television and media culture that offer points where these temporary identities can be momentarily defined. So the theory rejects political projects that are based on a claim that an identity is stable, such as claiming rights for equality based on being a woman, a Muslim or a black person. Postmodern theory would regard this kind of identity politics as an attempt to shore up a notion of the self that is incommensurate with the shifting identifications offered by music television, for example. But since there are obvious inequalities in the participation of women, Muslims or black people within the television industry, and also in their representation in programmes, there has been a critical rejection of postmodernist thinking by those who wish to use identity politics as a way of advancing their cause. For example, feminism has always valued the connections between everyday lives and political theories of inequality. It values active subjectivity, especially the subjective experience of women, and therefore some feminist theorists have seen postmodernism as a means to disempower feminist struggle. Meaghan Morris (1993) has pointed out that the leading thinkers about postmodernism are white European or American men. Despite the argument that postmodernism overthrows the hierarchies of the past, celebrates difference and rejects the dead hand of cultural authority, a select band of male theorists have become the new authorities, at the head of a hierarchy of theory. Despite the fact that postmodernism and feminism share many emphases, postmodernism can appear to be either a taking over of feminists' theoretical and political efforts, a diversionary sidetrack from feminism, or a strategy to deprive feminists of their hard-won academic distinction. In British television, there will be continuing struggles for under-represented groups to find a place in the television industry and for programmes to reflect diverse kinds of identity.

## Interactivity and convergence

Convergence refers to the way new media – basically the internet and website technology – interact with television and video technology via a broadband connection. The theory is that because everything is digital, everything can mix with everything else. The supposed benefit to the consumer is interactivity. This means that you can bank online or download films and watch entertainment on your computer via a broadband connection. Many observers think that as the cost of broadband goes down so more and more homes will subscribe to a broadband connection giving always-on access to the internet, video streaming and online movies, not to mention online advertising. However, broadband runs at different speeds. Always-on internet access at the lower speeds is perfectly acceptable for surfing the web and using email, but still pretty slow for downloading music and video. The fully fast-wired community is still some way off.

Both within the television industry and in academic work, people are coming to terms with the importance of the convergence of television with the interactive media of telephony, the internet and cable and satellite transmission. These recent developments in the means of reception suggest ways of thinking about television as a popular medium in which the notion of multi-accentuality (the different reception of the same material by different audiences) can be studied in new empirical and theoretical ways.

There have already been some studies of interactive programmes in the factual genre of Reality TV (and especially *Big Brother*) where these technologies were first significantly developed (see Tincknell and Raghuram 2004, for example). When Channel 4 planned its second series of *Big Brother* in 2001, it introduced interactive services accessible through its digital television channel E4, as well as on the world wide web. Since the programme already had established brand recognition, and viewers of the first series had already been able to interact with the programme on the internet, Channel 4 was able to enhance the second series in ways that audiences already understood. *Big Brother* has a large audience among the 18–34 audience, and this group is more likely than others in the British population to have access to interactive television technology (and also to the internet). Viewers of *Big Brother* were able to take part in interactive games using their remote control handsets, and could also vote for the exclusion of contestants, take part in quizzes, and gain access to additional information and video coverage. So *Big Brother 2* had numerous benefits for Channel 4 in attracting and maintaining a valuable youth audience, stimulating the use of and demand for digital interactive services, and promoting the brand identity of a programme closely identified with the channel.

Thinking about the ways that interactivity functions for audiences offers possibilities for updating the theoretical work begun in the 1970s on television as a mass broadcast medium addressing audiences as relatively homogenous wholes. Even when audiences have become fragmented by the different channels and viewing experiences that are now possible, television texts are deeply embedded in the popular culture of regions and nations, social groups and communities. Studying interactivity encourages researchers and programme makers to find out how television reconfigures and enables these audience cultures and communities. The discipline of Television Studies has always been interested in critiquing television's role in ideology and its relationship with the forces of social control. The increased valuation of ordinary viewers in both the television industry and in academic work will lead to further attention being paid to new modes of delivery and interaction with television.

The convergence of television with computer equipment and telecommunications technology is based on the common standards of data transmission and manipulation that are shared between equipment that treats content as a stream of digital data. These technologies were first developed in television production, but have now become sufficiently cheap

and user friendly for them to make inroads into domestic television technology and habits of media interaction. In the television industry, the digital
revolution made it possible to manipulate images and sound in new ways.
Editing systems treat camera pictures as a flat two-dimensional surface.
This enables the system to appear to move images by flipping them over,
lifting the corners or edges of the picture, enlarging or reducing the size
of the image, and distorting the image as though it were being turned at
an angle, folded, squeezed or torn. Because the image has been decom-
posed into digital data, and these numbers can be manipulated mathe-
matically by the computer and then turned back into an image, the image
is 'plastic'. Similar processes are used to record and process sound. The
editing systems used in television production are therefore a concrete
example of media convergence: they can access a wide variety of analogue
and digital information sources operating in different formats and standards, and integrate and store these various kinds of input information. By
integrating all these sources in digital form, they are able to treat them in
the same way, manipulate them, and produce a new output.

Once this possibility of manipulating television is in the hands of viewers
as well as programme makers, television can no longer be assumed to be
a fixed artefact or an unchangeable institution. The television material is
demystified and can be altered, distributed and used in new ways.
Contemporary digital technologies for recording and editing television, and
for transmitting it over networks, pose a potential challenge to the conventional expectations about television realism. These digital processes unfix
the image from what was shot, from its maker, and from its social and
historical contexts. Television will no longer be dominated by a broadcast
model whereby unalterable audio-visual material from a central institutional
source is transmitted to a passive mass audience.

Certain genres of programme have led the penetration of digital television in Britain. The most significant of these is sport. So far it has not
been profitable for television programme makers to invest in interactivity
in fiction programmes. Making a drama programme that has multiple
simultaneous plot lines, each of them accessible to viewers making choices
through their remote-control handsets and thus composing different
programmes according to the choices they have made, is an extremely
expensive and complicated business. The programme makers would be
asked in effect to write and produce the equivalent of several different
conventional programmes, and find ways of linking up narrative segments,
plot events and character development so that the choices made by the

*Figure 24.2* Editing HD pictures on 'Quicktime' digital editing system

viewer would continue to result in a meaningful and enjoyable programme. There is a long way to go before fully interactive TV becomes common across all genres, but the process has begun.

## Race, multiculturalism, future representations

Because of the centuries of movement of populations of different races to nations and regions that they do not consider to be their homelands, modern nations are not homogeneous in terms of race. British Asians have ancestors who came to Britain from India, Pakistan, and African nations to which they had previously emigrated, so there are not necessarily shared histories of place, language, history or culture among them. Racial identities do not primarily derive from a sense of belonging to an original place. Instead, they derive from social and cultural factors that have led a dominant racial group to regard, for example, black people as different and other from a white majority. A consequence of this, in turn, may be that black people may have come to identify themselves as different in a defensive strategy that allows them to create a sense of their own collective identity in resistance to a dominant culture. The racial categories identified by programme texts or by viewers do not have a direct connection to physical, linguistic or psychological facts about a particular group. Instead, the notion of a racial group is culturally produced by the categories and divisions between people that operate in a particular society. Multicultural Britain is still exploring the issue of race in its programmes, and will continue to do so.

For example, the BBC sketch show *Goodness Gracious Me* was a surprise hit with audiences in the late 1990s. The programme drew on a conscious engagement with the stereotypical representations of black and Asian people on British television, especially in comedy, going back at least as far as the 1970s. *Goodness Gracious Me* relies on the comic strategies of exaggeration and reversal in order to draw attention to stereotypes in a critical way. For example, in an often repeated dramatic sketch, younger middle-class Indians were shown 'going for an English' after an evening of heavy drinking in an Indian city, reversing the stereotype that young British people meet for a curry dinner after drinking in Britain. Being rude to the white British waiter, and challenging each other to eat the most exotic food (in this case, the most bland rather than the most spicy), drew attention to the ways in which some British people abuse the staff of Indian curry restaurants and challenge each other to consume the hottest dishes. The sketch ridiculed the behaviour of the Indian diners, but more significantly, drew attention to the racism and loutishness that British Asians often suffer.

When the programme was devised and first scheduled, both its performers and producers were concerned about whether there was a significant audience that might be drawn to it. Since *Goodness Gracious Me* relies on a degree of cultural competence among the audience not only about a television tradition of racial stereotypes, but also about the traditions, religions, family structures and economic positions of British Asians, they were anxious that it might only appeal to British Asian viewers themselves. For this reason, the series was first scheduled on the BBC's minority channel BBC2. However, very quickly, favourable press coverage and word of mouth drew large and diverse audiences to the programme. It seems likely that there were two main reasons for the success of *Goodness Gracious Me*. One of these is the relatively simple comic strategies employed by the programme, which most often consist of the reversal of stereotypes and exaggeration. A very wide range of viewers are sufficiently literate in the codes and conventions of British comedy to find these

strategies and structures familiar and entertaining, and the series' engagement with the history of representations of race and ethnicity in television
comedy supports this. Second, the long history of the integration of Asians
into British culture provides white British television viewers with suffi-
cient understanding of British Asian culture for the jokes in *Goodness
Gracious Me* to be comprehensible. It is also worth noting that the sketch
show format of the programme has a long history. While in some respects
*Goodness Gracious Me* was a new departure in British television, it also
engages with television formats that are deeply embedded in it. In future,
racial and ethnic identities will continue to be explored across many genres,
partly as a result of PSB obligations, and will manipulate existing genres
and formats as well as developing new ones.

## DIY scheduling with hard discs

Technologies themselves do not produce change in television culture, since
they first need to become marketable and attractive because of the possibilities they offer in extending existing ways of using television.
Technologies have to be integrated into the institutional and regulatory
structures that shape television production, delivery and economics. In 2000,
two digital video recorder products were introduced, TiVo and ReplayTV,
and in 2004 the Sky Plus box offered similar functions. These set-top boxes
were first introduced to the American market and quickly became available in Britain. They digitally record and store television as programmed
by the viewer (like a VCR) but can also automatically create a profile of
their user's preferences by analysing his or her previous viewing patterns.
They can then trawl multiple channels, and selectively store programmes
according either to the user's instructions or the machine's expectations
about what he or she might wish to view. This capability is referred to
as 'Me TV': the creation of a tailored repertoire of programmes for an
individual viewer.

 This technology can time-shift any programme, for viewing whenever
the user wishes, and can record several programmes simultaneously. It
becomes possible never to watch broadcast television at all, and instead
instruct the machine to create a library of programmes that are always
available. The set-top boxes can be programmed to omit or fast-forward
through commercials, thus threatening the funding basis of advertiser-
supported programmes. Digital video recorders suggest that the channel

identities and channel loyalty may become largely irrelevant, as would scheduling, since the time of broadcast has little impact on when programmes could be viewed. Television would largely cease to consist of must-see programmes when audiences view the same programme at the same time. The notions of liveness and the conception of the audience as a mass that have characterised the development of television would cease to apply. Viewer choice would be taken to a dramatic extreme. This is an exciting prospect for the consumer, but at a price. Even so, many people are beginning to see the benefits of such a flexible recording device. In the US, 30 million households are expected to have a DVR by 2007. Digital video recorders are likely to alter the way audiences use television, though exactly how is not yet clear.

Digital video recorders have caused anxiety among television executives whose channels are funded by advertising, since the recorders can omit ads. One response is virtual digital advertising. Rather than screening commercials in the intervals between programmes or programme segments, advertisers can buy virtual product placement, where digitally created logos, products or posters are pasted into specific shots or sequences in programmes. For example, a scene in which characters stand in a city street might have poster hoardings, or a soft-drink dispensing machine, inserted into the background of the shot as an advertisement for the soft drink. This technique was pioneered in the American CBS News programme's coverage of the New York millennium celebrations in Times Square in 2000, for example, where a large logo for the rival NBC television network was digitally 'pasted out' of the television pictures broadcast by CBS. Virtual hoardings already appear inserted digitally into the images of pitch-side advertising barriers on some American sports coverage. So the distinctions between advertising and programme content, and between 'live' images and virtually enhanced ones are eroded, in order to preserve the links between programme production funding and commercial advertising.

The advent of these techniques of digital image manipulation may challenge the expectation that television images are records of a reality that existed in front of the camera, and the expectation that programme content and advertising are identifiably different. But in their attempt to deal with this new technology and its challenge to current funding models and conceptions of what the television image is, television institutions put that technology to work in ways that preserve the economic structure of commercially funded television systems. This shows how much inertia there is in the system, and how it responds to change by looking for ways of reproducing and preserving the distribution of economic power and institutional relationships in television culture.

## Programming trends

Programmes featuring ordinary people have become commonplace on British television since the BBC series *Video Nation* (1995–2000) focused on the detail of people's everyday lives, their work and leisure, worries and attitudes. In the last 20 years, the video diary format has been introduced in Reality TV and documentary. The 'makeover' genre in programmes such as *Changing Rooms*, *Looking Good* and *Ground Force* denotes the transformation of homes, gardens, meals, clothing, hair etc. by 'experts'. The climax is a dramatic moment of revelation when the transformed house, garden or person is presented to an internal audience (such as members of a family) and the television audience. The reaction to the transformation highlights the public nature of a normally private process. In *Stars in Their Eyes*, members of the public transform themselves into imitation celebrities, seemingly transformed into public figures. These programmes combine dramatic and documentary modes, and blur the boundary between private and public experience, between ordinariness and celebrity.

When certain genres of programme are recognised as attracting large or valuable audiences, broadcasting executives are quick to imitate these popular formats for their own channel. Especially among young adult viewers, programmes featuring 'ordinary people' in competitive Reality TV formats have been successful recently. In 2001, Channel 4 launched its interactive cable and satellite channel E4, whose most successful programme was not the expensive imported first run showings of the hospital drama *ER* or the long-running sitcom *Friends* but, instead, continuous footage of *Big Brother*. In makeover shows, members of the public are advised, but importantly, they are also abused by a team of experts who guide their transformation. In some cases the objective of the transformation is explicitly public fame and recognition, as in *Pop Idol*, and the narrative progress of the serial is from ordinariness to extra-ordinariness, from alignment with the television audience to separation from the audience when the central figure becomes a star. But even in programmes where the objective is simply to become more attractive by losing weight, or to begin a satisfying relationship with a member of the opposite sex, in all cases the focus is on the often aggressive moulding of the subject. The assumption behind these programmes is that the self is a malleable and transformable object, that can be worked upon with the assistance of experts and with personal self-discipline. These conceptions of the self are likely to produce new variations on the makeover show and Reality TV formats in the future.

The search for novelty is an imperative for television producers, and the genres of television have become highly unstable (though there is also a debate to be had about how stable they ever were). Contemporary programmes and formats mix genre characteristics, dismantling and recombining genres within and across the episodes of a series and between programmes of both the present and the past. Genres rise and fall in profile and popularity as producers seek what is new. But, on the other hand, there is a strong presence of the past in television since past programmes are always being repeated, and contemporary programmes communicate about their genre and how they should be watched by referring to programmes that viewers already know. Television classics such as the sitcoms *Dad's Army* or *Porridge* return every few years and attract large audiences. On cable and satellite, channels such as UK Gold and Granada Plus have entire schedules of repeated programmes. Channels also repackage television from the past in order to sell it to a new audience, ironically repackaging past programmes for a new younger audience. Media choices and patterns of television consumption define social role. Identities constructed in this way are necessarily temporary as cultural fashions change, and the sense of the individual continuity of identity becomes more difficult to sustain. In this situation nostalgia allows viewers to remember a sense of themselves in the past, to connect the present with the past by using memories of television. The popularity of such programmes as *100 Best Kids' TV Shows*, *I Love the Seventies* etc. is a result of this. The search for the new will continue to happen at the same time as television from the past is recycled, repackaged and repeated.

## Audience trends

BARB, the television audience research body, introduced a new audience panel on 1 January 2002 covering 5,100 households selected so it is as representative as possible of the whole British television audience. About £3 billion a year in advertising revenue is traded on the basis of BARB figures. BARB's new household panel is the first entirely new panel to be recruited in more than 30 years. Opportunities to commission, continue or cancel a television programme are significantly determined by BARB research. Although new forms of programme such as docusoaps and Reality TV have been very popular with British audiences in recent years, fiction programmes have always attracted the largest audiences, and programmes in the long-established genres of the sitcom, soap opera and police drama, for example, are still the most popular according to BARB ratings. John Ellis (2000: 28), considering the changing significance of audience ratings and targeted niche audiences, explains:

> Numbers still matter in that they provide the bench-mark for the performance of the channel as a whole. But overall audience numbers can only be increased by a subtle strategy of targeting particular sections of the audience on competing channels and providing something that will appeal to or satisfy them more. . . . audiences can be specified according to age, class, gender, region, pattern of viewing and even by their degree of appreciation of the programme.

Television means different things for different age groups, and in a multichannel environment, it is often difficult for viewers to share viewing experiences with people of different generations and interests. As well as measuring audience sizes, both television industry researchers and academics are interested in the contexts in which programmes are watched, and how the situation of viewing can be accommodated by the forms that programmes take, and the effects of the multichannel, multi-receiver household. Some programmes assume, encourage and reward family viewing, whereas others are directed at age-specific or gender-specific groups or individuals. As well as trying to conform to the ways that people watch television now, programme makers and programmes contribute to changes in viewing habits.

The problem for British television now and in the immediate future is the gradual fall in average hours of weekly viewing, drifting downwards towards about 20 hours per week. Just as importantly, more affluent and younger audiences tend to watch less, because they have plenty of other things to do. Marketing programmes to valuable audiences is already very important in British television, and is likely to become more so.

# Marketing trends

The fragmentation of audiences in the multichannel environment, and the falling number of hours of viewing, means that already television institutions are trying to market programmes to audiences in new ways. As John Caldwell argued in his significantly titled book *Televisuality: Style, Crisis, and Authority in American Television* (1995), contemporary television develops fandom and supports programmes by marketing their public image. That brand image is made up of elements such as imagery and characters, and is disseminated in TV and across other media in spin-off publications or websites, for example. The purpose of creating fan audiences is to produce intense involvement in the programme and sometimes also in the related texts that are produced. In the future, the branding of programmes and the creating of loyal fan audiences will continue, largely for economic reasons. Some recent TV formats achieve this by drawing on and representing relationships that already happen outside of television, such as dating, friendship networks and gossip. Created formats in Reality TV place a lot of emphasis on getting along with others who are not part of an intimate family circle, though sometimes characters are assimilated into familial roles. Getting along and conflicts among the group involve rivalries, jealousy and competition. For the relatively youthful viewers (and the same is true of fictional drama such as *Sex and the City* or the sitcom *Coupling*), it seems likely that the participants are understood in comparison with their own friendship networks, and identification with the characters takes place on a 'horizontal' plane of substitution rather than in relation to a 'vertical' structure in which characters have relative positions in a hierarchy. More broadly, other genres such as sitcom, drama serials such as *Queer as Folk*, and teen dramas such as *Charmed* or *Daria*, all deal with questions of identity, especially for female characters. Soap operas focus on the formation of couples and have an increasing concern with younger characters, as in *Hollyoaks*. Contemporary TV targets audiences by age group or generation, and by gender, aiming to match the preoccupations of the performers or characters with the preoccupations of their intended viewers.

A notable aspect of this is the emphasis on the body, sexuality and self-development in factual and fictional programmes. A significant focus of interest in *Big Brother* was the question of whether any of the participants would have sex with each other. The nudity of participants early in the first series of *Big Brother* was a prominent part of its public image and in the second series the producers installed a hot-tub in the house, thus providing further opportunities for the display of the participants' bodies. Partly because there was little else for them to do, participants spent a lot of time exercising and sunbathing, at the same time presenting their physicality for the cameras. Sexuality is a particularly intimate aspect of social behaviour, it also corresponds to the programme's emphasis on the construction of identity, and potential conflicts over matters of desire and the formation of relationships. The enforced hothouse situation was somewhat like a scientific laboratory experiment in which sexual behaviour could be observed. The inclusion of gay, lesbian and transsexual participants in later *Big Brother* series places further strains on these individuals and their fellow participants, because of the still prevalent homophobia of British society. Streaming video on the internet, almost in real time, gave the opportunity of interaction and gossip, and the programme's pseudo-documentary realism encouraged viewers to feel they knew the contestants. The programme consisted largely of sequences of the participants interacting and conversing, with frequent close-ups reinforcing apparent intimacy with the audience. For Graeme Burton (2000: 146): 'The dominance of this way of using and experiencing television gives the illusion of physical closeness, invokes those rules of social interaction which demand attention and which create some sense of social proximity.' New TV formats attempt to draw audiences by focusing on sex and relationships, and finding ways of connecting the audience to programmes through interaction and gossip. As the quest for audiences continues in the multichannel world, this marketing trend is likely to persist.

Changes in genres including the talk show, makeover programmes and 'Reality TV' exemplify an uneasy shift from a liberal emphasis on personal empowerment and public service issues to the aggressive surveillance of individuals and a process of stigmatisation, competition and risk. It is appropriate that the participants in the first *Big Brother* were all aged between 22 and 38, and that its audience mainly comprised viewers in the 16–34 age group, of whom 75 per cent watched the programme during its first run. This is the audience most attractive to television advertisers. For this younger generation, free market individualism is apposite to their lives. Student grants have been abolished, low-paid work is common, conspicuous consumption and excessive behaviour are conventional, illegal activity such as drug use is accepted, and threats such as sexually transmitted diseases and violence against the person are more likely than for other age groups. In future, the edginess and cruelty that can be seen in some recent programmes is likely to develop further, but there may also be a backlash against it. The cosiness and predictability that can already be seen in some factual and fictional forms (such as sitcoms, gardening programmes and Sunday-night drama series) is distinctively different and may appeal especially to older viewers.

# 25 Programme making in the future

One of the main changes in the future will be to do with the acquisition and storage of pictures and sound for television. Footage will be captured and stored on professional disc, or other form of tapeless digital storage that is compatible with a fully digital environment.

The BBC is leading the way, and intends to remove videotape from the production process by 2010. A project is under way to devise a tapeless production system based around the computer desktop. Already postproduction is digital and non-linear, and file storage on computer is the way things are going.

At present television programmes, except some high-cost TV dramas, which are made on super 16 mm or 35 mm film, are recorded onto videotape. Digital formats mean the videotape no longer stores analogue frames. The tape holds only the digital data, offering extensive storage and largely error-free playback. However tape is on the way out. Even DV tape is a relatively bulky item to load and carry with you on location. Playback machines require tape transport mechanisms that can be heavy and can break down. The other drawback of tape systems is that it takes time to download the material into a non-linear editing system. Tapeless production overcomes all these drawbacks.

## News

To speed up the process, particularly for news gathering in the field, Sony and other camera makers are bringing out professional disc camcorders. These cameras, such as Sony XDCAM, integrate with the latest digital editing systems using a single sided five-inch rewriteable disc. This allows random access recording of high resolution pictures and sound, as well as metadata and associated PC project files all on the same disc. This sort of system can transform the way television programmes are made, because the same physical medium is used for acquisition, editing and archive. The disc holds 85 minutes of DVCAM broadcast-quality pictures and sound, or 45 minutes of MPEG IMX. The makers claim the blue laser technology eliminates physical wear of the disc surface, so that the disc can be used over 1,000 times, and all for about £20 per disc.

The BBC is shooting programmes such as *Top Gear* on SONY's XDCAM, a tapeless camera. The files can be loaded straight into a computer for desktop editing, and then stored in a server for later transmission and archiving. The BBC's natural history unit in Bristol used a semi-tapeless environment in the production of its blockbuster series *Planet Earth*. This system allows up to 24 users to access 500 hours of digitally stored pictures and sound. From their desktop users can browse, catalogue, storyboard and rough cut any of the material.

Modern editing systems such as Apple's Final Cut Pro or AVID mean that all the editing and sound mixing can be done on the desktop. Modern editing stations use high grade, flat, widescreen ratio monitors, and computers with a very large storage capacity.

## High definition television (HDTV)

The BBC's major factual series *Planet Earth* is being largely shot in High Definition (HD) format. Many more programmes will be made in HD as the costs of equipment continue to come down. HD cameras are becoming smaller and much more affordable. As tapeless production becomes the norm, it will be possible to transmit the superb quality offered by HD at lower cost. As with all the technical revolutions in TV, it is only when the consumer HD television set becomes affordable that the system will really become the standard.

High Definition Television is popular in the US, Canada and Japan, but is only just beginning to catch on in Europe. Most North American networks require productions to be shot in the HD widescreen format. HD has very high screen resolution of up to 1080 lines and can run at 24 frames per second (fps). This is ideal for showing movies, as standard film projection speed is 24 fps. To benefit from this high-quality transmission, programmes have to be videoed with HD cameras. Sony has led the way with its HDW–750P HDCAM. By the beginning of 2004 there were over 100 of these HD cameras in use in Europe.

## Benefits of HD

Many production companies with an eye on the US, Japanese and Canadian markets are shooting on HD. The BBC has experimented with using HD on drama serials such as *Holby City*. This can give programmes a new 'look', and move away from the perceived flatness of standard video. The BBC's outside broadcast of the Last Night of the Proms in 2003 was shot and edited in HD.

Major manufacturers Panasonic and Thomson offer HD cameras. AVID have an HD postproduction system in the form of an HD expansion module. This uses 10-bit encoding technology for collaborative HD editing.

The HD specification most often quoted is 1080-line widescreen format, which is compatible with HD broadcasters in the US. This uses progressive scanning – that is, it uses a non-interlaced signal. A desktop computer monitor works in the same way giving sharp, non-flicker, picture quality. (Domestic TV pictures are scanned with an interlaced system. This scans

*Figure 25.1* High Definition (HD) camcorder

alternate lines with one pass, and then fills in the 'missed' lines on a second pass.)

More and more programme makers worldwide are shooting and editing their shows in HD to ensure a long shelf life and global sales, even though the extra costs are considerable. The HD format has been proposed as a worldwide, universal production format. It has a resolution of 1920 × 1080, like the US 1080i format, but runs at 24 fps like film. Its key advantage is that all world TV standards – PAL, NTSC, DTV and HDTV – can be down-converted from a single digital master without the loss in quality associated with PAL/NTSC transfers. Some are suggesting this 24P format could replace film for high-quality drama, commercials and even movies. It is possible that the format could also be used for theatrical distribution via satellite – a move that would eradicate duplication expenses as well as improving security.

## Home viewing

One thing that will definitely change in the next ten years is the way we receive our television pictures. The UK government is committed to all-digital transmission before 2010, and the US government by 2007.

*Figure 25.2* Editing for an HD television production

Makers of home TV sets will soon be required to include a digital receiver in the majority of their TV sets. High Definition, already available on satellite, will become more available, as more and more programmes are made in this format. High Definition will be a marketing ploy used by pubs and clubs to attract customers to a big flat screen and surround sound. Plasma and LCD flat screens will become more attractive to consumers as the price comes down. The large box taking up floor space in the sitting room will give way to the large moving picture on the wall.

Television pictures are already available on your computer, but with only limited take-up. The computer will be used more as a source of broadcast television as more channels can be streamed. Already millions listen to radio stations from around the world on their computer. There will be increased use of the Digital Video Recorder. This already exists in various guises such as TiVo, and a similar version available from BSkyB. A whole 13-week series of the successor to *Friends* can be automatically recorded onto a high-capacity hard disc. It can record programmes without recording commercials – a very big worry for the TV industry. It can also record High Definition programmes if you have an HD receiver and television set to view them on.

## Home entertainment

The biggest revolution in home video distribution was the introduction of DVD in 1997. It is now possible to pick up a DVD player for around £20 at your local supermarket. The discs offer movie extras, high-quality pictures and sound and are slimmer and easier to store than VHS videos. In spite of on-demand films from cable and satellite television companies, the home rental market is still buoyant. DVDs take up less space on the shelves so a greater selection can be offered. VHS video is all but dead, though many homes still record television programmes on VHS. The cost of DVD recordable machines has come down, but they are not yet cheap enough for most people to throw out their VHS recorders. Recording TV programmes on hard disc with a Sky or TiVo system is attractive to TV buffs but still too expensive for most subscribers.

# DVD and beyond

In North America over 3 billion DVD discs have been distributed. You might think that this format is so successful that it is here to stay, but there is a continual quest for more digital storage. The next technical advance will be in the capturing of High Definition images. Big-name live concerts are already recorded in the HD format, which also has greatly enhanced high-specification sound reproduction.

The entertainment industry is actively seeking a new improved DVD format that will store all programmes made in High Definition format. These require more storage space and standard DVD discs cannot cope. A typical DVD disc stores 8.5 gigabytes (GB) of digital data on one side. New formats are being developed that can store a minimum of 15 GB of information, and some analysts predict the possibility of 150 GB on one disc. Rival systems are competing for this new market. Sony, JVC and Philips are involved with the Blu-ray Disc. In Japan, Blu-ray recorders from Sony are already available. The rival system is known as HD-DVD and comes from Toshiba and NEC. Although not yet in the marketplace, HD-DVD has been endorsed by Microsoft who have agreed to make it compatible with its next-generation operating system. Both formats will be backwards compatible in that they will play current DVDs.

The manufacturers are always looking for something new. The Japanese company Optware Corporation say they have developed a holographic recording disc with 200 times the storage capacity of a conventional DVD. This could make viewing horror films a whole new experience.

# Cinema

Film distribution companies are experimenting with projecting digital images in the cinema. They would like to do away with the expensive distribution system of moving large spools of 35 mm film around the country. They would like to beam their encoded films to a satellite that could be accessed by any individual cinema around the world. This would be most cost effective and would reduce the incidence of film theft and piracy that cost the film industry over 2 billion dollars a year.

Each year more feature films are shot digitally with cameras capable of significantly higher quality images than HD television pictures. Digital film production is popular with some directors and producers as it means that all the digital effects can be fully integrated with the live action on one technical platform. *Star Wars Episode II: Attack of the Clones*, released in 2002, was the first all-digital feature film shot without a single roll of film. A digitally produced, or digitally converted, film can be distributed to cinemas via satellite, physical media, or fibre optic cable networks. The digital film is stored by a computer server that is linked to a digital projector. In 2004 over 200 cinemas worldwide had installed digital projectors based on DLP Cinema™ technology. Research suggests that cinema audiences are happy with the image quality. Cinema projection and distribution will complete the digital loop begun in television production.

If the digital revolution does remove celluloid from the cinema it opens up the possibility that anyone could hire a digital cinema projection facility to show their own digitally shot home videos. Television already broadcasts a great deal of digital video shot by non-professionals. This is not just footage in those programmes of compilations of supposedly humorous disaster clips from home movies, but in all types of access programmes, and reality shows. Participants in access television want to make their own contributions shot without the intrusion of a camera crew. Digital video makes this easy. Soon individuals and groups may want to edit, schedule and distribute their own contributions.

## Television postproduction

The postproduction industry in the UK is large and highly regarded worldwide. It is worth £1.39 billion to the UK economy. Over 150 companies operate in this sector and work in international filmmaking as well as television production, satellite broadcasting, the internet, and broadband. London companies such as The Mill, Smoke and Mirrors and Framestore CFC also have overseas offices and offer the very latest technology. Mike Luckwell, Chairman of the trade association UK Post, sees a rosy future for postproduction in the UK: 'The producer's priorities are the creativity, reputation, ability, reliability and cost of the post and digital effects company.' He believes that the excellent reputation of UK companies means they are well placed to exploit overseas markets, especially the US which is the world's biggest film and broadcast product consumer.

Television producers, film companies and advertising agencies are the main clients of postproduction facility houses. Television producers need to be well versed in the evolving technology of postproduction.

Compressed video files can be sent for a client's approval as email video attachments via specialist services such as Beam TV and Sohonet, or BT Broadcast Services.

Digital effects and computer-generated imaging (CGI) can revolutionise your production, but be warned that all the high-end technology also comes at a high-end price.

# Further reading

Barker, C., *Global Television: An Introduction* (Oxford: Blackwell, 1997).

Bignell, J. and S. Lacey, 'Afterword', in J. Bignell and S. Lacey (eds), *Popular Television Drama: Critical Perspectives* (Manchester: Manchester University Press, 2005).

Boyd-Barrett, O. and T. Rantanen, *The Globalization of News* (London: Sage, 1998).

Bruzzi, S., *The New Documentary: A Critical Introduction* (London: Routledge, 2000).

Burton, G., *Talking Television: An Introduction to the Study of Television* (London: Arnold, 2000).

Caldwell, J., *Televisuality: Style, Crisis and Authority in American Television* (New Brunswick: Rutgers University Press, 1995).

Dovey, J., *Freakshow* (Cambridge: Polity, 2000).

Ellis, J., 'Scheduling: The Last Creative Act in Television', *Media, Culture & Society* 22: 1 (2002), pp. 25–38.

Ellis, J. *Seeing Things: Television in an Age of Uncertainty* (London: I. B. Tauris 2000).

Liebes, T. and E. Katz, *The Export of Meaning: Cross-Cultural Readings of 'Dallas'* (New York: Oxford University Press, 1990).

Lyotard, J.-F., *The Postmodern Condition: A Report on Knowledge* (Manchester: Manchester University Press, 1979).

Mackay, H. and T. O'Sullivan (eds), *The Media Reader: Continuity and Transformation* (London: Sage, 1999).

Morris, M., 'Feminism, Reading, Postmodernism', in T. Docherty (ed.), *Postmodernism: A Reader* (Hemel Hempstead: Harvester Wheatsheaf, 1993), pp. 368–89.

Mosely, R., 'Makeover Takover on British Television', *Screen* 41: 3 (2000), pp. 299–314.

Orlebar, J., *Digital Television Production* (London: Arnold, 2002).

Sinclair, J., E. Jacka and S. Cunningham, 'New Patterns in Global Television', in P. Marris and S. Thornham (eds), *The Media Reader* (Edinburgh: Edinburgh University Press, 1999), pp. 170–90.

Tincknell, E. and P. Raghuram, '*Big Brother*: Reconfiguring the "Active" Audience of Cultural Studies?', in S. Holmes and D. Jermyn (eds), *Understanding Reality Television* (London: Routledge, 2004), pp. 252–69.

Tunstall, J. (ed.), *Media Occupations and Professions: A Reader* (Oxford: Oxford University Press, 2001).

Webster, F., *Theories of the Information Society* (London: Routledge, 1995).

# Glossary of key terms

...........................................................................................................

**180 degree rule** – the convention that cameras are positioned only on one side of an imaginary line connecting two performers in a scene. This produces a coherent sense of space for the viewer, and is also known as 'not crossing the line'.

**active audience** – television audiences regarded not as passive consumers of meanings, but as negotiating meanings for themselves that are often resistant to those meanings that are intended or that are discovered by close analysis.

**actuality footage** – television pictures representing an event that was shot live. The term usually refers to pictures of news events.

**adaptation** – transferring a novel, theatre play, poem etc. from its original medium into another medium such as television.

**aesthetic** – a specific artistic form. Aesthetics means the study of art and beauty.

**affiliates** – local television stations (normally in the US) that have made agreements (affiliations) with a network to broadcast programmes offered by that network rather than another.

**AFM** – assistant floor manager. In a television studio the AFM works to the floor manager and looks after the actors, checks the props and helps co-ordinate studio production. He or she wears headphones to hear talkback with the studio Gallery.

**ambient noise** – the background sound present at any location recording such as the rumble of traffic or air conditioning.

**analogue** – representation in electrical terms of a physical quantity. Analogue broadcasting signals are in waves of varying frequency which require greater space or 'bandwidth' than digital signals, and do not allow interactive response from viewers.

**animation** – a style of filming that creates movement from still images. Drawings, computerised images or models are filmed or videoed frame by frame. Modern animation is computer-generated animation (CGA) where 3D images are created on computer, and the animation process is digitised.

**animatronics** – electronically and mechanically controlled puppets, models and prosthetics.

**Annan Report** – the report of the government committee (1977) chaired by Lord Annan whose recommendations included the retention of the BBC's licence fee and the setting up of a fourth television channel.

**anthology** – a series of separate unconnected programmes broadcast under a shared title.

**anthropology** – the study of humankind, including the evolution of humans and the different kinds of human society existing in different times and places.

**aperture** – controls the amount of light that enters a camera by enlarging or reducing the hole formed by the iris surrounding the lens. This alters the exposure and also controls the depth of field. A large 'opened up' aperture such as f-2 allows more light through the lens but reduces the depth of field. A small 'stopped down' aperture such as f-16 admits less light but gives an increased depth of field.

**archive** – film, video or sound recording that is stored in a film archive or library.

**art video** – the use of video technology in artistic work intended for gallery exhibition.

**aspect ratio** – the ratio of width to height in a television picture. The standard TV aspect ratio is 4:3, but modern widescreen broadcasting has an aspect ratio of 16:9. All new UK terrestrial programmes are shot in 16:9.

**Aston** – the industry standard text and graphics generator usually found in a TV studio or in a postproduction facility.

**audience share** – the percentage of viewers estimated to have watched one channel as opposed to another channel broadcasting at the same time.

**authorship** – the question of who an author is, the role of the author as creator, and the significance of the author's input into the material being studied.

**Autocue** – the brand name and colloquial term for prompting equipment that uses mirrors to project a presenter's script onto a glass screen in front of a TV camera lens. This allows the presenter to read the script while looking straight at the camera.

**avant-garde** – work aiming to challenge the norms and conventions of its medium, and the group of people making such work.

**AVID** – the brand name of a broadcast-standard computer video editing system, widely used in the UK and US.

**back lighting** – lighting the subject of a shot from behind, to provide an impression of depth by separating the subject from the background.

**balance** – the requirement in television news and current affairs to present both sides of an argument or issue.

**BARB (Broadcasters Audience Research Bureau)** – the independent body that gathers and reports viewing statistics on behalf of UK television institutions.

**barn doors** – moveable side flaps fitted to a portable or studio TV lamp, used to restrict the amount of light that spills into unwanted areas.

**BCU** – big close-up, typically showing only a person's face.

**Betacam SP** – a broadcast-quality analogue videotape format developed by Sony.

**binary opposition** – two contrasting terms, ideas or concepts, such as inside/outside, masculine/feminine, or culture/nature.

**blimp** – a sound-proof cover for a camera.

**blonde** – a 2,000 watt, variable-beam, portable lamp used in television and film, so called because of the yellow colour of the lamp's head or metal casing.

**blooper** – a mistake by a performer in a programme, or a technical error. The term often refers to humorous mistakes.

**bluescreen** – blue sheet or screen that allows an image or series of images to be overlaid on part of another image, also known as Chromakey. An actor or presenter is videoed against a blue background in a studio. The blue is used as an electronic key to be replaced by other relevant moving images including computer-generated images (CGI).

**boom** – a long adjustable telescopic pole, or arm, that holds a microphone or camera. It can be a portable fishpole boom for a microphone, or a large boom with adjustable extensions mounted on a moveable base and usually found in a TV studio.

**bourgeoisie** – the middle class, who are owners of property and businesses.

**brand recognition** – the ability of audiences to recognise the distinctive identity of a product, service or institution and the values and meanings associated with it.

**broadband** – a fast internet connection with permanent access, suitable for video streaming, good-quality video downloads on demand, and other multimedia functions.

*Broadcast* **magazine** – the leading weekly trade magazine for the UK broadcasting industry, www.broadcastnow.co.uk.

**broadcasting** – the transmission of signals from a central source, so that signals can be received by dispersed receivers over a large geographical area.

**Broadcasting Standards Commission (BSC)** – the regulatory body set up by government to monitor the standards of BBC broadcasting services, superseded by Ofcom.

**budget** – the money allocated to the making of a particular programme or series of programmes, controlled by the producer.

**cable television** – originally called Community Antenna Television (CATV), the transmission of television signals along cables in the ground.

**camcorder** – a video camera that also records video either digitally onto disc, tape or hard disc, or onto analogue video tape.

**capitalism** – the organisation of an economy around the private owner-ship of accumulated wealth, involving the exploitation of labour to produce profit that creates such wealth.

**CCD** – charge coupled device. A rectangular grid of detectors that are able to sense light, and are the picture sensing elements in a digital camera. The light arrives through the lens onto the CCDs. The millions of tiny pixels that make up the CCD convert this light into electrons which are then measured and converted to a digital value.

**CEEFAX** – the text-based information service provided by BBC and carried by analogue television signals.

**censorship** – the omission of sensitive, prohibited or disturbing material at any stage in the production process from the initial idea to its trans-mission.

**churn rate** – a ratio setting the numbers of new subscribers to a paid-for television service against the number of subscribers cancelling their subscription.

**class** – a section of society defined by their relationship to economic activity, whether as workers (the working class) or possessors of economic power (the bourgeoisie), for example.

**classic serial** – the dramatisation in serial form of literature written in the past, most often in the 19th and early 20th centuries, where the literary source already has high cultural status.

**closed-circuit television** – a small-scale television system where the images and sound are not intended for broadcast, for example a network of security cameras.

**close-up** – a camera shot where the frame is filled by the face and neck of a person, showing just the top of the shoulder. Close-ups may also show details of an object or place.

**CNN** – Cable News Network, the first international satellite news channel, operating from the US.

**code** – in semiotics, a system or set of rules that shapes how signs can be used, and therefore how meanings can be made and understood.

**commercial television** – television funded by the sale of advertising time or sponsorship of programmes.

**commissioning** – the process by which an idea for a programme is selected to go into production.

**committed** – a term used in the study of the politics of culture, implying that a person or a text has a commitment to positive and progressive social change.

**commodity** – a raw material or product whose economic value is established by market price rather than the intrinsic qualities or usefulness of the material or product itself.

**computer-generated animation/imaging (CGA/CGI)** – the creation of images by programming computers with mathematical equations that can generate realistic pictures mimicking the appearance, movement and proportions of actual objects or people.

**connotations** – the term used in semiotic analysis for the meanings that are associated with a particular sign or combination of signs.

**consensus** – a shared and accepted opinion or attitude among a certain group of people.

**conventions** – the frameworks and procedures used to make or interpret texts.

**convergence** – the process whereby previously separate media technologies merge together. For example, computers can now send faxes, show DVD films, and play music.

**copyright** – the legal right of ownership over written, visual or aural material, including the prohibition on copying this material without permission from its owner.

**couch potatoes** – a derogatory term for television viewers supposedly sitting motionless at home watching television passively and indiscriminately.

**crane** – counterweighted long metal arm with a flexible camera mounting that can raise or lower a camera to show high shots of the action.

**crew** – skilled technical personnel who operate equipment on a television set. This colloquially refers to the camera crew on location.

**cue** – a signal to an actor or presenter to start talking, or to begin the action specified in the script.

**cultural imperialism** – the critical argument that powerful nations and regions (especially those of the Western world) dominate less developed nations and regions by exporting values and ideologies to them.

**cultural studies** – the academic discipline devoted to studying culture, involving work on texts, institutions, audiences, and economic contexts.

**culture** – the shared attitudes, ways of life and assumptions of a group of people.

**cut** – the moment at which one camera shot ceases and another begins, where no transitional visual effect (such as a fade or a dissolve) is used.

**cutaway** – in fictional dialogue or interviews, shots that do not include people speaking. Cutaways often consist of details of the setting or of interviewees (such as hands).

**cyclorama** – a large backing cloth or curtain that covers the entire back wall in a TV studio and can be pulled on rails to surround and give a background to the set.

**DA Notice** – an instruction to the media not to broadcast material that could undermine national security.

**demography** – the study of population, and the groupings of people (demographic groups) within the whole population.

**denotation** – in semiotics, the function of signs to portray or refer to something in the real world.

**deregulation** – the removal of legal restrictions or guidelines that regulate the economics of the television industry or the standards that programmes must adhere to.

**diegesis** – the distinction between showing (mimesis) and telling (diegesis) suggests the way a story may be told in images. Diegetic sound is sound material that directly relates to the scene and is recorded, or appears to be recorded, at the same time as the pictures.

**digital television** – television pictures and sound encoded into the ones and zeros of electronic data. Digital signals can also be sent back down cables by viewers, enabling interaction with television programmes.

**digitise** – to convert an analogue electronic signal into a digital form as a series of electronic impulses that can be saved in a computer. The term is used in digital video editing.

**director** – the person responsible for the creative process of turning a script or idea into a finished programme, by working with a technical crew, performers and an editor.

**discourse** – a particular use of language for a certain purpose in a certain context (like academic discourse, or poetic discourse), and similarly in television, a particular usage of television's audio-visual 'language' (news programme discourse, or nature documentary discourse, for instance).

**dissolve** – the gradual merging and replacing of one shot with another, also called a mix.

**documentary** – a form aiming to record actual events, often with an explanatory purpose or to analyse and debate an issue.

**docusoap** – a television form combining documentary's depiction of non-actors in ordinary situations with soap opera's continuing narratives about selected characters.

**dolly** – a wheeled camera platform. A 'dolly shot' is a camera shot where the camera is moved forward or back using this platform.

**drama-documentary** – a television form combining dramatised story-telling with the 'objective' informational techniques of documentary. Abbreviated as 'drama-doc' or 'docudrama'.

**dry run** – a complete run-through of a television show before transmission to iron out any problems.

**dubbing** – replacing the original speech in a programme, advertisement etc. with speech added later, often to translate speech in a foreign language.

**dumbing-down** – the notion that television has reduced in quality as compared to an earlier period, showing programmes that are more 'dumb' or stupid and addressing its audience as if they were stupid.

**duration** – the exact length in minutes and seconds of a television programme.

**DV** – Digital Video. A video recording format widely used in television location production, and in domestic camcorders.

**DVD** – Digital Versatile Disc. A 12 cm disc that stores high-quality digital video and audio for playback and recording, and is rapidly superseding VHS as the preferred domestic video format.

**DVE** – Digital Video Effects. Electronic equipment typically located in a TV studio gallery for creating video effects such as wipes and bluescreen (Chromakey).

**ing** – the process of selecting and placing together different images and sounds to tell a factual or fictional story for television. Nearly all video editing for television is now non-linear, and is done on a computer using a proprietary video editing system such as AVID or Final Cut Pro.

**effects** – measurable outcomes produced by watching television, such as becoming more violent or adopting a certain opinion.

**electronic news gathering (ENG)** – the use of lightweight cameras and digital technology, such as portable satellite transmission dishes, to record and transmit news pictures and sound.

**embargo** – a date before which a certain news item, or defined commercial information, cannot be broadcast or published in the press.

**ethnicity** – membership of a group with a specific identity based on a sense of belonging, such as British Asian, or Italian-American for example.

**ethnography** – the detailed study of how people live, conducted by observing behaviour and talking to selected individuals about their attitudes and activities.

**exposure** – the amount of light that enters the lens of a camera through the aperture.

**exterior** – this term denotes that the location of a scene in a television programme is outside, and not inside a building or studio.

**eyeline** – the direction in which the eyes of an actor or contributor are looking as seen by the camera. It is important that the eyelines of two characters talking to each other are matched, otherwise they will not appear to be talking to each other but to someone else outside the frame.

**fade** – a fade-out is the gradual darkening of the shot until the image disappears leaving a blank screen. A fade-in is where the shot emerges from a black screen.

**fan culture** – the activities of groups of fans, as distinct from 'ordinary' viewers.

**Federal Communications Commission (FCC)** – the government body in the US that regulates the operations and output of television companies and other broadcasters.

**feminine** – having characteristics associated with the cultural role of women and not men.

**feminism** – the political and theoretical thinking which, in different ways, considers the roles of women and femininity in society and culture, often with the aim of critiquing current roles and changing them for the better.

**final cut** or **fine cut** – the final edited version of a programme that is delivered to the television institution for broadcast.

**flashback** – a television sequence marked as representing events that happened in a time previous to the programme's present.

**flow** – the ways that programmes, advertisements etc. follow one another in an unbroken sequence across the day or part of the day, and the experience of watching the sequence of programmes, advertisements, trailers etc.

**fly-on-the-wall** – a documentary form where the subject is observed without the programme-maker's intervention.

**focal length** – the distance, in millimetres, that a camera lens takes to focus the parallel rays of light from a subject.

**focus groups** – small groups of selected people representing larger social groupings, such as people of a certain age group, gender or economic status, who take part in discussions about a topic chosen for investigation.

**foldback** – sound played through a speaker or headphones on the TV studio floor that can be heard by performers, but does not form part of the final sound mix.

**format** – the blueprint for a programme, including its setting, main characters, genre, form and main themes.

**found footage** – television or film sequences 'found' in previously made programmes or films, and which can be incorporated unchanged into the programme being made.

**frame** – a rectangular image that is the basic unit in a film or video sequence. In video, a frame is a complete, scanned video image. The PAL video system used in the UK runs at 25 frames per second (fps).

**franchise** – the right to broadcast in one of the terrestrial ITV regions for a set number of years, secured by paying a fee to government.

**Frankfurt School** – a group of theorists, notably Theodor Adorno and Max Horkheimer, centred in Germany in the mid-twentieth century who worked on theories of contemporary culture from a Marxist perspective.

**freelance** – self-employed worker of any category in the media industry.

**free market** – a television marketplace where factors such as quotas and regulations do not restrict the free operation of economic 'laws' of supply and demand.

**free-to-air** – television programming for which viewers make no direct payment.

**f-stop** – the measurement of the size of a camera lens aperture. The smaller the stop number the larger the aperture, e.g. f-2 lets in more light than f-11.

**gallery** – the control room in a television studio where the studio director, vision mixer, and the sound and video supervisors observe the shooting of a programme, and control the activities of camera operators, sound technicians, performers and other personnel.

**gatekeepers** – the critical term used for the people and institutions (such as television commissioning producers, or regulatory bodies) who control access to television broadcasting.

**gender** – the social and cultural division of people into masculine or feminine individuals. This is different from sex, which refers to the biological difference between male and female bodies.

**genre** – a kind or type of programme. Programmes of the same genre have shared characteristics.

**globalisation** – the process whereby ownership of television institutions in different nations and regions is concentrated in the hands of international corporations, and whereby programmes and formats are traded between institutions around the world.

**graphics** – images and words created by drawing, lettering, or by computer, and used in a television programme.

**grip** – the member of the camera crew who sets up the camera dolly, controls it, and lays track for it to run on.

**gun mic** – a long, thin unidirectional microphone often seen encased in a hairy wind shield and used by a news film crew.

**HDTV** – High Definition Television. Widescreen television with a very high resolution of at least 720 progressive vertical lines and 1280 horizontal lines, roughly twice as many lines as conventional television and thus producing a more detailed image.

**hegemony** – a term deriving from Marxist theories of society, meaning a situation where different social classes or groups are persuaded to consent to a political regime that may be contrary to their benefit.

**hertz (Hz)** – the units for measuring the electrical frequency of radio or sound waves.

**high angle shot** – a shot where the camera is placed high above the eyeline of the action.

**HMI** – a large film or television light that is designed for shooting in daylight conditions.

**hype** – publicity and public relations effort aiming to raise interest in a television programme or an aspect of one.

**iconic sign** – in semiotics, a sign that resembles its referent. Photographs, for example, contain iconic signs resembling the objects they represent.

**identification** – a term deriving from psychoanalytic theories of cinema, which describes the viewer's conscious or unconscious wish to take the place of someone or something in a television text.

**idents** – the symbols representing production companies, television channels etc., often comprising graphics or animations.

**ideology** – the set of beliefs, attitudes and assumptions arising from the economic and class divisions in a culture, underlying the ways of life accepted as normal in that culture.

**IEEE 1394** – also known as Firewire. A special connecting cable and plug that creates a fast digital link between a camera or other accessory, and a computer. It is often used in video editing.

**independent production companies** – businesses making television programmes that can be sold to television networks that transmit and distribute them.

**Independent Television Authority (ITA)** – the first official body set up to regulate commercial television in Britain.

**Independent Television Commission (ITC)** – the regulatory body set up by government to monitor the standards of commercial ITV broadcasting companies, superseded by Ofcom.

**indexical sign** – in semiotics, a sign that is the result of what it signifies, in the way that smoke is the result of fire.

**information society** – a contemporary highly developed culture (especially Western culture) where the production and exchange of information is more significant than conventional industrial production.

**interactive** – offering the opportunity for viewers to respond to what is broadcast, by sending signals back to the broadcaster (along a cable or phone line, for example).

**interior** – an indication that the location of a scene is inside a building or other interior space.

**insert tape** – a video tape containing all the pre-recorded items that will be inserted into a television programme.

**intertextuality** – how one text draws on the meanings of another by referring to it, by allusion, quotation or parody, for example.

**iris** – the iris in a camera is made of overlapping metal flaps and controls the aperture or opening through which the light reaches the CCD or unexposed film.

**jump cut** – a cut in continuous action from one shot to another shot of the same shot size, disturbing the visual continuity of the scene.

**key light** – the main light source in any television lighting set up that provides the 'key' to the scene's appearance.

**libel** – the legal term for broadcasting a statement that is an unfair, untrue, or an unreasonable defamation of a person's character.

**licence fee** – an annual payment by all UK owners of television sets, which is the main source of income for the BBC.

**lighting cameraman** – the leading male or female cameraperson in a television location production, who is responsible for the framing and lighting of each scene so that it conforms to the director's intention.

**lip sync** – the synchronisation of an actor's lip movements so that speech recorded at an earlier time will match a shot of the speaker's mouth moving.

**location** – any place in which television images are shot, except inside a television studio.

**long shot (LS)** – a shot showing the full length of a person in a wide field of vision including the setting and background.

**long take** – an imprecise term denoting a longer than usual uninterrupted camera shot.

**low angle shot** – a shot where the camera is placed below the eyeline looking up at the subject, often giving the impression of the subject's power.

**magazine programme** – a television programme made up of a number of different items and stories, often in genres such as travel, business or sport.

**market research** – the collection of information about consumers and their preferences, used to identify products that can be sold to consumers likely to buy them.

**Marxism** – the political and economic theories associated with the German nineteenth-century theorist Karl Marx, who described and critiqued capitalist societies and proposed Communism as a revolutionary alternative.

**masculine** – having characteristics associated with the cultural role of men and not women.

**master shot** – a wide shot in a drama production that includes all the main action in a scene.

**media imperialism** – the critical argument that powerful nations and cultures (especially the US) exert control over other nations and cultures through the media products they export to them.

**media literacy** – the skills and competence that viewers learn in order to easily understand the audio-visual 'languages' of media texts.

**Mediawatch UK** – (formerly the National Viewers And Listeners Association). An organisation devoted to monitoring the activities of British broadcasters, with a special interest in upholding standards of taste and decency. www.mediawatchuk.org.

**medium close-up (MCU)** – a camera shot much used in television studio interviews and chat shows. Wider than a close-up, it includes the head and shoulders of the subject with the bottom of the frame along the line of the top pocket on a man's jacket.

**medium shot (MS)** – a shot of the top half of a person with the bottom of the frame running along the waist. Also called a mid shot.

**melodrama** – a form of drama characterised by exaggerated performance, a focus on reversals of fortune and extreme emotional reactions to events.

**merchandising** – the sale of products associated with a television programme, such as toys, books or clothing.

**metaphor** – the carrying-over from something of some of its meanings onto another thing of an apparently different kind. For example, a television narrative about life aboard ship could be a metaphor for British social life (the ship as metaphor for society).

**metonymy** – the substitution of one thing for another, either because one is part of the other or one is connected with the other. For example, 'the Crown' can be a metonym for the British state.

**microwave link** – the transmission across large distances of digital signals carried by high frequency microwaves, to ground stations or to satellites.

**mise-en-scène** – literally meaning 'putting on stage', all the elements of a shot or sequence that contribute to its meanings, such as set design, costume, lighting and camera position.

**mix** – a gradual transition from one shot to another, where the first shot gradually dissolves into the incoming shot. The sound mix of a television programme is where all the sounds in a scene, including the dialogue, music and sound effects, are mixed together.

**mixer** – this usually refers to audio equipment that combines different sound sources, either a portable unit or in a sound suite.

**modality** – the fit between a fictional representation and the conventional understanding of reality. High modality describes a close fit, and weak modality a distant one.

**monitor** – a high-quality television set used to view or monitor television pictures.

**monopoly** – control over the provision of a service or product by one institution or business.

**motivation/motivated** – a camera movement or cut is described as motivated when it follows an action, or is prompted by an event within the scene. A camera movement or a cut that follows no logic is described as unmotivated.

**multi-accentuality** – the situation where meanings are able to be read in different ways by different groups of viewers because a text offers multiple meanings at the same time.

**multiplex** – agencies that carry many disparate digital television and radio channels, using less bandwidth than conventional terrestrial television transmissions.

**music copyright** – any broadcasting of published music, including all commercial CDs, requires copyright clearance and the payment of royalties to royalty collection societies such as MCPS and PRS.

**mute** – means silent, and refers to when a video or film recording is made with no diegetic sound.

**name super** – the conventional way of naming a contributor to a television programme is the superimposition of the name over the person's image in the lower third of the screen. Also known as a caption.

**narration** – the process of telling a story through image and sound. Narration can also refer to the spoken text accompanying television images.

**narrative** – an ordered sequence of images and sound that tells a fictional or factual story.

**natural break** – a vague term meaning a point at which a programme can be interrupted without causing undue disruption to it.

**naturalism** – originally having a very specific meaning in literature and drama, this term is now used more loosely to denote television fiction that adopts realistic conventions of character portrayal, linear cause and effect narrative, and a consistent and recognisable fictional world.

**negotiated reading** – a viewer interpretation of a television text where the viewer understands meaning in relation to his or her own knowledge and experience, rather than simply accepting the meaning proposed by the text.

**network** – a television institution that transmits programmes through local or regional broadcasting stations that are owned by or affiliated to that institution.

**news agency** – a media institution that gathers news reports and distributes them to its customers (who include television news broadcasters).

**news value** – the degree of significance attributed to a news story, where items with high news value are deemed most significant to the audience.

**Nicam** – (Near Instantaneous Companded Audio Complex). The standard for UK and European stereo television broadcasts that provides high-quality digital stereo sound for domestic viewers.

**niche audiences** – particular groups of viewers defined by age group, gender or economic status, for example, who may be the target audience for a programme.

**noddy shot** – in television interviews, shots of the interviewer reacting silently (often by nodding) to the interviewee's responses to questions.

**non-linear editing** – video or film editing where the shots are assembled and reassembled in any order. Video editing is now done on a computer where all the images and audio are digitised and assembled in a non-linear way.

**non-sync** – a recording made on film or video with no synchronised sound. This is different from 'out of sync', which means that the sound is not correctly synchronised with the picture.

**NTSC** – (National Television Standards Committee). The standard colour television system used in the US, Japan and some South American countries.

**OB** – *see* outside broadcast.

**observational documentary** – a documentary form in which the programme maker aims to observe neutrally what would have happened even if he or she had not been present.

**Ofcom** – the independent regulator and competition authority for the UK communications industries. It is responsible for television, radio, telecommunications and wireless communications services. www.ofcom.org.uk.

**off-line editing** – the first stage of editing a completed programme, where the sequence of shots, sounds and music are established, using inexpensive copies of the original high-quality pictures and sound. Largely replaced by non-linear computer editing.

**off mic** – when a recorded sound is audible but muffled or obscure it is said to be off mic. Often this is because the sound source is not close enough to the microphone.

**online editing** – the final stage of editing a completed programme, where effects are added and a high-quality version of the programme is produced.

**ORACLE** – the text-based information service provided by ITV and carried by analogue television signals.

**outside broadcast** – the television transmission of outdoor events such as sport or ceremonial occasions, using equipment set up in advance for the purpose. Abbreviated as OB.

**outsourcing** – obtaining services from an independent business rather than from within a television institution, usually as a means of cutting costs.

**out-take** – a shot or sequence that was omitted from a finished programme, because of a mistake during production or an artistic decision.

**overlay** – the combining of two picture sources to make one composite image, usually through a TV gallery DVE console.

**PACT** – Producers' Alliance for Cinema & Television. The trade association that represents the interests of independent television and film producers. www.pact.co.uk.

**PAL** – Phase Alternate Line transmission of television pictures, a German technical standard introduced in the 1960s enabling improved picture quality and colour pictures.

**pan** – a shot where the camera, mounted on a tripod or dolly, is moved in a horizontal arc from left to right, or right to left. The term derives from the word 'panorama', suggesting the wide visual field that a pan can reveal.

**pan-and-scan** – capturing a section of an image and enlarging it to fill the TV frame, a technique used to fit wide film images into the square TV screen.

**pantograph** – a moveable arm with a lamp attached, which is part of a TV studio lighting rig enabling the lamp to be hoisted up or down.

**pastiche** – the imitation of forms or conventions in another text. The term can convey a negative view that the imitation is less effective or valuable than the original.

**patriarchy** – a social system in which power is held by men rather than women, and masculine values dominate.

**pay-per-view** – specific television programmes (such as sports events, or films) offered to subscribers on payment of a fixed one-off fee.

**pedestal** – a steady camera mounting on wheels, for a heavy studio television camera. The camera can be raised or lowered on the pedestal, as well as allowing camera movement in all directions.

**people meter** – a device resembling a TV remote control, used in sample households to monitor what viewers watch. Viewers record which channels they watch for how long.

**period drama** – television fiction set in the past, most often the nineteenth or early twentieth centuries.

**permits** – special permission forms, supplied by the production company or the broadcaster, that have to be signed by anyone offering services or locations for a television production.

**personalities** – people appearing on television who are recognised by audiences as celebrities with a media image and public status beyond the role they play in a particular programme.

**picture editor** – another name for a video editor, often working in news.

**Pilkington Report** – the report of a government committee chaired by Lord Pilkington (1960) whose recommendations included the setting up of a second BBC television channel.

**pitch** – a very short written or spoken outline for a programme, perhaps only a few sentences, often used to persuade a commissioning producer to commission the programme.

**pixel** – the grid of very small coloured electronic squares that create the picture on a TV screen or computer monitor. Pixels are the light sensing elements of a CCD in a digital camera.

**point of view shot** – a camera shot where the camera is placed in, or close to, the position from where a previously seen character might look.

**polysemia** – the quality of having multiple meanings at the same time. Texts like this are described as 'polysemic'.

**pool system** – in journalism, grouping journalists together to share information so that not all of them need to be present at a news event.

**popular culture** – the texts created by ordinary people (as opposed to an elite group) or created for them, and the ways these are used.

**postmodernism** – the most recent phase of capitalist culture, the aesthetic forms and styles associated with it, and the theoretical approaches developed to understand it.

**postproduction** – the work done on a programme after the video recording or filming has taken place, leading to the completion of the production.

**preferred reading** – an interpretation of a text that seems to be the one most encouraged by the text, the 'correct' interpretation.

**preproduction** – the work done on a television programme before any video recording or filming takes place, especially planning and research.

**prime-time** – the part of a day's television schedule when the greatest number of viewers may be watching, normally the mid-evening period.

**private sphere** – the domestic world of the home, family and personal life.

**privatisation** – the policy of placing industries or institutions in the hands of privately owned businesses, rather than state ownership.

**producer** – the person working for a television institution, or independent production company, who is responsible for the budget, planning and making of a television programme or series of programmes.

**production values** – the level of investment in a television production, such as the amount spent on costumes, props, effects and sets.

**progressive** – encouraging positive change or progress, usually implying progress towards fairer and more equal ways of organising society.

**PSC** – Portable Single Camera describes a camera operator working in the field with a camcorder, usually for acquisition of news material.

**psychoanalysis** – the study of human mental life, including not only conscious thoughts, wishes and fears but also unconscious ones. Psychoanalysis is an analytical and theoretical set of ideas as well as a therapeutic treatment.

**PTC** – (piece to camera) a television presenter on location looking straight into the camera reading autocue, or delivering a memorised script.

**public service broadcasting** – in television, the provision of a mix of programmes that inform, educate and entertain in ways that encourage the betterment of audiences and society in general.

**public sphere** – the world of politics, economic affairs and national and international events, as opposed to the 'private sphere' of domestic life.

**public television** – television funded by government or by private supporters, rather than solely by advertising.

**quality** – in television, kinds of programme that are perceived as more expensively produced and, especially, more culturally worthwhile than other programmes.

**quota** – a proportion of television programming, such as a proportion of programmes made by a particular nation rather than imported from abroad.

**ratings** – the number of viewers estimated to have watched certain programmes, as compared to the numbers watching other programmes.

**realism** – the aim for representations to reproduce reality faithfully, and the ways this is done.

**reality TV** – a vague term for programmes where the unscripted behaviour of 'ordinary people' is the focus of interest, where documentary observation is often combined with elements of the game show, makeover or talent contest.

**recce** – to recce a location is to check it out both for suitability for the programme, and for practical considerations such as the availability of an electrical power source or parking.

**red head** – a lightweight, variable beam, 800 watt television light.

**reflexivity** – a text's reflection on its own status as a text, for example by drawing attention to generic conventions, or revealing the technologies used to make a programme.

**register** – a term in the study of language for the kinds of speech or writing used to represent a particular kind of idea or to address a certain audience.

**regulation** – the control of television institutions by laws, codes of practice or guidelines.

**release form** – a form signed by a contributor to a television programme giving permission for his or her contribution to be broadcast. Most release forms cover all known rights so that the programme can be used in different formats and regional markets.

**representation** – the way people of different genders, races, ethnicities and from different backgrounds are portrayed on television.

**resistance** – the ways audiences make meaning from television programmes that is counter to the meanings thought to be intended, or that are discovered by close analysis.

**rostrum camera** – a video camera set up on an overhead rig to record drawings, still photos or any object that can be placed on a flat platform. The camera and the platform can be programmed to do a variety of moves, such as record an object rotating, or zoom in on detail in a photograph.

**rough cut** – the first edited version of a television programme which needs further editing because it may be too long or ineffectively structured.

**runner** – the most junior member of a television or film production team.

**running order** – a list of the duration, source and description of the items in a television programme in the order in which they will appear in the programme.

**rushes** – all the audio and visual material that has been shot during the production period, including bad takes and other unwanted material. The rushes are the raw material for the editor.

**satellite television** – television signals beamed from a ground transmitter to a stationary satellite that broadcasts the signal to a specific area (called the 'footprint') below it.

**satire** – a mode of critical commentary about society or an aspect of it, using humour to attack people or ideas.

**scanner** – the large vehicle housing the mobile control room for an outside broadcast.

**schedule** – the arrangement of programmes, advertisements and other material into a sequential order within a certain period of time, such as an evening, day or week.

**screenplay** – a script that is written specifically to be made into a television drama or film.

**semiotics** – the study of signs and their meanings, initially developed for the study of spoken language, and now used also to study the visual and aural 'languages' of other media such as television.

**serial** – a television form where a developing narrative unfolds across a sequence of separate episodes.

**series** – a television form where each programme in the series has a different story or topic, though settings, main characters or performers remain the same.

**set** – the arrangement of scenery in a studio, or on location, where scenes for a television programme will be shot.

**set-top box** – the electronic decoding equipment connected to home television sets that allows access to digital television signals.

**shooting ratio** – the number of minutes of film used to film a scene or complete programme as compared to the screen-time of the finished scene or programme.

**shot** – a single shot runs from the point at which the camera is turned on to where it is paused or turned off. A shot can be identified by the time code on the video, or by using a clapperboard.

**shot, reverse shot** – the convention of alternating a shot of one character and a shot of another character in a scene, producing a back-and-forth movement which represents their interaction visually.

**shot size** – the size of the subject within the frame of a shot. Standard shot sizes are used throughout television production and are referred to by their abbreviations such as CU for close-up.

**sign** – in semiotics, something that communicates meaning, such as a word, an image or a sound.

**simulation** – a representation that mirrors an aspect of reality so perfectly that it takes the place of the reality it aims to reproduce.

**Skillset** – the national training and careers advice organisation for the film, broadcasting, video and multimedia industries. www.skillset.org.

**slot** – the position in a television schedule where a programme is shown.

**soap opera** – a continuing drama serial involving a large number of characters in a specific location, focusing on relationships, emotions and reversals of fortune.

**sociology** – the academic study of society, aiming to describe and explain aspects of life in that society.

**sparks** – the colloquial name for the electricians who are responsible for the lights on a production. They take their instructions from the lighting cameraperson.

**spectacle** – a fascinating image that draws attention to its immediate surface meanings and offers visual pleasure for its own sake.

**spin-off** – a product, television programme, book etc. that is created to exploit the reputation, meaning or commercial success of a previous one, often in a different medium from the original.

**sponsorship** – the funding of programmes or channels by businesses, whose name is usually prominently displayed in the programme or channel as a means of advertising.

**sound effects (fx)** – the extra sounds that are added in the editing process to the natural sounds in a scene.

**status quo** – a Latin term meaning the ways that culture and society are currently organised.

**steadicam** – a camera mounting that straps the camera to the body of the operator and incorporates a device that keeps the image steady.

**stick mic** – a long, stick-like, hand-held microphone typically used by a presenter on location.

**stills** – static images used in a television production such as photographs or still frames from a television programme or film.

**sting** – a brief musical or visual insert used as punctuation in a programme.

**stock footage** – video and film that is kept in a archive or library and can be used as illustrative material in a programme.

**storyboard** – a sequence of drawn images showing the shots to be used in a programme.

**strand** – a linked series of programmes, sharing a common title.

**stripping** – in television scheduling, placing a programme or genre of programme at the same time on several days of each week.

**structure of feeling** – the assumptions, attitudes and ideas prevalent in a society, arising from the ideologies underpinning that society.

**subject** – in psychoanalysis, the term for the individual self whose identity has both conscious and unconscious components.

**subscription** – payment to a television broadcaster in exchange for the opportunity to view programmes on certain channels that are otherwise blocked.

**subtitle** – written text appearing on the television screen, normally to translate speech in a foreign language.

**sungun** – a hand-held television light that runs from belt batteries and can give an intense beam.

**super-cardioid** – a highly directional microphone used in a gun or rifle mic.

**superimpose** – to introduce a new image or graphic and superimpose it over an existing picture. This is normally done by the vision mixer in a TV studio gallery.

**symbol** – a representation that condenses many meanings together and can stand for those many meanings in a certain context. For example, a brand-new car could be a symbol of wealth, social status and masculine prowess.

**symbolic sign** – in semiotics, a sign that is connected arbitrarily to its referent rather than because the sign resembles its referent. For example, a photograph of a cat resembles it, whereas the word 'cat' does not: the word is a symbolic sign.

**sync sound** – abbreviation for synchronised sound, meaning sound that is shot simultaneously with the pictures, and matches the lip movements of the actors or contributors.

**syndication** – the sale of programmes for regional television broadcasters to transmit within their territory.

**syntagm** – in semiotics, a linked sequence of signs existing at a certain point in time. Written or spoken sentences, or television sequences, are examples of syntagms.

**take** – a repetition of the action when recording a scene. Each recording of the same scene will have a take number.

**talking heads** – the term used for interviews or other head and shoulder shots of contributors to a programme.

**taste and decency** – conformity to the standards of good taste and acceptable language and behaviour on television, as required by regulations.

**teaser** – a very short television sequence advertising a forthcoming programme, often puzzling or teasing to viewers because it contains little information and encourages curiosity and interest.

**terrestrial** – broadcasting from a ground-based transmission system, as opposed to broadcasting via satellite.

**text** – an object such as a television programme, film or poem, considered as a network of meaningful signs that can be analysed and interpreted.

**textual analysis** – a critical approach that seeks to understand a television text's meanings by undertaking detailed analysis of its image and sound components, and the relationships between those components.

**three-point lighting** – the standard way to light an interview or small scene for television, so called because it uses three lights in different positions – a key light, back light and fill light.

**three shot** – a shot with three people in the frame.

**time code** – the electronic process that gives each frame of video its own numerical identification. This can be displayed on the screen as a series of numbers that show the tape number, hours, minutes, seconds and frames.

**timeline** – a visual reference for computer video editing, showing video tracks, edit points, and audio tracks along a time reference scale.

**title sequence** – the sequence at the opening of a television programme in which the programme title and performers' names may appear along with other information, accompanied by images, sound and music introducing the programme. Colloquially known as 'titles'.

**tracking shot** – a camera shot where the camera is mounted on a dolly and records while moving along a track similar to a miniature railway track, often parallel to a moving subject.

**trailer** – a short television sequence advertising a forthcoming programme, usually containing selected 'highlights' from the programme.

**transition** – a change from one shot to the next different shot, sometimes using a dissolve or wipe.

**transmission** – the process of broadcasting a television programme to an audience.

**treatment** – a short written outline for a programme, usually for a commissioning producer to read, specifying how the programme will tell its story or address its subject.

**tripod** – a three-legged camera mounting used to obtain professional-looking shots.

**tungsten lamp** – a television lighting lamp with a tungsten filament that has to be colour balanced for daylight using a blue gel.

**turn over** – the instruction given by the director to start the camera and sound recording.

**uplink** – the electronic system that beams television signals from the ground to a satellite for onward transmission to a television institution elsewhere.

**uses and gratifications** – a theoretical approach that assumes people engage in an activity because it provides them with a benefit of some kind.

**utopia** – an ideal society.

**variety programmes** – entertainment programmes containing a mix of material such as songs and comedy sketches.

**VCR** – video cassette recorder.

**vérité** – a French word (meaning 'truth') describing observational shooting that follows events, rather than reconstructing them or using other conventions from fictional cinema or TV.

**vertical integration** – the control by media institutions of all levels of a business, from the production of products to their distribution and means of reception.

**vision mixer** – the operator of the vision mixing desk in the gallery of a multicamera TV studio.

**voice-over** – speech accompanying visual images but not presumed to derive from the same place or time as the images.

**vox pop** – literally meaning 'the voice of the people', short television interviews answering just one question, conducted with members of the public, usually in the street.

**voyeurism** – gaining sexual pleasure from looking at someone or something that cannot look back.

**VU meter** – Volume Unit meter found on audio equipment, displaying the intensity (measured in decibels) of a sound source.

**watershed** – the time in the day (conventionally 9.00 pm) after which programmes can be shown with content that may disturb children.

**whip-pan** – a very rapid panning shot from one point to another.

**white balance** – a way of making the colour of the pictures from a camcorder accurately represent the true colours of the scene, by pointing the camera at a white surface that reflects the light temperature of the scene.

**widescreen** – the standard broadcasting format for television programmes with an aspect ratio of 16:9, instead of the previous standard of 4:3.

**wildtrack** – sound recording taken at the time of shooting on location but without pictures. The wildtrack sound is used in editing, sometimes as background sound.

**zapping** – hopping rapidly from channel to channel while watching television, using a remote control (a 'zapper').

**zoom lens** – a lens with a variable focal length, enabling the camera operator to choose and vary the shot size by 'zooming in' or 'zooming out'.

# Index

........................

broadcasting laws and guidelines 254, 255, 258–66

Broadcasting Standards Commission (BSC) 9, 304

*Brookside* 123, 127, 128

Brunsdon, Charlotte 121

Bruzzi, Stella 116

BSkyB 296

budgets 38, 202–3

*Buffy* series 186, 201

*Buried* 66

Burton, Graeme 112, 290

*Cabin Fever* 71

cable television 20, 113, 137, 270, 287, 304

Caldwell, John 289

Caleb, Ruth 131

camcorders 206–7, 304; *see also* Sony

camera: digital video 21–3, 203; High Definition 293–4, 294; practical tips for programme making 206–7; professional disc systems 292–3; set-up 214–15; and three-point lighting 212–14; used in documentary 174

camera angles: describing shots 224–6; *mise-en-scène* 228; non-traditional postmodern style 219; for sporting events 25–6, 152

camera assistant 39–40

camera card 240

camera movement 226–7; framing shots 221, 224; *mise-en-scène* 228

camera operator 39, 41–2, 234

camera script 32, 239

camera shots: break down in camera script 239; importance of angles 224–6; *mise-en-scène* 102–3, 104; narration 91; paper edit 250–2; shot reverse shot 216, 248–50, 320; sizes 219–22, 228, 320

camera supervisor 234

Campbell, Naomi 258

Canada 273, 293

Canal Plus 111

Cannes Film Festival 174

capitalism 304; American values in MTV 165

*Cardiac Arrest* 66

Carlton 9

The Cartoon Network 59

cartoons 63

*Castaway* 115

casting director 230

*Casualty* 61, 100

*Cathy Come Home* 66

Caughie, John 111, 121

CBBC 270

CBeebies 270

CBS News 285

CCD (charge-coupled diode) 21–3, 304

celebrities: guests in studio shows 238; making factual programme with 185; transformation of ordinary people into 175, 286

celebrity culture: characters from docusoaps 112, 175; media discourses 164–5; pop performers on MTV 159–60; and Reality TV 70, 115

censorship 304; films before watershed 11; news about war 137

*Changing Rooms* 286

Channel 4 51, 286; digital transmission systems 19–20; drama series 66, 122; placing and scheduling of *Big Brother* 75, 82, 280; public service provision 13, 14, 18, 271; relocation programmes 176; viewers of factual programmes 110

Channel 5 *see* Five

channel controller 244, 256

characters: *mise-en-scène* 228–9; ordinary folk in docusoaps 112, 175; scripting 186–9, 191, 193; television acting ability 230; viewers' identification with 289

*Charmed* 289

chat shows 43, 233; *see also* talk shows

childhood: contrasting conceptions of in West 84

children: channels for 270; and concerns about television 84, 255; making factual programme with 185

children's programmes 43, 273

China 135

chromakey 46, 240–1; *see also* bluescreen

*Related titles from Routledge*

# Freelancing for Television and Radio

## Leslie Mitchell

*Freelancing for Television and Radio* explains what it means to
be a freelance in the world of the audio visual industries.
From an outline of tax and employment issues it goes on
to describe the ups and downs of the world in which the
freelance works. Radio, television and related sectors
like facilities and video production are assessed for the
opportunities they offer the aspiring freelance, and there's
also an analysis of the skills you need for a successful
freelance career.

Freelancing for Television and Radio includes:

- Practical advice on how to make a start; where to find
  work; writing the right kind of CV, networking and
  making contacts
- Important section on maintaining and developing a
  freelance career as well as a chapter on the challenges
  and responsibilities of setting up and running a small
  business.
- A significant chapter on the basics of writing and
  submitting programme proposals to broadcasters as well
  as a substantial section of useful contact information.

Hb: 0–415–34101–9
Pb: 0–415–34102–7

Available at all good bookshops
For ordering and further information please visit:
www.routledge.com

*Related titles from Routledge*

# Writing for Broadcast Journalists

## Rick Thompson

*Writing for Broadcast Journalists* guides readers through the differences between written and spoken language in journalism, helping broadcast journalists at every stage of their career to steer past such pitfalls as pronunciation, terms of address, and Americanised phrases, as well as to capitalise on the immediacy of the spoken word in writing broadcast news scripts.

Written in a lively and accessible style by an experienced BBC radio and TV journalist, *Writing for Broadcast Journalists* provides an invaluable guide to the techniques of writing for radio, television and online news sources.

Sections include:

- guidance on tailoring your writing style to suit a particular broadcast news audience
- advice on editing agency copy
- tips on how to avoid cliches, 'news-speak' and Americanisms
- an appendix of 'dangerous' words and phrases, explaining correct usage and advising when to avoid certain terms.

Hb: 0–415–31796–7
Pb: 0–415–31797–5

Available at all good bookshops
For ordering and further information please visit:
www.routledge.com